First World War
and Army of Occupation
War Diary
France, Belgium and Germany

31 DIVISION
92 Infantry Brigade
East Lancashire Regiment 11th Battalion,
Brigade Machine Gun Company
and Brigade Trench Mortar Battery
1 January 1916 - 31 August 1916

WO95/2358

The Naval & Military Press Ltd
www.nmarchive.com
Published in association with The National Archives

Published by

The Naval & Military Press Ltd
Unit 10 Ridgewood Industrial Park,
Uckfield, East Sussex,
TN22 5QE England
Tel: +44 (0) 1825 749494

www.naval-military-press.com

www.nmarchive.com

This diary has been reprinted in facsimile from the original. Any imperfections are inevitably reproduced and the quality may fall short of modern type and cartographic standards.

© **Crown Copyright**
Images reproduced by permission of The National Archives, London, England, 2015.

Contents

Document type	Place/Title	Date From	Date To
Heading	94th Brigade 92nd Brigade 31st Division Battalion Transferred To 92nd Brigade 11th February 1918		
War Diary	Front Line Acheville Sector L2 Hudson Post	01/02/1918	04/02/1918
War Diary	Ecurie	05/02/1918	16/02/1918
War Diary	Neuville St Vaast	16/02/1918	16/02/1918
War Diary	Front Line	22/02/1918	22/02/1918
War Diary	Ecurie	28/02/1918	28/02/1918
War Diary	Front Line Acheville Sector L2 Hudson Post	01/02/1918	04/02/1918
War Diary	Ecurie	05/02/1918	16/02/1918
War Diary	Ecurie	11/02/1918	11/02/1918
War Diary	Neuville St Vaast	16/02/1918	16/02/1918
War Diary	Front Line	22/02/1918	22/02/1918
War Diary	Ecurie	28/02/1918	28/02/1918
Heading	31st Division 92nd Infantry Brigade. 11th Battalion East Lancashire Regiment March 1918		
War Diary	Ecurie Spolingvale Camp	01/03/1918	02/03/1918
War Diary	Bray	03/03/1918	03/03/1918
War Diary	Marquay and Bailleul	04/03/1918	04/03/1918
War Diary	Cornailles	04/03/1918	21/03/1918
War Diary	Cornailles	12/03/1918	12/03/1918
War Diary	Cornailles	05/03/1918	05/03/1918
War Diary	Marquay	15/03/1918	22/03/1918
War Diary	Marquay	21/03/1918	21/03/1918
War Diary	Bailleulval	22/03/1918	22/03/1918
Heading	1 Am 23rd Should Apparently read "1 am 24"		
War Diary		23/03/1918	25/03/1918
Heading	10 E York-Top Line		
War Diary		25/03/1918	27/03/1918
War Diary		31/03/1918	31/03/1918
War Diary		27/03/1918	28/03/1918
Heading	92nd Brigade 31st Division 1/11th Battalion East Lancashire Regiment April 1918		
War Diary	St Amand	01/04/1918	01/04/1918
War Diary	Sus St Leger	01/04/1918	01/04/1918
War Diary	Bailleul Aux Cornailles	02/04/1918	12/04/1918
Miscellaneous			
War Diary		12/04/1918	14/04/1918
War Diary	Hondeghem	14/04/1918	30/04/1918
War Diary	81st Division 92nd Infy Bde 11th Bn East Lancs Regt Feb 1918-Jly 1919		
Heading	War Diary 11th Battn E Lancs Regiment May 1918		
War Diary	Hondeghem	01/05/1918	09/05/1918
War Diary	Caestre	09/05/1918	15/05/1918
War Diary	Meteren Sector	15/05/1918	20/05/1918
War Diary	Caestre	21/05/1918	24/05/1918
War Diary	Lumbres.	25/05/1918	31/05/1918
War Diary	Val De Lumbres	01/06/1918	08/06/1918
War Diary	Racquinghem	08/06/1918	15/06/1918
War Diary	Wallon Cappel	15/06/1918	15/06/1918
War Diary	Blaringhem	17/06/1918	21/06/1918

War Diary	Grand Hasard		25/06/1918	28/06/1918
War Diary	Grand Hasard		30/06/1918	16/07/1918
War Diary	Grand Hasard		11/07/1918	30/07/1918
War Diary	La Motte Sector		01/08/1918	03/08/1918
War Diary	Grand Hazard		03/08/1918	09/08/1918
War Diary	Front Line		09/08/1918	10/08/1918
War Diary	La Motte		10/08/1918	13/08/1918
War Diary	Resell		13/08/1918	14/08/1918
War Diary	Front Line		15/08/1918	19/08/1918
War Diary	Reserve		19/08/1918	20/08/1918
War Diary	Wallon Cappel		21/08/1918	21/08/1918
War Diary	La Brearde		24/08/1918	24/08/1918
War Diary	Fletre		24/08/1918	01/09/1918
War Diary	Reserve		03/09/1918	03/09/1918
War Diary	Front Line		04/09/1918	13/09/1918
War Diary	La Brearde		13/09/1918	23/09/1918
War Diary	Hazebrouck		23/09/1918	28/09/1918
War Diary	Hill 13 Ploegsteert		01/10/1918	04/10/1918
War Diary	Neuve Eglise		04/10/1918	05/10/1918
War Diary	Bailleul		06/10/1918	12/10/1918
War Diary	Ploegsteert		12/10/1918	16/10/1918
War Diary	Quesnoy		17/10/1918	19/10/1918
War Diary	Turcoing		19/10/1918	29/10/1918
War Diary	Harlebeke		01/11/1918	01/11/1918
War Diary	Halluin		03/11/1918	03/11/1918
War Diary	Kloosterhoek		07/11/1918	07/11/1918
War Diary	Avelghem		08/11/1918	09/11/1918
War Diary	L'Escaut		09/11/1918	09/11/1918
War Diary	Amougies		10/11/1918	10/11/1918
War Diary	Quesnau		11/11/1918	11/11/1918
War Diary	Guefferdinge		11/11/1918	11/11/1918
War Diary	Quesnau		13/11/1918	13/11/1918
War Diary	Banhout Bosch		15/11/1918	15/11/1918
War Diary	Marke		16/11/1918	16/11/1918
War Diary	Menin		25/11/1918	25/11/1918
War Diary	Vlamertinge		26/11/1918	26/11/1918
War Diary	St Eloi		27/11/1918	27/11/1918
War Diary	Renescure		28/11/1918	28/11/1918
War Diary	St Omer		29/11/1918	31/12/1918
War Diary	St Omer		01/01/1919	29/01/1919
War Diary	Calais		29/01/1919	31/01/1919
War Diary	St Omer		01/02/1919	28/02/1919
War Diary	Abbeville		16/03/1919	30/04/1919
War Diary	Abbeville		01/04/1919	15/04/1919
War Diary	Abbeville		01/05/1919	26/05/1919
War Diary	Abbeville to Havre		27/05/1919	31/05/1919
War Diary	Le Havre		01/06/1919	30/06/1919
War Diary	Harfleur		01/07/1919	15/07/1919
War Diary	Harfleur		01/07/1919	31/07/1919
War Diary	Harfleur		16/07/1919	31/07/1919
Heading	31st Division 92nd Infy Bde 92nd Machine Gun Coy Jly 1916-Feb 1918			
Heading	92nd Bde. 31st Div 92nd Brigade Machine Gun Company 1st to 31st July 1916 Feb 1919			
Heading	War Diary Of 92nd M. Gun. Coy 1st July To 31st July 1916 Vol 3			

War Diary		01/07/1916	31/07/1916
Heading	War Diary Of 92nd Machine Gun Coy Aug 1916		
War Diary		01/08/1916	31/08/1916
Heading	War Diary 92nd Machine Gun Coy 31st Division September 1916 Vol 5		
War Diary		01/09/1916	30/10/1916
Heading	War Diary Of 92nd Machine Gun Company From 1st Oct 1916 To 31st Oct 1916 Volume X		
War Diary		01/12/1916	31/12/1916
War Diary	Confidential War Diary Of From 1st Nov 16 to 30th Nov 16 volume Volume		
War Diary	In The Field	01/11/1916	30/11/1916
War Diary	War Diary of From 1st Decr 16 To 31st Decr Volume XII		
War Diary	In The Field (Coigneux 59 D NE 1/20000)	01/12/1916	31/12/1916
Heading	War Diary Of 92nd Machine Gun Company From 1st Jan 1917 To 31st Jan 1917 Volume XIII		
War Diary		01/01/1916	31/01/1916
Heading	War Diary Of 92 Machine Gun Company Volume 14 From 1-2-19 to 28-2-19 Vol 10		
War Diary		01/02/1917	28/02/1917
Heading	War Diary Of 92 Machine Gun Company From 1st March 1919 To 31st March 1919 Volume IV		
War Diary		01/03/1917	31/03/1917
Heading	War Diary Of No 92 Machine Gun Company From 1st April 1917 To 30th April 1917 Volume XVI		
War Diary		01/04/1917	07/04/1917
War Diary	BEF	07/04/1917	09/04/1917
War Diary	2/Lt Thomson Cook Over Transport Duties From 2/Lt Jackson	09/04/1917	30/04/1917
Heading	92nd Machine Gun Company War Diary. 1st May. 1917 to 31st May 1917. Volume 17		
War Diary	B.E.F.	01/05/1917	31/05/1917
Miscellaneous	Appendix II		
Miscellaneous	Appendix III		
Miscellaneous	Appendix IV		
Miscellaneous	Appendix V		
Miscellaneous	Appendix VI		
Miscellaneous	Appendix VII		
Miscellaneous	Appendix VIII Order For Relief 15/4/17	15/04/1917	15/04/1917
Miscellaneous	Appendix IX To Accompany 93rd Infantry Brigade Operation Order No.		
Miscellaneous	Appendix X Recommendation For Award	20/05/1917	20/05/1917
Miscellaneous	Appendix I		
Heading	War Diary For 92nd M.G. Coy From June 1st June 30th 1917 Volume XVIII		
War Diary	France	01/06/1917	30/06/1917
Operation(al) Order(s)	Special Orders No 10 Remove To Ecoivres		
Miscellaneous	Programme of Training 4th To 10/6/17		
Operation(al) Order(s)	Appendix III 92nd M.G. Coy Special Order No. 11	10/06/1917	10/06/1917
Operation(al) Order(s)	Appendix 4 Special Orders No. 14 Jan 16-6-17	16/06/1917	16/06/1917
Miscellaneous	Appendix 5	20/06/1917	20/06/1917
Miscellaneous	Appendix VI		
Miscellaneous	Appendix VII	23/06/1917	23/06/1917
Miscellaneous	Appendix VIII	26/06/1917	26/06/1917

Heading	War Diary Of 92nd Machine Gun Company From 1st July 1917 To 31st July 1917 (Volume 19)		
War Diary	BEF	01/07/1917	31/07/1917
Operation(al) Order(s)	Order for relief of 92nd M.G.Coy by 92nd M.G. Coy Appendix I	01/07/1917	01/07/1917
Miscellaneous	Situation Report Appendix 2		
Miscellaneous	Training Programme 92nd M.G. Company Appendix	07/07/1917	07/07/1917
Operation(al) Order(s)	92nd M.G. Coy Order No. 20 Appendix 4	11/07/1917	11/07/1917
Operation(al) Order(s)	92 M.G Coy Order No. 2 Appendix 5	20/07/1917	20/07/1917
Operation(al) Order(s)	Report on Action Of M.Gs of 31st Div in Conjunction with Operation by 3rd Canadian Division night of 22/23rd July 1917 Appendix 6	22/07/1917	22/07/1917
Miscellaneous	Order for Relief of 92nd Coy by 243 Coy Appendix 4	23/07/1917	23/07/1917
Miscellaneous	Programme ? of work of 92nd M.G. Coy Whilst Out of the line at Mont St Eloy Appendix 8	25/07/1917	25/07/1917
Heading	War Diary 92nd Machine Gun Company 31st Division August 1917 Volume 1917 Vol 16		
War Diary	BEF	01/08/1917	31/08/1917
Miscellaneous	Proposed Programme Of Work Of 92nd M.G. Coy Whilst Out of the line at Mont. St. Eloy. Appendix I	25/07/1917	25/07/1917
Miscellaneous	Orders For Relief Of 243 M.G. Coy By 92 MG Coy Night 4th/5th Aug. 17 Appendix 2		
Miscellaneous	Orders For Relief Of 92 MG Coy By 243 Coy By Capt R.N. Ekins Commdg 92 MG Coy Appendix 3	15/08/1917	15/08/1917
Miscellaneous	Orders For Relief Of 243 M.G.Coy By 92 Coy Night 29th/30th Aug. Appendix	29/08/1917	29/08/1917
Miscellaneous	Programme of Training Period 18th To 29th Aug Appendix 4	18/08/1917	18/08/1917
Heading	War Diary Of 92 Machine Gun Coy From 1st Sept. 1917 To 30th Sept. 1917 (Volume 21) Vol 17		
War Diary	BEF	01/09/1917	04/09/1917
War Diary	Being In Position	05/09/1917	30/09/1917
Operation(al) Order(s)	Operation Order For Relief Of 92 M.G. Coy By 9th & 15th Canadian M.G. Coys On Night 4/5 Sept 1917 Appendix 1	09/09/1917	09/09/1917
Operation(al) Order(s)	Operation Orders No 29 By Capt E.N. Ekins Commdg. 92 M.G. Coy Appendix 2	06/09/1917	06/09/1917
Miscellaneous	Appendix 1		
Miscellaneous	Operation Report On Night Training 10/11/1917 Appendix. 4	10/09/1917	10/09/1917
Miscellaneous	Operation Report Night Firing 11/12/ 9/17 Appendix 5	11/09/1917	11/09/1917
Miscellaneous	Report On Machine Gun Operations On Night Of 12/13 Sept 1917 Appendix 6	12/09/1917	12/09/1917
Miscellaneous	Operation Report-Gas Projection-13th-9-17	13/09/1917	13/09/1917
Miscellaneous	Operation Report Night 14/15 9.17 Appendix 8	14/09/1917	14/09/1917
Miscellaneous	Operation Report 24 Hours Ending 9 a.m.17.9.17 Appendix 9	17/09/1917	17/09/1917
Miscellaneous	Operation Order 3/4 1/4 Appendix 9	15/09/1917	15/09/1917
Miscellaneous	Operation Report Night 16/17 Sept Appendix 10	16/09/1917	16/09/1917
Miscellaneous	Operation Order For Relief Of 92nd MG Coy By 92 M.G. Coy On Afternoon 18. Sept 1917	18/09/1917	18/09/1917
Miscellaneous	Programme of Training 19th Sept To 1st Oct 19 Appendix 12	09/09/1917	09/09/1917
Miscellaneous	Operation Orders No 36 by Capt NA Johns Commdg 92 MG Coy 29th Sept 1917 Appendix 13	29/09/1917	29/09/1917

Heading	War Diary Of 92 Machine Gun Company From 1st Oct. 1917 To 31st Oct. 1917 Volume XXII		
War Diary		01/10/1917	31/10/1917
Miscellaneous	Operations From 1-10-17 To 12-10-17 Appendix 1	01/10/1917	01/10/1917
Miscellaneous	App 2		
Miscellaneous	App 3		
Miscellaneous	Relief Orders App 4		
Miscellaneous	Programme of Training 15/10/17 To 23/10/17 App 5	15/10/1917	15/10/1917
Operation(al) Order(s)	Operation Orders No 26 By Capt NA Johns Commdg 92 MG Coy Appendix 6	23/10/1917	23/10/1917
Miscellaneous	Operation Report From 25-10-17 To 31-10-17 Appendix 7	25/10/1917	25/10/1917
Heading	War Diary Of 92 M.G. Coy For Month Of November 1917 Volume XXIII		
War Diary		01/11/1917	30/11/1917
Miscellaneous	Operation From 2-11-17 to 7-11-17 (Inclusive) App 1	02/11/1917	02/11/1917
Miscellaneous	Report On Operation of the Two Batteries of 92 MG Coy On 8-11-17 App 2	08/11/1917	08/11/1917
Operation(al) Order(s)	Group Orders No. 1 Group App 3	04/11/1917	04/11/1917
Miscellaneous	Orders With Reference to Operations on Nov 8th 1917 App 4	06/11/1917	06/11/1917
Miscellaneous		10/11/1917	10/11/1917
Miscellaneous	92 M.G Comp		
Miscellaneous	Operation Orders By Capt G.S. King Commdg 92 M.G. Coy App 6		
Operation(al) Order(s)	Operation Order No. 201 20.11.17 By Capt G.S. King Commdg 92 M.G. Coy	20/11/1917	20/11/1917
Operation(al) Order(s)	Operations From 22-11-17 To 30-11-17 (Inclusive) App 8	22/11/1917	22/11/1917
Operation(al) Order(s)	Operation Order No. 202 By Capt G.S. King. Commdg 92 M.G. Coy. App 9		
Miscellaneous	Report On Operation Under 31st /0.2.3 92 Inf Bde 0.184 28/11/17 App. 10	28/11/1917	28/11/1917
Heading	War Diary 92nd Machine Gun Company 31st Division December 1917 Volume XXIV Vol 20		
War Diary		01/12/1917	31/12/1917
Miscellaneous	Operations From 1-12-17 To 7-12-17 (Inclusive) Appendix 1	01/12/1917	01/12/1917
Operation(al) Order(s)	Operation Order No. 205 By Capt G.S. King Commdg 92 M.G Coy App 2		
Miscellaneous	Company Orders No For 8.12.17 By Capt N.A. Johns Commdg 92 MG Coy	08/12/1917	08/12/1917
Miscellaneous	Company Orders No. 4 For 9-12-17 By Capt N.A Johns Commdg 92 Mg Coy.	09/12/1917	09/12/1917
Miscellaneous	Company Orders No. 63 For 10-12-17 By Capt N.A Johns Commdg 92 MG Coy	10/12/1917	10/12/1917
Miscellaneous	App 6 Vol 19		
Miscellaneous	Cooperation Of M.G's With a Vanguard Scheme in Conjunction With 12th East Yorks App 6 Vol 19		
Miscellaneous	Operation Order For 22-12-17 Capt N.A. Johns Commdg 92 M.G Coy. App 7 Vol 19		
Miscellaneous	Appendix 8 Vol 19		
Heading	War Diary Of 92 Machine Gun Coy For Month Of January 1918		
War Diary		01/01/1918	31/01/1918

Miscellaneous	Operation Orders By Capt N.A. Johns Commd 92nd M.G. Coy. App No. 1		
Operation(al) Order(s)	Operation Order No. 207 By Lieut. W.N.U. Dunlop Commg 92nd MG Coy App 2		
Miscellaneous	Training Programme App No. 3		
Operation(al) Order(s)	Operation Order No. 208 by LIeut. W.N.U Dunlop Commdg 92nd MG Coy App 4		
Heading	War Diary Of 92nd Machine Gun Coy For Month Of February 1918 Vol 22		
War Diary		01/02/1918	28/02/1918
Operation(al) Order(s)	Operation Order No 209 By Cap I N.A. Johns Commdg 92 M.G. Coy	16/02/1918	16/02/1918
Operation(al) Order(s)	Operation Order No. 210 By Capt N.A. Johns Commdg 92nd M.G. Coy		
Operation(al) Order(s)	Operation Order No 208 By Lieut. Dunlop W.N.U. Commdg. 92 M.G. Coy.		
Heading	31st Division 92nd Infy Bde Trench Mortar Bty May-Aug 1916		
War Diary	Colincamps Trenches Continued	11/05/1916	31/05/1916
War Diary	Bus-Les-Artois	06/05/1916	06/05/1916
War Diary	Collin Camps Trenches	07/05/1916	14/05/1916
War Diary	Bus-Les-Artois	15/05/1916	26/05/1916
War Diary	Bus-Les-Artois	25/05/1916	31/05/1916
War Diary	Bus-Les-Artois	06/05/1916	06/05/1916
War Diary	Colincamps Trenches Re Trench Map	06/05/1916	06/05/1916
War Diary	Hebuterne 57D NE 304 (Ports of) Second action Seale 1:10,000	04/05/1916	10/05/1916
War Diary	Colincamps Trenches Continued	11/05/1916	31/05/1916
War Diary	Bus-Les-Artois	06/05/1916	06/05/1916
War Diary	Colincamps Trenches Ref Trench Map	06/05/1916	07/05/1916
War Diary	Hebuterne 57d NE 304 (Ports of) Second action Seale 1:10,000	08/05/1916	10/05/1916
Heading	War Diary Of 92 TMB From The 1/6/16 To 30/6/16 Vol 2		
War Diary	Trenches E Of Collincamps	01/06/1916	04/06/1916
War Diary	Bus	04/06/1916	06/06/1916
War Diary	Bus-Les-Artois	11/06/1916	11/06/1916
War Diary	Colincamps	12/06/1916	30/06/1916
Heading	92nd Bde. 31st Div. 92nd Brigade Trench Mortar Battery 1st To 31st July 1916		
Heading	War Diary Of 92nd I. Mortar Battery 1st July To 31st July 1916		
War Diary	Trenches E. of Colincamps	01/07/1916	30/07/1916
Heading	War Diary Of 92nd Trench Mortar Battery August 1916		
War Diary	Richeborg St Vaast	01/08/1916	31/08/1916

94th Brigade
92nd Brigade
31st Division

BATTALION TRANSFERRED TO
92nd BRIGADE 11th FEBRUARY
1 9 1 8

1/11th BATTALION

EAST LANCASHIRE REGIMENT

FEBRUARY 1 9 1 8

WAR DIARY
or
INTELLIGENCE SUMMARY.

Army Form C. 2118.

(Erase heading not required.)

Place	Date	Hour	Summary of Events and Information	Remarks and references to Appendices
	Nov 1917		VIIme XXV	
			H⁰ R.E. Jerusalem Regt	
Front line RAMEVALLE RIDGE N.85W 2966	October G.	1-4	All (Battlry) for on company 1/5th Q. Your Lancaster Reg. leaving the Four line.	
			Relief by 1/4th Yorks and Lancs Regt by 1/5th Yorks Fer Reg on night [?] R. Polished horses who [B] left scale at SAINTE MARIE	
E.1.B.6.	5	b.t.	Camp. Employed on laundry fatigues and training.	
			Reinforcements of 3 Officers and 460 O.R.s joined [?] Battalion E Jarrett [?] Regt. B Battalion. attached 146 and 147 Infant Company.	
			4 15- 148 Infty B.C. Battalion (Liest) no 943 Infantry Bn	

WAR DIARY
or
INTELLIGENCE SUMMARY
(Erase heading not required.)

Army Form C. 2118.

Place	Date	Hour	Summary of Events and Information	Remarks and references to Appendices
	11.		to the Spt Infantry Brigade on Ex from Huyton. We split up.	W/L
NEWSHAM ST MARIE	16.		Major Lane H.C. proceeded on leave. The Relieving arrived at 10: E. York Regt in support in Rouge – Croix (Kensville). 2 Companies and HQ in the Bailleul – Sector (Kensville). 2 Companies at Neuville – St – Marie. Villermaine and 2 Companies at the Junction Ld (Achevolle).	W/L
				W/L
FONT LINE	22.		Relieved the 10: E. York Regt. in the Junction Ld (Achevolle). Working over the Support Line. 10-10: E.York Regt. 227 Bn Regt. GUARDS on the Right 43 Rn Canadian Mounted Infantry on the Left.	W/L
				W/L
CORIC ST.	27.		Relieved by the 10: E. York Regt. Moved to Royal Rouen at Springvale Camp. Roads Condr. during the night 3 Bn killed 11 OR wounded. Draft – 97 OR & 4 Offrs. 9 rejoined or Corps H. + B. Camp.	W/L

Army Form C. 2118.

WAR DIARY
OR
INTELLIGENCE SUMMARY.
(Erase heading not required.)

(1st Bn East Lancs Regt)

Hour. Date. Place.	Summary of Events and Information.	Remarks and references to Appendices
1918 Nord lin Acheville Sector L.2. HUDSON POST 1–4"	The Battalion plus 1 Company 12th Bn York & Lancs Regt holding the front line.	
ECURIE 5"	Relieved by 14th York & Lancs Regt + 1 Coy 13th York & Lancs Regt. On relief the Battn moved into Brigade Reserve at "SPRINGVALE" Camp.	
5" – 16"	Employed on working parties & training. Reinforced by 2 officers & 400 men from 8th Battn East Lancs Regt. Battalion reorganised in 4 H.Q. & 4 fighting Companies. On 16th February the Battalion passed from 86th Brigade to the 92nd Infantry Brigade as the former Brigade was split up.	
11"	Lt Col W.D. LOWE MC proceeded on leave.	

Army Form C. 2118.

WAR DIARY
OR
INTELLIGENCE SUMMARY.
(Erase heading not required.)

Instructions regarding War Diaries and Intelligence Summaries are contained in F. S. Regs., Part II, and the Staff Manual. respectively. Title pages will be prepared in manuscript.

July 1915

Hour. Date. Place.	Summary of Events and Information.	Remarks and references to Appendices
Neuville St Vaast 16th Feb.	The Battalion relieved the 11th East York Regt. in support in 42 Sussex Tren (Acheville) 2 Coys & HQ in the BAILLEUL WILLERVAL line. 2 Coys at NEUVILLE ST VAAST	
22nd Northern	Relieved the 11th East York Regt. in the front line 42 (Acheville) having over the support to 10th E. Yorks Regt. 2nd Bn. Brit Guards on the Right. 4th Battalion Canadian M.G. Infantry on the Left	
ECURIE 25th	Relieved by the 10th E. Yorks Regt. marched viâ Bogue Hincum at SPRINGFIELD Camp. Batln. carried during the month 3 OR killed 15 OR wounded	
	Draft :- 97 OR (includes 7 returned) or Coys M. & R. Coys.	
	(Sgd) J.V. KERSHAW, Major Commanding M.E. R.P. Regt.	

31st Division.
92nd Infantry Brigade.

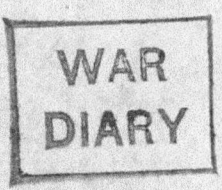

11th BATTALION

EAST LANCASHIRE REGIMENT

MARCH 1918

WAR DIARY
or
INTELLIGENCE SUMMARY.
(Erase heading not required.)

Army Form C. 2118.

11 # East Lancs Regt
Vol 25

Place	Date	Hour	Summary of Events and Information	Remarks and references to Appendices
			11th Battn East Lancashire Regt.	
			Volume XIII No 3. March 1917.	
ECURIE Camp P.	1.		Battalion bathing & refitting after tour in the trenches.	aur
	2.			
BRAY	3.		Battalion (less 2 offrs and QM.) moved by march route to BRAY	aur
MEAULTE	4.		moved by march route to MEAULTE (HQ & 2 Coys) and BAIZIEUX &	aur
BAIZIEUX and CORBIE GC			CARNAILLE! (2 Coys).	
	4-21		Battalion employed training – Route marching – Battalion and Brigade attack Schemes – Musketry – Bombing.	aur
	12.		2 Officers and 100 O.R. drafts taken as working party to BATTEUX – INTERVAL line reprints the Battalion.	aur
	5.		Temp. Col. W.B. HUCKE DSO took over command of the Battalion from Col. B [LD/NTE] MC returning to IV B D.L.I. on his return from [leave]	aur sitt

WAR DIARY
or
INTELLIGENCE SUMMARY.
(Erase heading not required.)

Army Form C. 2118.

Instructions regarding War Diaries and Intelligence Summaries are contained in F. S. Regs., Part II. and the Staff Manual respectively. Title pages will be prepared in manuscript.

Place	Date	Hour	Summary of Events and Information	Remarks and references to Appendices
HAPLINCOURT			Active.	
	14		Lieut D/ LEWIS JONES left Battalion for 6 months tour of duty in England	ans.
	15		a/Lt J.A. EDMONDSON returned to England for duty with the Machine Gun Corps.	ans.
	20		Lieut - Col. A.O. RICKMAN DSO rejoined the Battalion and took over command. 1st Bn Lee & 2/Lt SAUNDERS rejoined from 94 L.T.M.B.	ans.
	22		Lt Col WITHERS left the Battalion for 2 months leave in England.	ans.
	21	10 p.m.	Battalion to be prepared to move by Bus at 9 GMS	ans.
			march by F.O.M.H. 21. 3. 17.	
BRULEUX VAL	22		Entrained in Lee St PAL - BIHUCOURT TRIS at 9 a.m. and moved to BAILLEULVAL	ans.
		11 p.m.	Orders to move up to march march and take up a position in the GREEN LINE E. of BOISLEUX ST MARCQ. An enemy attack was found that this position had already been taken over by the Guest Division and the Battalion returned	ans.

"I am 23." should apparently read "I am 24."

tmm

Army Form C. 2118.

WAR DIARY
or
INTELLIGENCE SUMMARY.
(Erase heading not required.)

Place	Date	Hour	Summary of Events and Information	Remarks and references to Appendices
	23	6 A.M.	Took position astride the Railway to S.W. of BOISEUX ST. MARC. (Shown on R.H. diagram).	Appx.
		9:15 A.M.	Was to push in support N. of ERVILLERS the 17th D.L.I. were on the Left and the 11th E. Yorks. Regt. on our right holding the front of ERVILLERS. Three companies were to take E. of the MANCHESTER — ERVILLERS Road and a fourth company and Battalion HQ to the SOMME DUMP Road.	Appx.
	14	11—	On was in this position until 14th inst.	Appx.
	24/25		3 two companies were ordered to take up a sugar line frame on the South facing from 15 court so we was reported as at the enemy had taken it up to S. of ERVILLE ERS. The company at Battalion HQ and one of the 3 forward companies were employed for the 24 hour. i.e. I remaining forward coy taking over the position previously held by these 3 coys. When this position was taken up it & forward coys	Appx.

10 E YORK – top line –
must mean 11 E. YORK.
 Dw?

WAR DIARY
or
INTELLIGENCE SUMMARY.
(Erase heading not required.)

Army Form C. 2118.

Place	Date	Hour	Summary of Events and Information	Remarks and references to Appendices
	25.		Had the 10th Yorks Regt on their Right and the Border Division on their Left. Also 2 companies from the Oyster Reserve Battn were in command with the 10th Yorks Regt on their Left.	AAR.
			During the morning of 25th the 2 coys from the Oyster Reserve Bn to the Sore were drawn to the Yorks on him S. of HAMEL INFORT and EAST of the railway line.	AAR.
		5/6/18	The enemy attack developed from trench trough on the South and heavy reports in 8 and 18 Corps. Battn moved to relieve the 2 companies in the YELLOW Line and 2 companies were in a front facing E. of COUTE CELLER LA ETITE and faces the railway. Companies were to drop into position in artillery formation the two companies were in the YELLOW Line moved to the green position in front of	AAR.

A 8534 Wt. W4973/M687 750,000 8/16 D. D. & L. Ltd. Forms/C.2118/13.

WAR DIARY or INTELLIGENCE SUMMARY

Army Form C. 2118.

Place	Date	Hour	Summary of Events and Information	Remarks and references to Appendices
			Facing South under the direction of Major C/ Lewis M.C. and the two companies previously N. of ERVILLERS moved to the YELLOW line. Battalion HQ was in the railway embankment near the Ropes on the BURCELLES – U – ENTE – HAMELIN CCPT Road.	aw.
	26	4 A.M.	Received orders to withdraw to a position N. of ABLAINZEVELLE – MOYENNEVILLE Road South of where it crosses the MOYENNEVILLE Road, MOYENNEVILLE Road South of where it crosses the Railway and wait until the BURCELLES – U – ENTE – AYETTE Road Battalion	aw.
			and to East of the Railway, and wait until the position East of the right Hamp Spot N. of ABLAINZEVELLE was taken up with the right Hamp Spot N. of ABLAINZEVELLE and the left on the BURCELLES – U ENTE – AYETTE Road. ABLAINZEVELLE was held by M.G.s of the 41st Division.	aw. aw.

Army Form C. 2118.

WAR DIARY
or
INTELLIGENCE SUMMARY.
(Erase heading not required.)

Place	Date	Hour	Summary of Events and Information	Remarks and references to Appendices
			but the right flank was in touch with the 11th E. York Regt. On the left there was any infantry in the line to the [rear?] have now [returned?] by the 11th E. York Regt. The 10th York Regt was in support to the Brigade. Battalion HQ was in the dugouts on the AVELETTE — ENGLEBELMER — ENGLEBELMER road.	ans.
	26/27		During the day 26 x 27. the enemy attacked in three ? ? but was driven off.	ans.
			On the night 26/27 the right company extended up right for a distance of 200 x to the Red Track with its battalion on the right.	ans.
	27	11:17 AM	Enemy attacked with a Division on the front MARTINSART — MESNIL. During the time half have been taken but the position was on the left gave a little ground but was retaken ? ? ?	ans.
	12 noon		Not held by a later counter-attack by 12 noon	

A5834 Wt.W4973/M687 750,000 8/16 D.D.&L. Ltd. Forms/C.2118/13.

WAR DIARY
or
INTELLIGENCE SUMMARY.
(Erase heading not required.)

Army Form C. 2118.

Place	Date	Hour	Summary of Events and Information	Remarks and references to Appendices
		12.30	our attack has recoiled and again the left Battalion fell back to its support line. Enemy (opposite?) in ABRAHAM FILE	Ack.
		11.45 pm	left battalion line restored, and held	Ack.
		3.0 pm	Attack again fell back to the support position to the Enemy Catapulted Onto J point on top of ridge to AYETTE — COLECULER — to ENEMY Road.	Ack.
		4.15 pm	Enemy had got into the hands of Brigade and the Brigade was required to withdraw. Battalion was formed up R. of AYETTE and would have to pass the PURPLE line E. of ADINFER Wood and was in position	Ack.
		7.0 pm	about 7.0 pm. Right resting on QUESNOY FARM. Remainder in position in PURPLE line between ESSARTS and the DOUCHY — MONCHY road were relieved in night 31/1 April and relieved by 1st Devon Regt.	Ack.
	—21			Ack.

WAR DIARY or INTELLIGENCE SUMMARY

Army Form C. 2118.

Place	Date	Hour	Summary of Events and Information	Remarks and references to Appendices
	27/3/18		On the night 27/28 the first reinforcements were sent up to the 4th Guards Brigade amounting to 4 W/Offrs but were returned to the battalion in the form PURPLE Line on report 29/3/18.	auth.
			During the next days amounting to 59 O.R. joined the Battalion including 1 O.R. from 94 = LTM. B.	auth.
			Casualties 10.3.1918. 1 O.R. wounded. 25 – 29 =. 4 Offrs killed (2/Lt HORSFALL, 2/Lt GARDNER, 2/Lt HILLINGHEAD + 2/Lt BELL).	auth.
			4 Offrs wounded (1)/Lt TIVER, 2/Lt TYLER, 2/Lt CARRUTHERS, 2/Lt PERKINS, 2/Lt REBAN, 2/Lt FULLER 2/Lt LOTT) auth.	
			329 O.R. killed wounded + missing.	

P.M. Pechym
Lt Col Cmdg
4E L.N.R.
11/4/18.

92nd Brigade.

31st Division.

1/11th BATTALION

EAST LANCASHIRE REGIMENT

APRIL 1918.

11 E Lan R 92/31
Army Form C. 2118.
Vol 26

WAR DIARY
or
INTELLIGENCE SUMMARY.
(Erase heading not required.)

Instructions regarding War Diaries and Intelligence Summaries are contained in F. S. Regs., Part II. and the Staff Manual respectively. Title pages will be prepared in manuscript.

Place	Date 1918	Hour	Summary of Events and Information	Remarks and references to Appendices
	April		11th Battalion East Lancashire Regt.	
			References to Maps:-	
			France and Belgium 1/100,000	
ST AMAND	1.		Sheets 36 A NW } 1/20,000	
			" 27 SE }	
			On the night 31st March/1st April the Battalion were on the PURPLE Line at ST AMAND the 11th Ch[eshire] route, reaching their [?] at 4.0 A.M. and was by march route to BUS-ST-LEGER.	ack.
BUS ST LEGER		4A.M.		
BAILLEUL and CORNAILLES	1.		Entrained on the FREVENT – AVECNES to COETIS Rd and proceeded to BAILLEUL and CORNAILLES.	
	2-10		Reorganising and Training at BAILLEUL and CORNAILLES.	ans
	10	11.15A.M.	Received orders to be prepared to entrain that day.	ans
		7 P.M.	Entrained on the ST POL – BETHUNE Rd and proceeded via LILLERS and HAZEBROUCK	
	11	5A.M.	to VIEUX BERQUIN Debussed on the STRAZEELE – VIEUX BERQUIN Rd and the Battalion	
			(Sheet 36 A). Packs were dumped and the Battalion marched to BLEU via LA COURONNE	
			le PARADIS. Position taken up defending BLEU with 2 companies on the Eastern side of the Village and 2 forming a flank on the South side.	ans

Place	Date	Hour	Summary of Events and Information	Remarks and references to Appendices

All map references refer to Sheet 36A NE — AuR.

11 continued.
12 noon. lines forward and took up a position with its right flank resting about F.27.c.05 and its left flank F.22.c.23. Between was the Battalion Support to the 10th and 11th Btns E. Yorkshire Regt which were holding a line west of DOULIEU.

On the evening the right two companies which formed as it extends the right of the 10th E. York. Regt to the Source from L.4.c.73 to L.3.a.40. The left two companies took new position in F.27 in support. previously held by the left two companies remaining in support in F.27. Later in the evening the 2 companies in support in F.27 extended the line west wall to L.16.

Just before dawn the line held by the Battalion was taken over by Battalions of 29th Division and the position occupied in F.27 + F.22 during the afternoon of 11th inst was taken up.

During the early afternoon of 11th inst Battalion HQ has been established at F.27.b.24 but was moved back to F.12.c.96.

AuR 1/20000
AuR
AuR

4 copies

WAR DIARY or INTELLIGENCE SUMMARY

Place	Date	Hour	Summary of Events and Information	Remarks and references to Appendices
	13	continued		
		9.15 AM	The enemy attacked our troops on our left flank gave way. The 2 right companies were unable met in artillery formation to extend the support line to the North through F13 c and to the Brigade was ordered to reinforce on the line of the PAU du LEET. The 11th E./Lan. R. was already forming from HAUTE MAISON to F13 central and the 10th E. York. Regt was on its left. The 11th E. York Regt were to extend the line with orders to the left had old up take up the position then heavily left up the East Yorks R. shrad. any machine gun fire received from the 10 E. York R. shrad. The enemy were advancing along the railway and consequently the 11 E. York R. Kresterin left trek and took up a line HAUTE MAISON — Railway F8d. As the same time the 11 E. Lan. R. endeavoured to advance their Right to rest on BLEU and link up with the 29th Div there. Information was received that the enemy were in	ans. ans.

A.5834   Wt. W4973/M687   750,000   8/16   D. D. & L. Ltd.   Forms/C.2118/13.

Army Form C. 2118.

WAR DIARY
or
INTELLIGENCE SUMMARY.
(Erase heading not required.)

Place	Date	Hour	Summary of Events and Information	Remarks and references to Appendices
OUTTERSTEENE	13.		Battalion marched to join Fwd. LINES — EIDGTZ will post in front of the Wood in Fwc. That was an extension of the 29ᵗʰ Div. which had a line running through VIEUX BERQUIN to the right and the 10ᵗʰ E YORK R. to the left. The 10 E York R. had attended on a line running W. of MERRIS Battalion HQ HE/on R. were established at EllESS. During the afternoon, the right flank troops Sasa way to the high ground of VIEUX BERQUIN and at dusk it was necessary to withdraw the right flank of E 19 Central. This was done upon receipt of orders from the Brigadier-General and was carried out after the enemy attack had been repulsed.	AWR AWR AWR

Army Form C. 2118.

WAR DIARY
or
INTELLIGENCE SUMMARY.
(Erase heading not required.)

Place	Date	Hour	Summary of Events and Information	Remarks and references to Appendices
	14		During the day the Australian Troops had established their running troops E11 to E22 b and ceased to Ath. the battalion to under orders withdrew to complete the line and marched to billets at PRADELLES.	Refer to map Sheet 36A NE 1/20000 aur.
HONDEGHEM.		4 p.m.	Marched to billets in V.10 (Sheet 27 SE Hazebrouck).	aur.
	14-19		Reequipping and refitting. A composite Brigade was formed from the 92nd and 93rd Bns. this battalion found 3 [?] and generated with the 1st BE York r Lanc: Regt to form the 94th Composite Battalion. 1 Coy and 2 Companies were formed by the 4/E Lan R and 2 Coy by B 4/L R. Major L'Estomin in command. 94 Composite Battalion that now took part in the HAZEBROUCK Defences (H0-2m) in I5 26 c and E1 and 2. the 2nd Iron Guards were on the Right and the 92nd Composite Battalion on the left Battn HQ L'HOFFAND (V23c).	Refer Sheets 36A NW and 27 SE box 1/20000 aur. aur.

WAR DIARY
or
INTELLIGENCE SUMMARY.

Army Form C. 2118.

Place	Date	Hour	Summary of Events and Information	Remarks and references to Appendices
	18		Took carriers out in HAREBROCK Dyke Rd.	ansr
	19		Carparts Baton split up and 11E/Lan R. recorganized into 4 companies forming 10 platoons. 11E.Lan.R. took over posns of front line held by 5th Australian Infantry Batt. Frontage held E21.c.90 – E16.d.91. 4 platoons in the front line – 2 in support and one in reserve. Battalion HQ E15.d.39.	ansr
	25/26		2nd Inst Guards on the Right and the 11E.York Regt on the Left. On the night 21/26 Batn in relieved by the 10E.York Regt and took over the support line previously held by York Battalion. Dispositions – 2 Coys holding support line E21.d.19 – E15.d.19 One company E20.a and one company E26 as Bat reserve. Counter-attack.	ansr
	27/28		Battalion relieved on the night 27/28: and moved into Camp Reserve in V10.	ansr
	28-30		Training and Baths. Working party of 200 OR provided daily to ansr	ansr

WAR DIARY
or
INTELLIGENCE SUMMARY.
(Erase heading not required.)

Army Form C. 2118.

Place	Date	Hour	Summary of Events and Information	Remarks and references to Appendices
			Work in the FAZEBROUCK Defences. Reorganisation carried out.	A.R.
			Casualties during the week.	
			Killed 2 Officers 33 O.R.	
			Wounded 9 Officers 149 O.R.	
			Missing 47 O.R.	
			4 Officers went to England sick	
			4 Officers and 271 O.R. joined the Battalion during the week.	

In the Field
May 1. 1918.

A.H. Pankhurst
Lieut. Col. comdg
11E. Lancashire Regt.

31ST DIVISION
92ND INFY BDE

11TH BN EAST LANCS REGT
FEB 1918 - JLY 1919

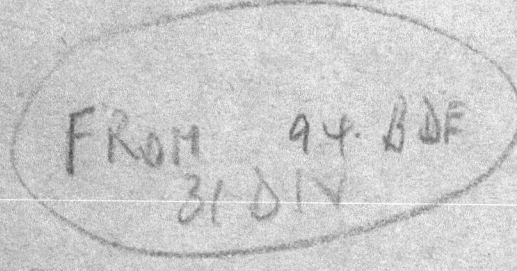

FROM 94 BDE
31 DIV

92/31.

Volume XXIX.

Vol 27

27. Z.
3 sheets

Confidential.

War Diary.

11th Battn. E. Lancs Regiment.

May. 1918.

Army Form C. 2118.

WAR DIARY
or
INTELLIGENCE SUMMARY.
(Erase heading not required.)

Instructions regarding War Diaries and Intelligence Summaries are contained in F. S. Regs., Part II. and the Staff Manual respectively. Title pages will be prepared in manuscript.

Place	Date	Hour	Summary of Events and Information	Remarks and references to Appendices
			11th Battalion East Lancashire Regiment	
			Vol III 1915	
			May 1915	
HONDEGHEM	1–8		Battalion remained in VIII Supply working parties for the Reinforce Division.	
	9		Battalion moved up into Reserve to the METEREN Ridge occupying trenches war ROUGE CROIX windmill and BAKERSHILLE switch line. Remain in Reserve.	MK
CAESTRE	9			MK
	"15		15 West York Regt & East Lancs to the Right. Battalion relieved 15 West York Regt. Front age from METEREN Begin Ruts–Seine METEREN.	
METEREN Sector	15/16		15 x 150 9.15. Into 1 coy. and 1 coy. in Support 1st Queenslanders 11/5 E York Regt to top by day. Remainder on the Right.	MK
	19/20		Left Company finished trenches now 15 18E York R. in artillery line.	MK

Army Form C. 2118.

WAR DIARY
or
INTELLIGENCE SUMMARY.
(Erase heading not required.)

Instructions regarding War Diaries and Intelligence Summaries are contained in F. S. Regs., Part II. and the Staff Manual respectively. Title pages will be prepared in manuscript.

Place	Date	Hour	Summary of Events and Information	Remarks and references to Appendices
Dressieré	9/1/21		Battalion left Boundary at ALBERT - MEAULTE Road (incl.) – Coys in billets in Dressieré.	
			Relieved by 1st Bn York & Lanc. Rgt in front line, and went to Reserve posn near Fort le Croix. Line now presently occupied.	
	30/11		Reduced to 9th Bde Reserve - 9th Div. and moved by Bus into Tramway Camp at LUMBRES.	
Lumbres	31-31		Battalion train up – Pursue drivers to Divisional School up Drive and Specialist training. Casualties during the month: Killed 6 OR. Wounded 1 offr. 15 OR. 1 OR. Drafts amounting to 15 officers and 154 OR joined during the month.	

June 30 1915. Lt. Col. in the Field.

signatures
Major Comdt
16 Regt.

WAR DIARY
INTELLIGENCE SUMMARY

Army Form C. 2118.

11 E Lanc Rgt
June 1918 V.I. 28

Place	Date	Hour	Summary of Events and Information	Remarks and references to Appendices
			11th Battalion East Lancashire Regiment.	
			Vol IV No 6.	
			June 1918.	
VIEILLE HEGAE	1-5		Battalion remained in camp at VAL de LUMBRES -	DHR
			musketry, company and battalion training -	
HANDESQUENT	6		Battalion moved by march route to camp at RACQUINGHEM.	DHR
	7-15		River divots to company and battalion training -	
WALLON CAPPEL	16		Battalion moved to WALLON CAPPEL - to an assembly position for taking up	DHR
			a line of defence either on LE PEUPLIER SWITCH or the WEST HAZEBROUCK defences	
			in the event of enemy attack.	
	17		Battalion moved to billets at BLARINGHEM.	DHR
BLARINGHEM	18		Battalion relieved the 2nd South Wales Borderers in front line - left sector	DHR
			right brigade - frontage E 23.c.0.7. – E 28.a.6.0.	
	25		Battalion relieved by 11th East Yorkshire Regt & moved into camp's near to	DHR
F.M. MOLARD			Grande Hazard east of HAZEBROUCK-MORBECQUE road.	
	24		Battalion moved into the line and took up assembly positions for	

WAR DIARY or INTELLIGENCE SUMMARY

Army Form C. 2118.

Place	Date	Hour	Summary of Events and Information	Remarks and references to Appendices
	28		attack. The attack was by the 5th & 31st Divisions the 5th Division on the right. The 92nd Inf. Bde. attacked with the 10th & 5th Yorkshire Regt on the right 11th East Yorkshire Regt in the centre and the 11th East Yorkshire Regt on the left. The objective of companies were - Z Coy - E 28 d 65.00 to E 28 d 64. W Coy - E 29 c 77.00 - E 29 c 55.90 - X Coy - E 29 d 5.0 - E 29 d 55. 34 (road inclusive) Y Coy E 29 d 55. 34 (road exclusive) - E 29 d 70.52. The formations were - Z Coy - 2 lines in extended order at 20 paces distance - W Coy - front of section on file distance 1+ 2 lines in extended order on W. Coy's front of section on file distance X & Y Coys - 2 lines of sections in file distance passing 2 Coys objectives. There was 50 yards between each on passing W Coy's objective. The Battalion attacked at 6 A.M. All objectives were taken. The following material was captured ———— 10 light machine guns, 2 heavy machine guns, 1 heavy trench mortar, 2 medium mortars, and 2 light field guns —	CHL CHL CHL CHL LHL LWL LWL
GRAND HASARD	30		The Battalion was relieved by the 24th R.W. Fusiliers and moved into camp near to GRAND HASARD - Casualties from 1/6/18 to 29/6/18 - Killed 2 officers [2/Lieut H.H. Saunders Capt. P.J. Torrand] Wounded 14 O.R.	LHL

WAR DIARY
or
INTELLIGENCE SUMMARY.
(Erase heading not required.)

Army Form C. 2118.

Place	Date	Hour	Summary of Events and Information	Remarks and references to Appendices
			Casualties from 2/6/18 to 30/6/18.	
			Killed 2 Officers (Lt R.H. Freeman) and 38 O.R.	DHL
			(Lt B.F. MacKenzie)	
			Wounded 9 officers (Capt G Hope Bentley M.C. and 195 O.R.	DHL
			(a)Capt Rob Chadwick M.C.	
			Lt G.B.W. Gyldher	
			Lt S.W. Pigott	
			2Lt G.H.J. Greenhill	
			2Lt R.D. Harley	
			2Lt J.R. Stolden	
			Missing 11 O.R.	DHL
			Drafts amounting to 8 officers and 129 O.R. joined the battalion during the month.	
			July 2nd 1918. In the field.	

L H Lewis
Major Commanding
11th E. Lancashire Regt.

July 1916

11 E Lan SG1

JSL 29

Army Form C. 2118.

WAR DIARY
or
INTELLIGENCE SUMMARY.
(Erase heading not required.)

Instructions regarding War Diaries and Intelligence Summaries are contained in F.S. Regs., Part II. and the Staff Manual respectively. Title pages will be prepared in manuscript.

Place	Date	Hour	Summary of Events and Information	Remarks and references to Appendices
GRAND HAZARD			11th Battalion East Yorkshire Regt. Vol III. No 7. July 1916.	Maps Maps France Sheet 36A 1/40,000 SH 1/10,000
	1-4		The battalion remained in Camp at GRAND HAZARD in Divisional reserve. Period occupied in specialist training.	
	7.		The battalion moved out of the line, relieving the 12th York & Lancasters Regt. in the front line sector.	
	8.		The battalion relieved the 10th Yorkshire Lancaster Regt. in the right subsector of the Left Brigade front. Two companies in front, 1 & 2 in support, hdqtrs from E 23 a 88 & E 29 b 44.	
	16.		The battalion was relieved by the 12th K.R. Royal Scots Fusiliers & proceeded to the Camp previously occupied at the GRAND HAZARD.	
	16/22		The battalion was in Divisional reserve. Period occupied in specialist training, musketry & rifle competitions.	
	22.		The battalion moved into the line in the left subsector of the Brigade front, relieving the 17th Battalion Durham Light Infantry.	
	30.		The battalion was relieved by the 11th East Yorkshire Regt. & proceeded unto Brigade reserve.	
			Casualties during period — killed — offrs —, O.R. 8 wounded 1 off., 35 O.R.	
			Drafts amounting to 11 offrs + 336 O.R. joined the battalion during the month.	

A.W. Peshawar
Lt Colonel
Commanding
11th E Lancashire Regt

August 1916
11 E Lanc [?]
Army Form C. 2118.

WAR DIARY or INTELLIGENCE SUMMARY

11th Bn. E. Lancashire Regt.

Vol III   Month of August 1916

Place	Date	Hour	Summary of Events and Information	Remarks and references to Appendices
LAMOTTE SECTOR	1–3		Battalion in Brigade Reserve.	Othw. N/R
GRAND HAZARD	3		Moved by billets to MORBECQUE – Brigade being in Div. Reserve – Training (cont'd not during the week)	L.H.L.
French line	3–9		Battalion relieved 15th Bn W. York. Regt. in Rt. Subsector. Battalion Hr	L.H.L.
LAMOTTE	9/10		61st Div. on R and 11E. York R on left. 2 Companies ill etc.	L.H.L.
	10–13		and 2 in "Z" line.	
Reserve	13/14		Relieved by 15th Bn KOYLI and moved into Battn. Reserve.	L.H.L.
French line	14/15		Relieved 10th E. York. R. in Front line. R. Subsector	
	15–19		on R and 13th Bn. Norfolk Regt. on L. 11E. York R.	P.H.L.
			line advanced about 200 yards during stay in line. Lost	
			First Casualty by shelling on night 17/18 inst.	
Reserve	19	9.00	Relieved by 13. By 10E York R and moved into Bre Reserve	P.J.L.
			at LE SOUVERAIN.	
HALLEN CAPPEL	21		And Nen camp near STACON CAPPEL (U176)	L.H.L.

30.Z
2 sheets

WAR DIARY
or
INTELLIGENCE SUMMARY
(Erase heading not required.)

Army Form C. 2118.

Instructions regarding War Diaries and Intelligence Summaries are contained in F. S. Regs., Part II. and the Staff Manual respectively. Title pages will be prepared in manuscript.

Place	Date	Hour	Summary of Events and Information	Remarks and references to Appendices
LA BREWARDE	23rd		March route to camp Via a 7, N. & HAZEBROUCK taking over from 13 Bn. NORFOLK R. Bryde + Div. Bomb.	J H L
FLÊTRE	24th		March by road route V13 d33 all all men ung to Dis. Bomb. nil were detach by enemy Aircraft. Reinforcement during march 10 O.R. 121 O.R. Casualties (other) Killed 11 O.R. Wounded 15 O.R. 79 O.R. Bn des d. + m. m. g. 3 O.R. being 1 OR.	J H L

Sept 25th 1915.

Major Commanding
11th Lancashire [Fus.]

WAR DIARY or INTELLIGENCE SUMMARY

11 E Lane
V.R. 31

Army Form C. 2118.

11th Bn. E Yorkshire Regt.
Vol III No 8 September 1918

Place	Date	Hour	Summary of Events and Information	Remarks and references to Appendices
FLÊTRE	1		Refer Maps Sheets 27, 28 and 36A 1/40000	
RESERVE	3		The Battalion marched in and moved to W.B.a. to relieve the 2nd Div. Boundary in Brigade sector –	
			Relieved the 10th S. Yorks Regt in the line – N Boundary the post line N of	
FRONT LINE	4/5		64. E5 – 73.6 – 3 Battalions and attacked and at 6.30 a.m. Patrols went out to	
	5		an enemy withdrawal was suspected. The front line about B.16.c.21 – D.13.b.7.9 – Forward	
			Indecisive to reach the front line about B.16.c.21 – These patrols went	
			forward under enemy machine gun fire until the boot place at 5 from	
			an extreme enemy outpost patrol position was reached. Late night – The enemy then	
			with 2 Coy on the 27 y in the evening 4 & on late night – The attack was answered up to	
			gained a foothold of the advancing forces. the first possibilities the fight	
			the left that attack was reached heavy machine gun fire considerable attack on the right	
			as far as their objective. Our enemy counter attack and 2 machine guns	
			Ground was given up – About 20 prisoners were captured	
	6/7		Relieved by the 11th E York Regt and proceeded to camp at A.11.d.7.3.	
	7/8		Battalion relieved the 10th E York Regt in the line.	
	8/9		Battalion relieved by the 10th E York Regt and the 11th E York Regt and	
			proceeded to camp at A.11.a.87.	
	10/11		Battalion relieved the 11th E York Regt and the 11th E York Regt in the	
			line, W & Y Coys in the front posts and Z Coy in support in the W.Staffs	

Army Form C. 2118.

WAR DIARY
or
INTELLIGENCE SUMMARY.
(Erase heading not required.)

Instructions regarding War Diaries and Intelligence Summaries are contained in F. S. Regs., Part II. and the Staff Manual respectively. Title pages will be prepared in manuscript.

Place	Date	Hour	Summary of Events and Information	Remarks and references to Appendices
	12/13		Battalion relieved by the 13th York Regt and moved by bus from BRILLIER to camp at V10 central.	
Our Brouwer	13/23		Battalion in divisional reserve – Company & Platoon training – Reclections training – Platoon tactical exercises – lectures.	
Hoogstraat	23		The battalion moved to Hoogstraat into billets.	
	24		The battalion bivouaced by Routten and then by smell Corps to Allanbrecht. During the 12th Norfolk Regt. in Brigade support – Company training.	
	26		The remainder of the Brigade were relieved northwards and the battalion bivouaced with boundaries as follows. Relieved front of ours 2/16 London Regiment – U13 b 29, W clong (rail bridge) to U 26 d 58. North – U9 central. U6 central – U Metherynel – T18 b 49. South – T18 M49. – T18 M43 – U 196 24 along light railway U15 a 21. T18 a 49. T18 a 44. – U14 d 80. Moved along railway E/W between square – an enemy withdrawal was expected & orders were issued for an attack to take place if enemy evacuation followed an attack further north. "Assembly positions" of Company W Cgy from U9 a 83 to U10 a 85. Z Cgy from U9 a 21 to U10 a 23. Y Cgy from U9 b 28.75 to U10 d 44. X & Y Cgys more suitable the front objective which was supported by W & Z Cgys for second objective. 1st objective was U 8.d.12. to 44.14. d. 99. 2nd objective was U 8 central to 2215.b.25.80 to 2215.b.9.5.
			(One Platoon of X Company was attached to the 2/16 London on the left & one platoon of Bret Wallis was attached to X Coy.)	

A.5834 Wt. W4973/M687 750,000 8/16 D. D. & L. Ltd. Forms/C.2118/13.

WAR DIARY or INTELLIGENCE SUMMARY

Army Form C. 2118.

Place	Date	Hour	Summary of Events and Information	Remarks and references to Appendices
	Oct 5th 1918		Zero was at 3 p.m. The 2/1th L Hants Regt were on the left the 10 th E York Regt on the right. The barrage was good but thin - advancing at the rate of 100 yds for 3 minutes - 2 sections of Machine Guns cooperated - was in port Nw.d of overhead fire per per from 2x3 right. At 3.34 pm informants from the O.P. that the first objective was taken. Prisoners reported Germans on the left objective were taken but on the right enemy resistance was heavy and a stubborn fight from his strong hold from 2.14 rendered forward the LA HUTTE - artillery were ordered to continue firing on the right for 15 minutes. The 10th E York Regt on the right was found most forward and the defensive flank on the left was unnecessary. The 92nd Bde with the object of blocking the enemy retreat through HOUTHEM to a junction forward over Lys feeder - in the 29th and 31 Bde were ordered to join the line reached about R 13 and respectively. RESERVES 15 & QUE sent the 10th E York Regt & the 12.12 E Lan. R. where to join on the night 29/30th and the instruction about the 11th E Lan Regt. They were to operate about St Pierres-Cappelle to the old front line. During the operations was to be withdrawn to fall [new] and 19 machine guns - 2 heavy mortars and were taken - capitulated and some rescued from Military Asylum of Ypres and anti-tank guns. Capitulated manages were received near Capinghem. About 40 horses.

Casualties - Army ranks
  13 offrs, 340 O.R.
  Wounded 3 offrs, 2/14 Alderson, 2/14 Clarke, 41 O.R.
  Missing 6 offrs, 258 O.R.
  4b O.R.

A.D. ull ____ Captain
Commanding 11 th E Lan. R. |

11 East Lancs Regt
32.Z
Hostels

WAR DIARY or INTELLIGENCE SUMMARY
Army Form C. 2118.

Place	Date	Hour	Summary of Events and Information	Remarks and references to Appendices
			11th Battalion East Lancashire Regiment Vol III. No 9. October 1916. Ref Maps Sheets 27, 28, 29, 36 & 37 1/40000	
HILL 63 PLOEGSTEERT	1/3		The battalion remained in Brigade support on Hill 63 with X and Z Companies in large dug outs at Hyde Park Corner and W Company at Petit Monque Farm. Salvage and carrying parties were supplied.	CJK
	3/4		The battalion relieved the 11th E. York Regt in C1 subsector (PLOEGSTEERT) into Headquarters at the Convent. X, Y, and Z Coys were in the front line and W Coy in support. The day and night were spent in patrolling the West bank of the LYS and in attempts to cross. 2/Lieut RICHMOND succeeded in getting down on the enemy bank in daylight and patrolled some distance on the East side. By night enemy machine guns prevented patrols from getting near now. Two more strong an considerable attempts of machine guns on the rest of the river.	CJK
MESSINES MESSINES	4/5		The battalion was relieved by the 15th W York Regt and proceeded to camp at T.10.d.01. (near NEUVE EGLISE)	CJK
BAILLEUL	6		The 92nd Bde. moved into Divisional Reserve and the battalion proceeded to camp at S.23.d.35. (near BAILLEUL) taking over from the 12th R. Scots Fusiliers.	CJK
	6-12		The battalion carried out daily training. A 30 yards range was constructed near the camp for rifle & Lewis Gun practice. Divl: Conway assumed command of the battalion on the 4th inst.	CJK
PLOEGSTEERT	12/13		The battalion relieved the 12th Norfolk Regt in C1 subsector (PLOEGSTEERT) moving off in Coys on Spinney by light railway. W and Z Coys were in the front line. HYDE PARK CORNER by battalion headquarters in LONDONFARM and X and Y Coys in support — with the LYS now in SUPPORT FARM. An enemy withdrawal was suspected and the extremely patrolled and efforts made to cross and form bridgeheads.	CJK

WAR DIARY
or
INTELLIGENCE SUMMARY.
(Erase heading not required.)

Army Form C. 2118.

Place	Date	Hour	Summary of Events and Information	Remarks and references to Appendices
	13/4		W Coy withdrew rats support 2 company taking over the whole of the battalion frontage two 500 yards which was taken over by the 10th P York Regt Patrols of 2 coy met considerable opposition the enemy having strong machine gun posts at or near all bridges. Valuable information concerning the position of enemy posts was brought in. the troops of the river and the enemy tanks of obtained —	DHR
	14/15		Patrols continued but the enemy was still in strength on the enemy tanks of the river — some in company were practically ended by 0700 in the River. Enemy activity decreased and red pyrotechnic lights were seen in the Machine headquarters during the night machine gun fire continued throughout the 14th inst —	DHR
	15		The patrols in front of enemy withdrawal was noticed on the first advance to a line made in two decades W and 2 Coys moving through strong points from to East of FRELINGHIEN – DOULIEUT and X and Y Coys passing through. On the night of the 15th R. the enemy the QUESNOY – COMINES Railway. Further advance was checked just near the river was very quiet and patrols pushed further ahead bank of the LYS at PONT ROUGE and 2 coys hqrs 500 yards further round. The river was crossed by rafts when their highpoints were established. companies crossed the river and W and 2 Coy established the first objectives reached opposition. X Coy formed though to the reserve objectives on the left and W Coy on the right	DHR
	16.		the QUESNOY – COMINES Railway was established and W Coy were ordered to hold the line. X Y and 2 Coys being in support the Nalen headquarters moved to PONT ROUGE on the 16th inst and later to the rat footing in QUESNOY – Rations were brought so far as the LYS by George	DHR

A5834 Wt. W4973/M687 750000 8/16 D. D. & L. Ltd. Forms/C.2118/13

WAR DIARY or INTELLIGENCE SUMMARY.

Army Form C. 2118.

Place	Date	Hour	Summary of Events and Information	Remarks and references to Appendices
QUESNOY	17		The Brigade continued its advance the Battalion moving into Brigade support. The river DEULE which runs Eastwards from the L41 was crossed by trestle bridges which the Battalion prepared by the aid of long planks spread over the bridges. The moving was by single file. All old bridges had been completely destroyed. The Battalion proceeded in an arc to E 15 E 22 and E 28 a confusion being caused in places. The Brigade outpost line formed by the 10th R. York R. was about two yards East of this area - the Brigade Battalion were ordered to meet a BONDUES this area was Battalion Headquarters was at the Chateau in LASSERRE.	L.W.R.
	18		The advance guard of the Brigade advanced through TURCOING Battalion formed two separate deal of TURCOING but was eventually forced through. The enemy had his artillery in position. The 2nd C. Batty 170 Bde R.F.A. and C. Bty 31 Medium Bty Battn left BONDUES at 5 am, and passed through the outpost line of 19th I York Regt w Company found the enemy gone. No opposition was encountered in TURCOING. The town was full of civilians who gave the Battalion with great enthusiasm. East of the river W.X. and Y companies advanced to their objective (Z company being in support) but met opposition east of WATTRELOS the enemy began to shell WATTRELOS very heavy and considerable machine gun fire. Every horseless shells and there was considerable machine gun fire. Every horseless ing gradually overcome and all companies reached their objectives Battalion headquarters moved to W. MAIRE WATTRELOS. some prisoners were captured. The line extended from from WERSEAUX through A.12 canal to the canal in A 27 A and was held and maintained with flank units. The 11 W.S. York Regt formed the advance from of the Brigade forming through TURCOING and 11 I Kar Regt in the morning of the 19th and the Battalion marching to Billets.	L.W.R.
	19			L.W.R.

WAR DIARY
or
INTELLIGENCE SUMMARY.
(Erase heading not required.)

Army Form C. 2118.

Place	Date	Hour	Summary of Events and Information	Remarks and references to Appendices
TOURCOING	10.25		The Brigade came into Tourcoing as Divisional support on the 20th and the battalion garrisoned Tourcoing. The inhabitants continued to show their appreciation of their relief from enemy control. Company and Platoon training was carried out until the 25th. when the Division was ordered to proceed next to relieve the 7th Division.	LHR
	25		The Battalion proceeded by road to EVERNE. The Corps Commander expressed his great satisfaction with the turn out and deception of the battalion on the march.	LHR
	26		The battalion relieved the Scottish Rifles and R. Scots Fusiliers in the line in the INGOYGHEM sector. W and Z Coys in the front line and X and Y Coys in support. The enemy was in great strength in machine guns and was very active in artillery fire. - especially any movement from turn to turn. A Coy proceeded by guns astride the road. Belgian civilians remained in their farms in many cases in the shelled area. The line of posts was advanced about 400 yards but the enemy maintained strong machine gun fire. The Battalion was relieved by the 12th R Scots Fusiliers and proceeded to billets in HARLEBEKE.	LHR
	27-?		Reinforcements during month :- 185 O.R. 6 offrs Casualties { Killed - - - - - - - - 5 O.R. Wounded - 2 offrs 2d.Lt. R.L. Munday, T.F, 2d.Lt. M. Shuttleworth T.F, 57 O.R.	LHR

L.H. Evans
Major Commanding
11th East Lancashire Regt.

11 A Hawes Vol 33

337
3 sheets

WAR DIARY
or
INTELLIGENCE SUMMARY.

Army Form C. 2118.

11th Battalion West Yorkshire Regiment   Ref Maps 27, 28, 29, 1/40,000
Vol III   No. 10.   November 1918   Hazebrouck Sh 1/100,000

Place	Date	Hour	Summary of Events and Information	Remarks and references to Appendices
WAREGEM	1		The Battalion had moved from HAERLEBEKE to billets near INGOYGHEM following up the advance of the 94th Brigade on the 31st ult., and started the battlefield capturing several prisoners & bringing in a considerable amount of material including 10 machine guns. The battalion received back 6 killed at WAREGHEM.	PH
HALLUIN	3		The battalion moved to billets in HALLUIN.	CHK
KLOOSTERHOEK	7		The battalion moved to billets near KLOOSTERHOEK in close support to the 12th Yorks Regt. W company moved forward by night through the 12th York Regt and secured the DEN AYTGRACHT CANAL at RUGEE with the object of establishing posts on the west bank of the ESCAUT. The resistance of the enemy was very bad and there were considerable losses. Posts were established on the East bank of the DEN AYTGRACHT.	AHK
VELGHEM	8/9		The battalion relieved the 12th Yorks. W, Y Coys & Coy. HQ. on the right, Y Coy on the left, and Z Coy in support at BOSCH. Battalion Headquarters were at DRIESCH. W company carried out a successful minor operation under the support of artillery, machine guns and trench mortars. They established a line of posts on the west bank of the ESCAUT.	AHK
ESCAUT	9		31st Division started an advance from the line of the railway running through P.11 Central - P3.d - P6.a - P3.b.a. The battalion moved forward. Information was received that the enemy were.	

WAR DIARY
or
INTELLIGENCE SUMMARY.
(Erase heading not required.)

Army Form C. 2118.

Place	Date	Hour	Summary of Events and Information	Remarks and references to Appendices
ATHUSIES	10		attempt and an attempt was made to cross the ESCAUT by the bridge of a Water bridge. There was successful without opposition. "Y" Company crossed at RUGGE X.day by rafts at ESCANAFFLES. Their conforming advanced to MT. de LEUCLUS which was occupied by men. The battalion reached the orders to halt and allow the 11th Bn. 6 Yorkshire Regt. to take up the advance. This battalion passed through and the 11th Bn. 6 Lancashire advance. This battalion passed through and the 11th Bn. 6 Lancashire Regt. came into support in WEETS at ANOUGIES.	LHR
QUESNAU	11		The brigade continued the advance the 11th Bn. 6 Lancashire Regt. being in support. By night the brigade had reached a line on the high ground east of MONT de KINOGS and the 11th 6 W. Lancashire Regt. was billeted in QUESNAU. In the early morning orders were received with the information that the enemy had accepted the terms on which the allied governments were prepared to grant an armistice and that hostilities would cease at 1100 hours. The battalion was ordered to take up a line of laverny posts east of QUEFFEDINES with advance to allow no one to pass further east and west from the enemy's lines. Precautions were allowed in the case of french troops and civilian audience. These posts were established by midnight.	LHR
QUEFFEDINES				LHR
QUESNAU	13		The brigade moved back to form the 37th Army and its battalion moved into WEETS at QUESNAU being relieved by a battalion of the 41st Division.	LHR

WAR DIARY
or
INTELLIGENCE SUMMARY.
(Erase heading not required.)

Army Form C. 2118.

Place	Date	Hour	Summary of Events and Information	Remarks and references to Appendices
BRANDHOEK BOSCH	15		The Battalion moved to BANHOUT BOSCH.	JHR
MORRE	16		The battalion moved to MORRE and remained in billets until the 23rd and battalion baths were completed. On the 22nd met a ceremonial parade of the Brigade was held when the Divisional Commander presented medal ribbons to officers & men who had received awards since June 27th last.	JHR
MENIN	23		The battalion received orders that the Division moved forward to the ST OMER area. The first day's march was to MENIN.	JHR
LOMMERTINGE	26		From MENIN the battalion moved to billets at VLAMERTINGHE 2 January through YPRES. The Divisional Commander sent the battalion round YPRES & congratulated the officers, warrant officers, NCOs & men on the host & soldierly bearing and the spirit in which they had endured a trying month.	JHR
ST ELOI	27		The battalion moved to billets on the ST ELOI area (STEENVOORDE)	JHR
REBECQUE	28		The battalion moved to billets at LA CROSIE (REBECQUE)	JHR
ST OMER	29		The battalion moved to the Cavalry Barracks ST OMER. 213 other ranks, 6 officers	JHR
			Reinforcements during month. (2nd L. Humphries, 2nd D. Brogdan, 2nd Lt. Whelan, 2nd Lt. Trenair, 2/Lt. H. Tapper and 2/Lt. R.H. Ward)	
			Casualties Killed Officers Nil Other ranks 3 Wounded Officers Nil Other ranks 24	

LewisMayer
Lt Col. Commanding
11th L. East Lancaster Regt.

11 E Lanc Regt

WAR DIARY / INTELLIGENCE SUMMARY

Army Form C. 2118.

Place	Date	Hour	Summary of Events and Information	Remarks and references to Appendices
			11th Battalion East Lancashire Regiment Vol III No 11. December 1918.	
ST. PIERRE	1-31		The Battalion remained in the Country Barracks St Pierre. Classes were formed under the direction of 2/Lieut Clarke on the 24th inst. a Brigade ceremonial parade was held & the Bgde Commander Bt. Col. Rev Ratcliff D.S.O. presented when the Bgde Commander Bt. Col. Rev Ratcliff D.S.O. presented the Croix de Guerre to 2/Lt F Handby 241229 Pte H. Wilkinson 240457 Pte O. Parkinson and 240851 Sgt. R. Helmet. During the month submarines were sent to Rifle Mat 11423 B Robin 522 — 7/100 ord.	LHK LHK LHK
			for dispersal & review work with their former employers. The following were mentioned in dispatches (November 8th): Major E H Lewis D.S.O. M.C., Capt Geo L.R. Freulan D.S.O. M.C., Capt. D.H.B. Stonefelt and No 36862 Pte T.D. Donnell D.S.O. M.C., Capt. D.H.B. Stonefelt.	LHK LHK
			Reinforcements 3 officers (Capt Hampson Capt Fardon D.S.O M.C. 2/Lt Kelley) 68 O.R.	LHK

EHKevan
Major
Commanding
11th Bn. E. Lancashire Regt.

Sh. 7.
1 sheet.

WAR DIARY
or
INTELLIGENCE SUMMARY.

(Erase heading not required.)

Army Form C. 2118.

11th Battalion East Lancashire Regiment
Vol III Nos 12 January 1919
Ref Major HAZEBROUCK S.A.
1/100,000

Place	Date	Hour	Summary of Events and Information	Remarks and references to Appendices
St Omer	1-29		The battalion remained in St Omer. Education classes were continued at the Army School. The battalion football XI was defeated by the R.E. in the 3rd round of the Divisional Cup Competition. On the 15th inst the battalion (less B Coy & transport) moved into the Prison of War Camp at Dover on the Sunday Parade, were inspected by the French authorities. On the morning of the 29th inst the battalion received S Zevers notice to proceed to CALAIS on account of disturbances there. The battalion entrained at St Omer at 07.40 and arrived at CALAIS at 12.00.	
CALAIS	29-31		Proceeded to a camp 3 kilometres N of CALAIS. In the morning of the 30th inst. The battalion proceeded towards CALAIS in support of the 35th Division but were not required. At 16.00 the 3rd inst. the battalion returned to camp. At 05.00 on 31st met the battalion entrained at CALAIS at 17.00 hrs and arrived at 21.00 hours. A/Lt A.W. Pickman D.S.O. returned to the battalion from the 92nd Inf Bde on the 13rd inst. He returned again to command the 92nd Inf Bde on the 23rd inst. Major E.M. Reuss D.S.O. M.C. Proceed to England for demobilisation on the 21st inst. Reinforcements. 21 O.R. Members demobilised. Major Leuris 223 O.R.	

H.E. LANCS.

36.2
1st May

Army Form C. 2118.

WAR DIARY
or
INTELLIGENCE SUMMARY.
(Erase heading not required.)

Vol 36

1st Batt. King's Lancashire Regiment
Vol V No 19 February 1919.

Ref Map HAZEBROUCK 5A
1/100,000.

Place	Date	Hour	Summary of Events and Information	Remarks and references to Appendices
ST OMER	Feb 1919 1-28		The Battalion remained in St Omer. Educational classes were continued at the Army School. 26 N.C.O's & men were concentrated and proceeded to the Battalion on the 14th inst. 26 were killed, an arrival & distribution to Coys. presided by Lieut Col A.C.O.D.S.O. — M.S. Jones returned from XIX Corps Demobilization camp on the 16th inst & T.R. was under of Transport Officer. That Birkenshaw O.S.O. returned to the Battalion from 92nd Inf Brigade on the 8th inst. Capt J.G. Ash proceeded to England Demobilization on the 9th inst. Numbers demobilized 4 Officers 226 Other Ranks.	[initials]

B.O.H Capt
Commanding 1st Batt...

Army Form C. 2118.

WAR DIARY
or
INTELLIGENCE SUMMARY.
(Erase heading not required.)

Instructions regarding War Diaries and Intelligence Summaries are contained in F.S. Regs., Part II. and the Staff Manual respectively. Title pages will be prepared in manuscript.

Place	Date	Hour	Summary of Events and Information	Remarks and references to Appendices
ABBEVILLE	16th		Nothing to record	P.1
	17th		Detachment of 17 men employed by 10 m.n. for A & M bags	P.1
	18th			P.1
	19th		Reinforcements (4) O.R.s for 2nd Batt. S.Lanc.R. At B Coy relieved by 61st Div, transit from Depot.	P.1 P.1 P.1
	21st		Lieut. A.H. Brindell proceeded to England on Demobilization	
	22nd		Capt N.D. Hampson returned from leave. Had taken over Adjutancy second in command	P.1
	23rd		A + B Coys paraded from 0900 hours to 1200 hours & toe taken in Close order Drill, Saluting, Salutes & Salutes	P.1
	24th			P.1
	25th		Pass meeting held. Full available officers. It was decided that the Sports Depot Officers' Mess should be taken on by the Batt. A + B Coys paraded from 0900 to 1200 hours.	P.1
	26th		The Commanding Officer inspected H.Q. Personnel	P.1
	27th			P.1
	28th		"B" Coy caught a new firing party at funeral of A.P.M. 61st Div. Killed by being thrown from his horse	P.1
	30th		The Commanding Officer inspected A + B Coys. The turn out was very good	

P.L. Ingles Lt Col
2nd Yorkshire Regt
Comd 11th Bn West Yorkshires

WAR DIARY
or
INTELLIGENCE SUMMARY

Army Form C. 2118.

11 E Lanc Regt
M 38

Place	Date	Hour	Summary of Events and Information	Remarks and references to Appendices
ABBEVILLE	April 1919	1-30	11th Battn. East Lancashire Regiment Diary Guarding & Escorting Prisoners of War. Vol. III No 15 April 1919	
	1st		The Battalion remained in ABBEVILLE. Capt. Duff M.C., Capt R. Thinkler T.O., O.C, Capt A.H. Mangules 2/17 J. Walker, 2/Lt J.A. Hrign, 2/Lt J.H. Tappin proceeds to England for demobilization. 2 reinforcements arrived from 2nd Battn posted to D. Coy.	P.L.1
	2nd		Lieut A. Fairclough M.C. took over command of B Coy vice 2/Lt. G.E. Long M.C. passed cross to U.K.	P.L.1
	3rd		Lieut W.A. Bell 1/6 Kings Liverpool Regt taken on Strength & posted to D. Coy. Lt. Jarosse took on command of C Coy.	P.L.1
	4th		Lie O.R. joined the Battn from Attachment to 2nd Bn. Somer posted to D. Coy.	P.L.1
	5th		L.T.S. Dragged took over Armoury duties of T.O. He held I.D. for posts bars to U.K.	P.L.1
	6th		He also carried out the "Indoors" Sam Rnn first Prem at CampTheatre which was a great success.	P.L.1
	7th		2/Lt Griffin proceed to England for Demobilization. The following draft arrived 28 O.R. from 11 Manchester Regt.	P.L.1
	8th		Capt Rogers 2/6 Burton Light Infantry to O.R. for G. Battn. Westmoreland Fusiliers posted to B Coy.	P.L.1
	9th		Two reinforcements arrived for 2nd Battn. posted to C Coy.	P.L.1
	10th		Capt H.A. Newark C.F. proceeded to Rhine Armies	P.L.1
	12th		21 Reinforcements arrived from 1/5 S. Lan R.	P.L.1
	14th		Lt J. Wild and 2/Lt T. Parson proceeded to England for Demobilization. Lieut Col P.L. Aspen DSO assumed Six reinforcements arrived from 1/5 th S. Lan R. 11/3 st Yorkshire Regt	P.L.1
	15th		Lieut Col P.L. Aspen DSO MC resumed command of Battn.	P.L.1

WAR DIARY
or
INTELLIGENCE SUMMARY.
(Erase heading not required.)

Army Form C. 2118.

11 E Lane Rgt

Place	Date	Hour	Summary of Events and Information	Remarks and references to Appendices
Athnele	1919 Aug 1st		A & B Coys were inspected by the Brigadier. It was not till 1pm the Transport was inspected, as was schedule	#513
	2nd		Training to A & B Coys	#513
	2nd		Captain H.S. Brickell taken on strength of Battn. 2nd in Command	#513
	4th		Officers served in Elmwat Col	#513
	5th		Training as usual	#513
	6th		The following Officers taken on strength of Battn. Capt H Wilson re to assume command of C Coy. Lt H McA Leiacon re posted to C Coy. 2nd Lt J.P. Ritchie posted to C Coy. Lt F.J. Hughes posted to D Coy	#513
	7th		Route march of A & B Coy to Mackellar & back via No. 2 Stationary hospital Capt OD Hampson and Capt HH Lowery OC'd B coys & of A coy	#513
	8th		Reported by the Commanding Officer I all employed men Returned Proceeded to Bde Detail	#513
	9/10		Training as usual	#513
	12			
	13th		2/Lt Thomas & 2nd Lt A Perry joined Battn. & posted to A Coy	#513

08.2
3 sheet

WAR DIARY
or
INTELLIGENCE SUMMARY.
(Erase heading not required.)

Army Form C. 2118.

Place	Date	Hour	Summary of Events and Information	Remarks and references to Appendices
Athies	14		A/Lt Rays Raction at Montfliers	#SB
	15		Teams personal. 1st & 2 Officers & 2nd Lts parade the Batt's	#SB
			2nd 2/Lts Smith	
	16		Short Swing apparas at 2045 for the train.	#SB
	17		Detachments V.C. Coy at 507 & 508 Pnrs. relieved by D. Coy	#SB
			" D. Coy at Wail " B. Coy	
	18		Church parade	#SB
	19		Training	
	20		"	#SB
	21		2/Lt A Hall Joined the Group for 16/8/19	#SB
			Capt Hastings for Vector in Shakespeare plays	
	22		Route march	#SB
	23		Training	#SB
	24		Relief of detachments at Wail & 196 Pnr. by 2/5 Lond Rgt	#SB
	25			#SB
	26		Detachments by 7/14 " Lond " at 507 & 508 Pnrs. detachment of N°2 Factory	#SB

Army Form C. 2118.

WAR DIARY
or
INTELLIGENCE SUMMARY.
(Erase heading not required.)

Place	Date	Hour	Summary of Events and Information	Remarks and references to Appendices
Athralla to Havre	27th		Batt̄n moved from Athralla to Havre. C & D Coys Transport left by train at 0940 hrs A & B Coys & HQ Staff by train at 2100 hrs	#5B
	28th		Arriv in Havre - Take on No 1 Dispatching Camp.	#5B
	29th		Day spent settling down to new camp.	#5B
	30th		Training from 0900 hrs to 12.30 hrs Visited by Div: Gunsiah	#5B
	31st		The Brigadier visited the Battn,	#5B

#5 Buckell
Captain
Commanding 11 Bn E Lancashire Regt.

A5834 Wt. W4973/M687 750,000 8/16 D. D. & L. Ltd. Forms/C.2118/13.

Instructions regarding War Diaries and Intelligence Summaries are contained in F.S. Regs., Part II. and the Staff Manual respectively. Title pages will be prepared in manuscript.

WAR DIARY
or
INTELLIGENCE SUMMARY

11 E Lancs Rgt

Army Form C. 2118.

Place	Date	Hour	Summary of Events and Information	Remarks and references to Appendices
Le Havre	June 1919		11 Bn East Lancs Regiment Training — Escorts to POW —	
	1	30	Sunday — Church Parade —	
	2		O. Musicoff and 17 Details proceeded for demobilization to England. Lieut. & 210 Thompson took over duties of Staff Ct Bn.	
	3		Holiday in Honour of HM King George V Birthday.	
	4		Reinforcements from 16 RB, 1 Bn & Reserve? Cadre arrived	
	5		OC Sequna notifies on L.G.O.C. and assumes command of the Coy	
	6		Vice Lt Col Bell & 163 RB.	
	7		Lt A.M. Malenzie and 1p Nurses NC proceeded to England for demobilization. RSM Bewitt, Regts Gounho, & Officer arrives from Base. Dems draft arrives and in billets for rest. 10 183 R.T. School.	
	8		Whit Sunday — Church Parade —	
	9		Whit Monday — Holiday —	
	10		1 Reinforcements arrive	

WAR DIARY
or
INTELLIGENCE SUMMARY
(Erase heading not required.)

Army Form C. 2118.

Place	Date	Hour	Summary of Events and Information	Remarks and references to Appendices
Lestrem	11		Route march	
	12		2/Lt Ashe return from 2/6 Warwick Regiment	
	13		2/Lt Haliwell handed over 1st Coy to B Coy	
			2/Lt Brown MR was appointed Honorary Bandmaster	
			33 OR to strengthen from Bns Base, nearly Coy Bt arrived	
			1 Col Pl Hupa 2 Lt Manson commanding & the Bn	
	14		Sunday	
	15			
	16		Bn Pl consisted of nine's consisting of 1 Col P.S. Capt L A Leslie DSO	
			Capt McAvevin - Capt + 2nd Lieut. llC and con'experantatives	
			R.S.M. Merritt	
	17		A Ashe proceeded to Boulogne for demobilisation	
	18		Route March - Lecture	
	19		lecture by Lt Lenn on "Arab Italian War"	
	20		Almany Running	
	21		Sunday - Church Parade	
	22			
	23			
	24		were sent for leave R. Hayllew home	

Army Form C. 2118.

WAR DIARY
or
INTELLIGENCE SUMMARY
(Erase heading not required.)

Instructions regarding War Diaries and Intelligence Summaries are contained in F. S. Regs., Part II. and the Staff Manual respectively. Title pages will be prepared in manuscript.

Place	Date	Hour	Summary of Events and Information	Remarks and references to Appendices
Lahore	25		Move to Rafflles - Bn housed In 2 be-batching camp -	ini
	26		L.i. Coffrast removes elsewr to new camp	ini
	27		Heavy cleaning up camp and barracks Capt L. Bromfus we Drient on leave to UK.	ini
	28		He Fancouf wc annue awke of Fash Peace Terms accepted - Paris Fautes to which saluts fill 23:59 hs	ini ini
	29		Sunday Church Parade.	
	30		Holiday in honour of Peace Terms being signed	ini
	31		Drawing - Capt HS Buckley President of a Court Martial -	ini

P. L. Ingham
LT. COL.
COMMANDING 11TH BATTALION EAST LANCASHIRE REGIMENT.

WAR DIARY or INTELLIGENCE SUMMARY

(Erase heading not required.)

Army Form C. 2118.

COMMANDING 11TH BATTALION EAST LANCASHIRE REGIMENT.

LT. COL.,

R.L. Aspin(?)

Place	Date	Hour	Summary of Events and Information	Remarks and references to Appendices
Hoyflion	Sept 1919			
"	1st		Usual Training	
"	2nd		Battalion went to Mailly-Maillet and took train to Amiens. Capt W.F. Neill & Capt WS Hasler left Baton on UK leave viz: Capt Million & C.	
"	3rd		Usual Training	
"	4th		Received 7 scout armlets to be issued by H. Glam RS	
"	5th		Commdg Officer inspected Coy Lines.	
"	6th		Church Parade. Capt Shepherd. R.S. Battery of Instructors left.	
"	7th		Training as usual.	
"	8th		Lecture on "Arming Coy MGs" was delivered by Mr Weller, S. Renshaw. There was a large attendance.	
"	9th		Route March.	
"	10th		Commanding Officers parade. Lt R.H. Moss joined Baton for duty. Lieut E.H. Jones transferred from C to B Coy.	
"	11th		Capt L.A. Dalton Stone. President of Cat. Martial. On ?? Court Martial.	
"	12th		Peace celebration Parade by Battn. Capt W.L. Bingfield in command. Officers inspected by Lieut Coy Colonel Commanding. @ H.R.T. Smith from Bate took over to D S J.	
"	13th		Church Parade.	
"	14th		General Holiday. Peace Celebrations. Lieut Gort Walton left Batn to take part in the Corps Boxing. L/Cpl B. Brown Commanded the Rifle Grenade Platoon.	
"	15th		The Company Capt H.S. Bickerth President of a Ct Martial.	
			Parade as usual.	

C.O. Maud(?)

WAR DIARY
or
INTELLIGENCE SUMMARY.

(Erase heading not required.)

Army Form C. 2118.

COMMANDING 11TH BATTALION EAST LANCASHIRE REGIMENT.
LT. COL.'S

Place	Date	Hour	Summary of Events and Information	Remarks and references to Appendices
Heufflize	July 1		Usual Training	R. Ingles
	2		Battalion made route march to Motreuillaring Forest took supper & finished	
	3		Ladies Cup kept & Known	
	4		Usual Training	
	5		Band I tried arms to Eglise by the greater art	
	6		Usual officer inspected Coy lines	
	7		Church Parade	
	8		Col J Henry R Berry J Saunders C/5	
	9		Thomas returned	
	10		Lt Col's w Aug'st Courtesy was relieved by Acherely & Rourke.	
			Three one "Camp"	
	11		Route march Parade & Mutton Spoons News of City.	
			Company officers stentered the C.O. to lay	
			Lut S.H. Yule stentered Present & Col. Hudson Coy. selected	
	12		Cpl LA Butter took Parados o Church Parade	
			& pasos clerdn entitled by Lnon Col. A. Professor about	
	13		Chandlin Green & H R & Amdh. Some land when army July 5	
			Cht Parade Prize Celebrated. Pass to B	
	14		Regimental school was. Cpl. Myth the Boots Bret in the Prom Ponce LCN & Bater	
	15		the Company Culture Funded fo Col. Michaelhead & Sgts Scott & Brown	
			Capt A.B. Nicholls to Home	

WAR DIARY
or
INTELLIGENCE SUMMARY

Bahn at Hopfent   July 1919

(Erase heading not required.)

Army Form C. 2118.

COMMANDING 11TH BATTALION EAST LANCASHIRE REGIMENT.
LT. COL.s
R.L. Ingle

Place	Date	Hour	Summary of Events and Information	Remarks and references to Appendices
Hopflint	16th July		Route march to Fort de Hoc. Regt'l Routine Parties & fatigues.	
	17th		Light horse event in stage. PRs Dudley & Jennings attested.	
	18th		D.C.M. under sgts 3/6/19.	
	19th		Commanding Officer's Parade. Lecture on Naval History by Major Burn RN.	
	20th		Posted to D. Coy. 2 Lieuts Chopley & Ripple Mulder to Baker Place Attachot Enroute.	
	21st			
	22nd		Arrangements made by SM & Seper. VOs 2/pas 100. 2/pas 1 Lectrier reported to Church Parade.	
	23rd		Court of Enquiry. Music up't Wendergrass Capt. Workhis. As President.	
	24th		Col. P. Ingram	
	25th		Route march to Post de Hoc 2/Lt. G. Hanan Scanford Hotty posted to D. Coy. 2/Lt. FR Port Moreau Bolton posted to H. Coy.	
	26th		Rehearsal of S.M.G.C.'s inspection +1000 them not.	
	27th		Church Parade.	
	28th		Parades as usual.	
	29th		""	
	30th		Maj'r General Jeren CMG. DSO inspected Battn. And was very pleased.	
	31st		Route March to Post de Hoc. Swimming Corporals & shooting event.	

C. Coy.

WAR DIARY
or
INTELLIGENCE SUMMARY
(Erase heading not required)

Instructions regarding War Diaries and Intelligence Summaries are contained in F.S. Regs., Part II. and the Staff Manual respectively. Title pages will be prepared in manuscript.

Army Form C. 2118.

Bn. of H.Q. [illegible] July 1919

Place	Date	Hour	Summary of Events and Information	Remarks and references to Appendices
Henflin	16 July		Route march to [illegible]. Hot. Revd. Ratns. B.H. of [illegible] pr Bully & Turnips	
	17"		OC's Coy Rifle [illegible]. Coy Cmdg Offers Parade.	
	18"		Posted to D Coy noting by Major Dre.	
	19"		Relief of Bttn Russ attend [illegible] 500 left me. [illegible] & [illegible] report to [illegible]	
	20"		[illegible] gone [illegible]	
	21"		Col. & Capt. Turner & [illegible] to [illegible]	
	22"		Capt. Rogers to [illegible] on return about 9 Mph	
	23"		Revd [illegible] to Bttn on the [illegible] Rogers returned to H.Q.	
	24"		Mr. J.W. Harris rejoined Bttn. [illegible] at Hq to [illegible]	
	25"		Mr. Potts rejoin	
	26"		[illegible] at [illegible] no [illegible]	
	27"		Returned to M.S.C's at [illegible]	
	28"		Chief Phase	
	29"		Parade as usual. Mr. G. Eastwood Mr. G Spratt	
	30"		"B" Cord B Coys on no repaired boards. Hot weary Parades	
	31"		11½ p.m. Heavy thunder storm. Rain & hail. Storming Capnd. & Marker can't [illegible]	

Pl. Taylor

31ST DIVISION
92ND INFY BDE

92ND MACHINE GUN COY
JLY 1916 - FEB 1918

92nd Bde.
31st Div.

WAR DIARY

92nd BRIGADE

MACHINE GUN COMPANY

1st to 31st JULY 1916

Confidential

War Diary

of

92nd M. Gun Coy

1st July to 31st July
1916

Vol. VI 3

Army Form C. 2118.

WAR DIARY or INTELLIGENCE SUMMARY

(Erase heading not required.)

92nd Machine Gun Company for the month of **July 1916**

Place	Date	Hour	Summary of Events and Information	Remarks and references to Appendices
	1/7/16	7-30 A.M.	The 92nd Bde being in Reserve the cancelment by the 93rd & 94th Bde took place at 7-30 A.M: 20 minutes later orders received from Bde Hd Qrs for (8) guns to move forward under O.C. Coy to Rolland Trench (Map Ref France 57 D: NE: K 28 B 28) for the purpose of keeping fire to bear on points where enemy might collect to counter-attack on the Trenches won. N. Flank fire was maintained at fragment until the Bde withdrawn from the Trenches - 2/Lt E.B. White who was in charge of 4 of these guns was killed by a Rifle bullet about 4 PM and the gun was ordered forward to stop enemy who were observed to be bayoneting & pushing our wounded at (Ref Map as before - K 29 D 22.) The result was successful. The remaining 7 guns were kept in Reserve only one other casualty was sustained (wounded) up to mid-night when orders were received to withdraw from the Trenches & proceed to Bus-les-Artois.	
	2/7/16		Coy bivouacked in Bus Wood with orders to hold itself in readiness to move at 1 hour's notice the Bde being in Corps Reserve. Urgent order received to collect at once for all deficiencies in equipment this was carried out. Horse rental for was supplied but very little Sulphy applied. Order to move into Trenches	
	3/7/16		2/Lt R.A. Blake was conducted act. Order to move into Trenches received.	
	4/7/16		Order to move into Trenches cancelled. Coy enabled to get a bath in Bus order that Bde would move back was received.	
	5/7/16		Coy marched to Beauval via Sarton. Trps of France Zns 11 troops.	
	6/7/16		Coy marched to Bernaville via Candas	
	7/7/16		3 reinforcements received from Base. Remainder of day Training.	

Army Form C. 2118.

WAR DIARY
or
INTELLIGENCE SUMMARY

(Erase heading not required.)

No. 97th Machine Gun Company
for the month of July 1916

Place	Date	Hour	Summary of Events and Information	Remarks and references to Appendices
	8/7/16		Company marched to AUXI-LE-CHATEAU and entrained for THIENNES (sheet Ref. France sheet 36A 2200)	
	9/7/16		Marched from there to ROBECQ. During the march only one man fell out	
	10/7/16		Coy. training	
	11/7/16		Coy. training. Special attention being paid to Company Drill and Elementary Gun Drill	
	12/7/16		Company bathed. It has been our experience out here that baths together with clean shirts etc. are easily and frequently obtained	
	13/7/16		Company carried on with set programme of training.	
	14/7/16		Coy. marched to RIEZ-BAILLEUL (sheet Ref. Bethune combined sheet Scale 1:40,000)	
	15/7/16		Two officers proceeded up to line to make a reconnaissance of positions Coy. were taking over. The two emplacements taken over from 183rd M.G. Coy. were N13c0005 & N24c45.10 (sheet Ref. Vanchicoup France 36SW Scale 1/20000) Six emplacements taken over from 182nd M.G. Coy. were M30a15. M30a23. M30a23. M2Hc91. Also three other support posts in rear these positions having been reconnoitred were occupied the same night. Remaining half of Coy. moved into billets in Pont du Hem. (in reserve)	
	16/7/16		Guns occupied in reconnoitring & choosing alternative positions.	
	17/7/16		Received two reinforcements. From 14th to 24th the main work of the guns in the front line consisted of keeping open set gaps in enemy wire	

Army Form C. 2118.

WAR DIARY
or
INTELLIGENCE SUMMARY
(Erase heading not required.)

192nd Machine Gun Company
In the Trenches
July 1916.

Place	Date	Hour	Summary of Events and Information	Remarks and references to Appendices
	18/7/16		Effective support given to patrols and wiring parties by overhead fire from all guns in front line. It was observed that enemy rifle fire was much less while the patrols were out, clearly owing to our overhead fire.	
	19/7/16		Effective support was again rendered by our overhead fire to patrols and wiring parties & guns in the salient fired 6 belts from parapet at enemy machine gun firing at/of our planes from front line. Enemy machine gun promptly changed its position and was stopped firing there also	
		19.20	A vigorous fire was opened by two guns in left sector to assist the assault made by the 2nd Div on enemy front line and support trenches. 2nd Lt HAWORTH was killed by a rifle bullet on night of 19th It was his work that was mainly responsible for the appreciatory message received by O.C. coy from the O.C. 2nd Div "Wounded R.O.R. Wellesy." During the attack a German machine gun mounted on the parapet, together with gun team, was knocked out by our fire. During these operations all guns were subjected to a heavy bombardment. During day and night over 15,000 rds were expended	
	21/7/16		Gaps in enemy wire & communication trenches fired on. It was again noticeable that number of muzzle caps that broke was very large.	
	22×23 / 7/16		Nothing of importance to record	
	24/7/16		Company moved to another billet just south of RICHEBOURG-ST VAAST.	

Army Form C. 2118.

WAR DIARY or INTELLIGENCE SUMMARY

192nd Machine Gun Company for the Month of July 1916.

(Erase heading not required.)

Place	Date	Hour	Summary of Events and Information	Remarks and references to Appendices
	24/7/16		Six guns took over emplacements from 116th Bde. 4 guns in front line from S.16.a.20.45 to S.22.c.00.4. 2 guns were in rear (Map Ref as before) 2 reinforcements joined on this date.	
	25/7/16		Y.O/o were and communication trenches kept under fire. It should be noted that during our operations in the 116 ARMY AREA VICKERS GUNS were much more frequently employed in the front line than before.	
	26/7/16 & 27/7/16		2 more guns were sent up to positions in rear. It was noticed about this time that the stronger the quality of the emplacement, the more quality of the fire from it. We sustained 1 O.R. casualty on this date. Lt. COOPE submitted to Bde. a recommendation for return to Grantham and command frame of M.G. Coy. Operations as before. It was found that when mules were picketed in an orchard very great care has to be taken that they are secured to the line in such a way that they cannot work up + down and damage the trees.	
	28/7/16 & 29/7/16		Operations as before.	
	30/7/16		Specimen Operation Report received from trenches. No 2 GUN fired 1600 rds at gap in wire S.22.c.66 No 6 GUN fired 1500 rds sweeping wire and parapet C.22.b No 4 GUN fired 1500 rds gap in wire S.16.c.88 to S.16.c.40.98 No 10 GUN fired 750 rds on gap S.16.a.48. FACTORY KEEP GUN fired 500 rds on communication trench	

Army Form C. 2118.

WAR DIARY or **INTELLIGENCE SUMMARY**
(Erase heading not required.)

No. 92nd Machine Gun Company
Infantry Bgd: Machine Gun Company
July 1916

Place	Date	Hour	Summary of Events and Information	Remarks and references to Appendices
	30/6/16		(Previous Operation Report from trench note) WINDY CORNER GUN fired 3000 rds in bursts day and night on communication trench	
			TUBE STATION GUN fired 1500 rds on communication trench	
			CADBURY TRENCH fired 1500 rds on ration dump))	
			L/CPL FORSTER A.P. (4th K.R.R.) sick from Grantham. Took over command of Coy.	
	31/6/16		2 guns in front line opened vigorous fire during 20 mins before and 20 mins after the commencement of raid on our right, to create a diversion. During the 15 days that we were in the trenches this month, our 120,000 rds were fired by 8 guns.	
			On this date the following officers joined us 2nd Lt. RODGER J, BOWN J.P. and ABERNETHY H.W.	

A.P. Donte
Capt
Lt. Gun M.G. Company

Confidential Vol 4
War Diary
of
92nd Machine Gun Coy
Aug 1916

Army Form C. 2118.

WAR DIARY

92nd MACHINE GUN COY

Month of August

VOLUME II
Page 1

Place	Date	Hour	Summary of Events and Information	Remarks and references to Appendices
	1916 Aug 1		The Company were billeted as at the end of previous month, in the villages of No 26 billet. RICHEBOURG-ST-VAAST (Sheet of France Sheet 36SW 1/20000) 8 guns were in the trenches and 8 in Bde Reserve. We carried out our own reliefs every 6 days. Co-ordinates of 8 Gun positions as follows – FrontLine S16a55.58 – S16a32 – S16c32 – S22a16 (4) Guns in Rear. S15C.8.4 – S21a.75.60 – S.15B.56 – S9a54 – (4) Operations Right gun in front line prevented enemy working party from doing anything during the night. Remaining guns in front line fired at gaps in enemy wire. Guns in rear fired on enemy communication trenches. Total rounds expended 8,800. During the shelling of LACOUTURE one horse and one mule were wounded. We relieved 4 O.R. reinforcements from the Base.	ANA
	2		One O.R. attached killed during afternoon.	
	3		Operations Enemy working party, suspected M.G. emplacement & gaps in enemy wire fired on by guns in front line Total rounds expended 6,250 9,650 rds expended	hrs.
	4		Arrangements made with Supply Officer for getting green forage for transport Coy keeping this became regular issue throughout the month. By keeping in close touch with habits, working parties etc. we were enabled to fire at working parties, gaps in enemy wire and guns in rear in communication trenches and cross roads Sgt Wigby killed whilst directing M.G. fire in NO MANS LAND Total rounds expended 11,300.	Letter. / Anno.

WAR DIARY

VOLUME IV
Part I

Army Form C. 2118.

92nd MACHINE GUN COY

Month of August

Place	Date	Hour	Summary of Events and Information	Remarks and references to Appendices
	1916 Aug 5		Right gun dispersed enemy working party. Total number of rounds expended 11,000. From this day onwards, guns were sent one and two at a time to be overhauled, to Divn. Armourers Shop, Lestrem.	MM3
	6		Guns in front gave overhead fire to wiring parties and swept enemy parapet. Total rounds expended 5,850.	MM3
	7		Operations Bren guns fired on cross roads and communications. Total rounds expended 4,800.	MM3
	8		6,900 rds fired by rear guns at enemy roads and cross roads. Guns in front line fired at gaps in wire. Total rounds expended 11,300. One OR wounded.	MM3
	9		9,950 rds expended. Bombing instruction for the boy commenced under Bde Bombing Officer. 3 OR wounded in front line.	MM3
	10		10,000 rds fired on cross roads and enemy trenches.	MM3
	11		Nothing of interest to report from trenches. Total rounds expended 8,500. In the evening 2nd Lt GARNER and 30 OR arrived from Corus near our billet.	MM3
	12		Camera. About 10 pm a few shells fell quite near our billet. Guns in front line assisted operations on our right by firing bursts at stated intervals about midnight. 139 men were transferred from E. YORKS to 92nd M.G. Co. Inefficients sent back to Base under 2/Lt JY 6.	MM3 #13 Aug

WAR DIARY

Army Form C. 2118.

92nd MACHINE GUN COY

Month of August

VOLUME IV, Page III

Place	Date	Hour	Summary of Events and Information	Remarks and references to Appendices
	12, 13		Two more men sent on course at Camiers. Guns fired at stated intervals as before. Work on the improvement of billets, wire entanglements, latrines etc. commenced with good results.	JWA JWA
	14		No operations of importance to note. 2nd Lt LAVENDER from Grantham reported in the evening for duty. The transport being now right back reported the most satisfactory billet they have yet had at MESPLAUX.	JWA
	15		Good rounds fired 4,800 considerable amount of work was commenced on all emplacements. Wiring and revetting parties went up every night for the remainder of the month. A special shield sent down through Ordnance from GHQ for trial, proved in every way satisfactory and was reported on to this effect. Three O.R. reinforcements were received. Two OR wounded.	JWA JWA
	16		Total rounds expended 1,800.	
	17		5,280 rds expended. Sufficient wire cots or billets were completed for 60 men. Light work in front line during this week consisted mainly of making each gun emplacement a stronghold, by building up a crescent shaped barrier of barbed wire in rear, closed with a knife rest.	JWA
	18		One of our guns dispersed an enemy working party 5,000 rds expended.	JWA

Army Form C. 2118.

VOLUME IV
Page IV

92nd MACHINE GUN COY.

WAR DIARY

Month of August

Place	Date	Hour	Summary of Events and Information	Remarks and references to Appendices
	18		3 Sergts and 4 O.R. reported for duty	
	19		1 O.R. rejoined from Rest Station	
	20		Operations - three enemy machine guns fired at near ruins of FME HUVI. COUR D'AVOUE. Total rounds expended 3,400.	
	21		Guns in rear swept rear roads in rear of enemy line. Guns in front line carried out usual programme against enemy wire and parapet. An enemy machine gun firing from NO MAN'S LAND, was silenced by our fire. Total rounds fired 4,650	
	22		6 O.R. reinforcements from Connaught Rangers reported for duty.	
	23		Our guns assisted with vigorous fire in the three artillery bursts which were opened at stated times, at midnight. Total number of rounds fired 4,650. Mens canteen opened, under the management of the Orderly Room Clerk and Artificer. It was decided that this should be run entirely in the interests of the men and all goods sold at cost price. The canteen fund was started on discount accruing from stores purchased at Expeditionary Force Canteen, Bethune.	
	24		Operations. There was little activity, owing to the successful raid fired.	

WAR DIARY

Army Form C. 2118.

VOLUME IV Page V

92nd MACHINE GUN COY

Month of August

Place	Date	Hour	Summary of Events and Information	Remarks and references to Appendices
	24		on our front, made by a company of the 12th E. Yorks R. What assistance could be given was vigourous and effective. One of our emplacements in the front line was blown in by enemy retaliation but no casualties were sustained. Yotal rounds expended 2850 MMR.	
	25		No operations of interest to report. Total rounds fired 1500 = MMR.	
	26		Working parties continued to do excellent work on emplacements at night, careful instruction in wiring being given during day and each man instructed in the portion of work to which he was detailed. 3250 rds expended	MMR.
	27		Our guns as usual were active by night, keeping open gaps in wire sweeping enemy parapet and searching cross roads. Total rounds fired 3250	MMR
	28		Operations as before 3750 rds expended. One O.R. wounded	MMR
	29		4750 rds expended	MMR
	30		Enemy working parties fired on with effect. Total Rounds fired 4,000	MMR.
	31		Enemy working party again fired on and dispersed. Total rounds expended 3,500. During this month there were considerably less breakages in muzzle cups; we returned a good number of barrels worn and torn. This months own guns showed practically no...	MMR. R. de Gruchy Capt M.G. Corps

Confidential   Vol. 5

War Diary.

92nd Machine Gun Coy.   31st Division

September 1916

WAR DIARY or INTELLIGENCE SUMMARY

Army Form C. 2118.

92nd MACHINE GUN COY
Month of Sept.

Place	Date	Hour	Summary of Events and Information	Remarks and references to Appendices
	1916 Sept 1		Dispositions of guns as in previous month. Our guns assisted with bursts of fire in the raid made on our left by the 94th Bde. Total rounds expended 8,950. Working parties went up regularly at nights throughout the month. 1 O.R. evacuated.	WAUA
	2		Total rounds expended 3,400. 1 O.R. evacuated.	WAUA
	3		Total rounds expended 4,550. Guns in front fired on enemy wire and parapet, guns in rear on cross roads as follows. LATOURELLE X RDS. LIGNY LE PETIT X RDS. LA BASSÉE X RDS and RUE DU MARAIS. 2nd LT. FORWARD, attached from 12th E.Y.R. left to join M.G.T.C. GRANTHAM. 4,000 rds expended.	WAUA WAUA
	4		Usual programme. 4,000 rounds expended. 1 O.R. wounded by rifle bullet.	WAUA
	5		3,500 rds expended. 1 O.R. evacuated	
	6		Guns in front line co-operated with bursts of fire from Artillery, which were fired shortly after midnight and again at 1-30am. Claim against transport for £4 for damage to lorry at ROBECQ was settled. 1 OR rejoined from CCS. Total rounds expended - 4,000.	WAUA
	8		2nd Lt RODGER admitted to hospital. This Officer was subsequently reported wounded on 15th through a supplementary casualty return from Bde. from Bde.	WAUA

WAR DIARY or INTELLIGENCE SUMMARY

92nd MACHINE GUN COY

Month of Sept

Volume 5 Page 2

Place	Date	Hour	Summary of Events and Information	Remarks and references to Appendices
	1916 Sept 9		Guns fired as before, expending 4,250 rds.	NONE
	" 10		Guns in rear fired on x rds, tracks & open fields behind enemy lines. Guns in front fired on trench junctions and enfiladed communication trenches. Total rounds expended 4,750	NONE
	" 11		1.O.R (A/G) reinforcement reported for duty. All guns co-operated with Artillery in sudden bursts of fire at stated intervals during night, with the object of causing casualties to enemy working parties etc. Total rounds expended 5,950.	NONE
	" 12		Guns in rear fired as usual. Guns in front line thoroughly swept enemy trench junctions and then depressed on to enemy wire and swept gaps. Total rounds expended 5,350. 4. O.R. were transferred to 465th M.G.Coy, 3rd DIVN, being surplus to our establishment. 2.O.R. wounded. 1.O.R returned to duty the same day. The men attached to the Coy from the E.Y. Regts, were returned to their units, with the exception of 5 per batln	NONE
	" 13		Guns fired as before, expending a total of 4,400 rds	NONE
	" 14		A long burst of fire was given by all guns at 2-50 am as per programme received from Bde. Total rounds expended 4,800 The Company moved out of billets in RICHEBOURG-ST-VAAST and proceeded to XII. b.18.20 [Map Ref FRANCE 36A.SE 1:40,000]	NONE

Army Form C. 2118.

WAR DIARY
or
INTELLIGENCE SUMMARY
(Erase heading not required.)

92nd MACHINE GUN COY
Month of Sept.
Volume V
Page 3

Place	Date	Hour	Summary of Events and Information	Remarks and references to Appendices
	1916 Sept 14		A large barn was employed as Orderly Room, Canteen, Stores & Sergts Mess then were billeted in barns with wire cots. 5,360 rds expended on usual targets. One sergeant returned to Base Depot [with AG No A/5856]	NWA.
	.. 15		Guns fired as usual, total rounds expended 5950. New positions for guns were selected as follows, at EMBANKMENT S15c8y. COPSE KEEP S10c56. LANSDOWNE TRENCH S10c64. LANSDOWNE KEEP S4a11. & another gun at S10c9089. No6 Position & WINDY CORNER were abandoned. This was consequent on the Bde extending its left flank to the ESTAIRES – LA BASSÉE RD. Total rounds expended 2250	NWA.
	.. 16			NWA.
	.. 17			NWA.
	.. 18		9685 rounds fired 3000. All guns gave vigorous assistance to the successful raid carried out by the 10th E.Y.R. Guns again commenced to be overhauled at Div Armourer's Shop. Total rounds expended 5950. 2.O.R. reported for duty from Base	NWA.
	.. 19		Total rounds fired 3000. 1.O.R. rejoined from G.C.S.	NWA.
	.. 20		Total rounds 3450 Guns at No 2, 4&10 positions fired on enemy wire and parapet. Also special bursts with the Artillery according to programme at LANSDOWNE POST fired 500 rds sweeping LA TOURELLE X rds and vicinity.	NWA.

Army Form C. 2118.

WAR DIARY
~~INTELLIGENCE SUMMARY~~

(Erase heading not required.)

92nd MACHINE GUN COY.

Month of Sept^r.

Volume V Page 4

Place	Date	Hour	Summary of Events and Information	Remarks and references to Appendices
	1916. Sept 22		Total rounds expended 3,500, at usual targets. Good progress made with house standings for winter. Indents submitted for struts & sandbags for loading.	W.W.D.
	23		4,250 rds expended. I.O.R. (attached) admitted to hospital	W.W.D.
	24		5,100 rds fired	W.W.D.
	25		TUBE STATION fired 1000 rds sweeping LA BASSÉE X RDS and vicinity POURVILLE fired 950 rds on REDOUBT ALLEY N. communication trench FACTORY KEEP fired 500 rds on FME DU BIEZ CROSS RDS. Drunk guns traversed enemy wire and parapet. Owing to information from German prisoners to the effect that all points which constituted our usual M.G. targets, were always avoided at night, our guns throughout the month were careful to search all intervening ground	W.W.D. to W.D.
	26		4,500 rds expended	
	27		4,100 rds fired from to-day, Oat Straw in lieu of Green Forage was issued to the transport	A.W.D.
	28		Total rounds fired 3,500	A.W.D.
	29		Total rounds expended 3,500. 3.O.R. Wounded. 1.O.R. rejoined from C.C.S. 3 O.R.'s rejoined from Farriery Course	A.W.D.
	30		4,000 rds fired on usual targets. Careful stock was taken of all kit & equipment in view of the possibility of moving.	M.A. [signature] Lt. OC Coy

2449 Wt. W14957/M90 750,000 1/16 J.B.C. & A. Forms/C.2118/12.

Army Form C. 2118.

VOL 6

WAR DIARY
or
INTELLIGENCE SUMMARY

(Erase heading not required.)

CONFIDENTIAL

WAR DIARY

of

92nd MACHINE GUN COMPANY

From 1st Oct. 1916 to 31st Oct. 1916

VOLUME X

WAR DIARY or **INTELLIGENCE SUMMARY**

(Erase heading not required.)

Army Form C. 2118.

VOLUME VI
PAGE I

No. 92 MACHINE GUN COMPANY.

MONTH OF OCTOBER

Place	Date	Hour	Summary of Events and Information	Remarks and references to Appendices
	Oct 1		3,500 rds expended on enemy x Rds & communication trenches.	WNUA
	2		3,500 rds fired. Preparations for move south; all excess stores disposed of	WNUA
	3		3,500 rds expended. Careful stock taken of boots, gas helmets, steel helmets	WNUA
			& iron rations.	WNUA
	4		3,450 rds expended. Billets & all M.G. positions handed over to 15 M.G. Coy.	
			Company moved into billets at VIEILLE CHAPELLE	WNUA
	5		Further move to CALONNE, where billets for Officers & men were very	WNUA
			comfortable	
	6		Company training	WNUA
	7		Preparations for move. Company moved as before, in 5 sections – HQ's	WNUA
			going first	
	8		HQs entrained at MERVILLE station 6.30am, arrived at CANDAS (54D)	WNUA
			in the afternoon. The 4 Sections arrived at intervals of 6 hrs	
			during the night & the following morning	
			2nd Lt BOWN injured as a result of fall from his horse outside CALONNE	
			station	WNUA
	9		Company bivouacked in a field at VAUCHELLES.	WNUA
	10		Company training	WNUA
	11		C.S.M. admitted to hospital	
	12		Special training in extended order.	WNUA

WAR DIARY or INTELLIGENCE SUMMARY

Army Form C. 2118.

No 92 MACHINE GUN COMPANY

MONTH OF OCTOBER

VOLUME VI
PAGE II

Place	Date	Hour	Summary of Events and Information	Remarks and references to Appendices
	14		Training as before. 2nd Lt HAMMOND & 20 O.R. rejoined from Course at CAMIERS. 2 O.R. proceeded on course. 2nd Lt SIPPE CR. [1st LINCOLNS] reported for duty.	KWD
	15		2nd Lt APPLETON + Servant proceeded on course from BELLE EGLISE. Company training as before. Lantern reopened. Warning received from Bde. that Company would move to SAILLY-AU-BOIS the following day.	KWD
	16		Information received that operations against PUISIEUX in which we were to have taken part, were cancelled. Company moved into billets at SAILLY. Taking over from #56 M.G.Coy 5 gun teams went into the line at HEBUTERNE. Positions as follows:— K22d.23.34, K16.58.08, K16b.00.40, K16a.85.45, K16c.34. No firing was done owing to darkness falling before relief was complete. Considerable work done on billets; baths were erected.	KWD
	17		We relieved 156 M.G.Coy. taking over 17 guns as follows. K23.52, K22b.32, K22d.3650, K23a.95.15 (54D), V1 (K23a.95.15) fired 500 rds at trench junction at L19a.16, V6 (K22d.3255) fired 250rds on trench junction at K18c.05.45, V4 (K22b.3550) fired 250rds on enemy line + copse at K17d.48, N.8. (K22d.23.24) 2nd rifle X rds at K18d.4.8 + vicinity firing 50rds, V9 (K16c5898), did not fire, V13 (K16b.040) fired 600 rds traversing	KWD
	18		K23.52, K22b.32, fired 250rds. V.2 fired 250rds on trench junction V.6 (K22d.3255) fired 250rds on enemy line + copse at K17d.48, V9 (K16c5898), K18d.94, V12 (K16a.85.45), Tramway fire on STARWOOD fired 500 rds sweeping fire in front of enemy 2nd line	KWD

2449 Wt. W14957/M90 750,000 1/16 J.B.C. & A. Forms/C.2118/12.

CEMETERY GUN (K16c.54.)

WAR DIARY

Army Form C. 2118.
VOLUME VI
PAGE III
No 92 MACHINE GUN COMPANY
MONTH OF OCTOBER

Place	Date	Hour	Summary of Events and Information	Remarks and references to Appendices
	18		Total rounds expended 6,250. Work continued on billets – baths used.	WNWD
	19		Approximately same targets were engaged by all guns. Sergt Tyndall proceeded to ENGLAND via BOULOGNE to join CADET SCHOOL. Programme of firing as before. 3000 rds. expended. 1. O.R. removed by motor ambulance suffering from diphtheria. 10 others were isolated infection spread no further than the one case.	WNWD
	20			WNWD
	21		Totals rounds 3,250. Company was relieved by 93 M.G. Coy. & proceeded into huts & tents a little to Eth. S. of COIGNEUX. 2nd Lt. HAMMOND left for GRAMMAM (Auth AG/6864FH)	WNWD
	22		Inspection of guns in the morning; cleaning in the afternoon.	WNWD
	23		2 Sections sent up to trenches to hold positions suitable for assisting the attack to be made by 92nd Inf. Bde. on 26th inst. These operations were subsequently postponed until the following month.	WNWD
	24		2nd Lt LEWIS reported for duty under authority of letter from G.H.Q. No CRF 1181 d.16.9.16. 8 Supernumerary privates now recognised as additional personnel to sections of a MACHINE GUN COMPANY previous to this we had had 5 attached men in each section from the 4 battns in the Bde. This was now increased to 8 Extra driver in addition also attached to transport for extra G.S. limbered wagon.	WNWD
	25		All supernumerary personnel reported for duty.	WNWD
	26 27 28		Company training in view of forthcoming operations.	WNWD

Army Form C. 2118.

WAR DIARY or **INTELLIGENCE SUMMARY**

(Erase heading not required.)

No. 92 MACHINE GUN COMPANY

MONTH OF OCTOBER

VOLUME 6 PAGE IV

Place	Date	Hour	Summary of Events and Information	Remarks and references to Appendices
	29		One O.R. under 18½ years of age, returned to Base. All G.C. Badges awarded.	WND
	30		Company moved into billets in WARNIMONT WOOD.	WND
	31		Company training as before + work on billets. During the latter half of the month the transport remained at COIGNEUX.	WND

Humph^t
Major
OC 92 MGCoy.

31.x.16.

Army Form C. 2118.

WAR DIARY
or
INTELLIGENCE SUMMARY.
(Erase heading not required.)

CONFIDENTIAL

WAR DIARY

OF

No. 92 MACHINE GUN COMPANY.

From 1st Nov 16 to 30th Nov '16.

VOLUME II

WAR DIARY

VOLUME XI
PAGE I

No 92 MACHINE GUN COMPANY
Date: NOVEMBER

Army Form C. 2118.

Place	Date	Hour	Summary of Events and Information	Remarks and references to Appendices
In the field	1916. Nov. 1st to 6th		Company in huts in WARNIMONT WOOD, weather continued very bad the whole time. Operations continued to be postponed.	WWD
	7th		10666 Sergt. A.J. Youens proceeded to England to join a Cadet Battn. with a view to obtaining a commission in the M.G. Corps.	WWD
	8		Working Parties commenced at new transport lines J.10.c.6.2. (57 D.N.E. 1/20,000)	WWD
	9.		Weather fine. XIII Corps M.G. Officer assumed his duties.	WWD
	10		Order received that "Z" day was 13th. 4 guns sent up into Sector from which Bde. was to attack. Instructions received about Divisional Laundry. Clean changes of underclothing available from this for the company, whenever Baths were to be had.	WWD
	11		Preparations for moving up to the attack.	WWD
	12.		Company proceeded into trenches via COIGNEUX & SAILLY, stopping at new transport lines for midday meal. 2nd Lt. LEWY & Sergt. Beadle remained in charge of rear party, which consisted of a few Hodgson details. No casualties.	WWD

WAR DIARY

Army Form C. 2118.

VOLUME XI
PAGE 2

No. 52 MACHINE GUN COMPANY
Date NOVEMBER

Place	Date	Hour	Summary of Events and Information	Remarks and references to Appendices
MAP Ref 57d N.E. 1/20,000	13		Transport moved into new lines. Zero hour for assault was fixed for 5·45 a.m. Company was distributed as follows —— No.1 Section in VAUBAN trench (K22d.) [57d.N.E.] No.2 Section in FORT BRIGGS (K22c.) } No.4 Section in VERCINGETORIX (K22a.) } These 10 guns were told off to cover the Bde front. No.3 & ½ No.4 Section were assembled in Du GUESCLIN trench & held in readiness to consolidate newly won positions. The Company was in position, with HQ in HOME trench nr VAUBAN by 5 pm on previous day. At zero hour the 5/10 guns covering Bde. front, opened fire on enemy communication trenches leading up to trenches that were being attacked & fire was maintained throughout the day. A total of 60,500 rds was expended by these guns. No. 3 & ½ No. 4 Section remained in their assembly trenches throughout, being heavily shelled at times & they lost 1 man killed & 4 wounded. 2nd Lt. GARNER, O.C. No.1 Section was killed by shrapnel in VAUBAN about 4 pm.	[initials]

WAR DIARY or INTELLIGENCE SUMMARY

Army Form C. 2118.

VOLUME XI
PAGE 3

No. 92 MACHINE GUN COMPANY.
Date NOVEMBER

Place	Date	Hour	Summary of Events and Information	Remarks and references to Appendices
	13.		ROSSIGNAL FARM, COIGNEUX, the lost section arrived there about 1am, 2nd Lt. GARNER & Pte Everingham were buried in the Military Cemetary at EUSTON DUMP (K53a24)	AWS.
	14.		Company moved into huts at WARNIMONT WOOD. The OC. Company & 2 OR. proceeded to the trenches in the afternoon to collect dead & wounded.	AWS.
	15.		50 OR. under 2nd Lt. ABERNETHY & LEVY proceeded to trenches to clear dead from NO MAN'S LAND. As there was little firing, the work was thoroughly done & no casualties occured.	AWS
	16.		Careful inspection of all kit & equipment. CSM. returned to duty from Base.	AWS
	17.		Inspection of kit continued, indents to cover deficiencies submitted to D.A.D.O.S.	AWS
	18.		2nd Lt. ANNIS reported for duty, 2 men under age returned to Base.	AWS
	19.		2nd Lt. ANNIS proceeded to Base to recover his kit.	AWS
	20		2nd Lt. ABERNETHY + 3 gun teams proceeded to trenches	AWS

VOLUME XI
PAGE IV

No. 92 MACHINE GUN COMPANY

Date: NOVEMBER

WAR DIARY
INTELLIGENCE SUMMARY
(Erase heading not required.)

Army Form C. 2118.

Place	Date	Hour	Summary of Events and Information	Remarks and references to Appendices
	20.		Dispositions as follows. 1 Gun at K.10.d.4.3. 1 Gun at K.10.d.1.3 & 1 Gun at K.10.d.4.6. No rounds fired.	NWR
	21.		No rounds fired.	NWR
	22.		Pte. Sock Laundry opened. A washerwoman & 100 hrs socks contributed. We were enabled by this to have a clean change of socks whenever required.	NWR
	23.		No. 9082 Pte Brookes + 34478 Pte Jones tried by Court Martial. Company moved into huts at the bottom of the hill in COIGNEUX. 2nd Lt. J.C.C. BEST reported for duty. No rounds fired.	NWR
	24.		2nd Lt LAVENDER relieved 2nd Lt. ABERNETHY. A Working Party under Lt. SIPPE. (30 men) proceeded to the trenches at 2pm for the purpose of wiring the "R" line in front of HEBUTERNE	NWR
	25		Working Party detailed as before was cancelled owing to rain. Sentence of 2 yrs I.H.L. on Ptes Brookes & Jones promulgated. This sentence was suspended on 30th inst. O.C. reconnoitred line in company with Corps M.G. Officer. 2nd Lt ANNIS reported back for duty. No rounds fired.	NWR
	26		Wiring Party under 2nd Lt. LEVY heavily shelled & had to leave their work incomplete.	NWR

WAR DIARY

INTELLIGENCE SUMMARY.

(Erase heading not required.)

Army Form C. 2118.

VOLUME VI
PAGE V

No. 92
MACHINE GUN
Date NOVEMBER

Place	Date	Hour	Summary of Events and Information	Remarks and references to Appendices
	26		2 Guns sent to Armourer's Shop for repairs. No rounds fired.	NWS
	27		2nd Lt. APPLETON & 4 O.R. proceeded on leave. Wiring Party under 2nd Lt. ANNIS. 40 rounds fired.	NWS
	28		2nd Lt. BEST conducted wiring. Lt. SIPPE relieved 2nd Lt LAVENDER in the trenches. No rounds fired.	NWS
	29		Wiring Party as usual. 1 O.R. of party wounded by stray rifle bullet. Line again reconnoitred with Corps M.G. Officer by O.C. 40 rounds fired. Dr Simmons rejoined from 2 months course of Gunnery at Abbeville.	NWS
	30		Wiring Party as usual. 2 O.Rs. reported for duty as reinforcements from Base.	NWS

Murphy wind
Major MGC

Army Form C. 2113.

WAR DIARY
or
INTELLIGENCE SUMMARY.
(Erase heading not required.)

Vol 8

CONFIDENTIAL

WAR DIARY

OF

No. 92 MACHINE GUN COMPANY.

From 1st Decr. '16 To 31st Decr. '16

(VOLUME ~~XII~~)

Army Form C. 2118.

VOLUME VII

PAGE I

No. 92 MACHINE GUN COMPANY

WAR DIARY
or
INTELLIGENCE SUMMARY
(Erase heading not required.)

Map Ref. 57d NE 1/20,000

Place	Date	Hour	Summary of Events and Information	Remarks and references to Appendices
In the field [COIGNEUX] 57d NE 2.a.6.0.0	1916 Dec 1		3 gun positions occupied in trenches as follows — K.10.c.4.3, K.10.d.1.3 & K.10.d.4.6. The remainder of the Company was billeted in COIGNEUX (5a.5.5). Transport lines were at T.10.c.6.2. Up to Decr. 5th Company continued to provide Wiring Parties for the "R" line in front of HEBUTERNE. No rounds fired. Wiring Party cancelled owing to bad weather. Application was received for Officers to be submitted for Instructional Staff, but no names were sent. 2nd Lt. BEST proceeded to the trenches for instruction in Section Duties.	WD WD WD
	2		nothing to report.	
	3		2nd Lt. KELAMENDER relieved 2nd Lt. ANNIS & 2nd Lt. BEST in the trenches. 2nd Lt. BEST conducted wiring party for that night. The duties of the wiring party consisted in making about 25" concertinas" during the morning & putting out from 25 to 50 nightly. The 92nd T.M.B. contributed 25 concertinas daily. We provided Transport. 6 reinforcements received from the Base.	WD WD
	4th 5 6		notification was received no further reliefs in future. 92nd Bde. to be 12 days in the line & 12 days out. M.G. Coy HQ remained at COIGNEUX the whole time	

A5834. Wt. W4973/M687. 730,000 8/16 D.D. & L. Ltd. Forms/C.2118/13.

VOLUME XII
PAGE 2

WAR DIARY

No. 92 MACHINE GUN COMPANY.
Date: DECEMBER

Date	Hour	Summary of Events and Information	Remarks
1916 8/9		No rounds fired	(own)
9		Bde was relieved. From this date until the next relief working parties consisting of one Officer + 50 OR were found by this Coy for roads in the back area	(own)
10		Weather continued bad throughout the month, but the Company was fortunate in not having a single case of trench feet. This was largely due to the use made of the Bde. Sock Laundry + regular parades for the washing + rubbing of feet with whale oil. 2nd Lt ABERNETHY was voted Treasurer + director of the Company Xmas Dinner fund.	(own)
11		2nd Lt APPLETON returned from leave	
12		2 guns detailed for A.A. Duties proceeded to HEBUTERNE to be under the orders of 143rd M.G.Co.	(own)
13		After spell of bad weather, camp was deep in mud + owing to fact that all "duck boards" were reserved for the trenches, none were available for us	(own)
14		Owing to Divisional Scheme for reduction of Transport on roads rations were drawn on 1st Line Transport from this day onwards from Dump close to Camp	(own)

Volume XII
PAGE 3

Army Form C. 2118.

WAR DIARY
or
INTELLIGENCE SUMMARY.
(Erase heading not required.)

No. 02 MACHINE GUN COMPANY.
DECEMBER

Place	Date	Hour	Summary of Events and Information	Remarks and references to Appendices
	1916 Dec			
	13		Small Drying Room erected in the camp. Company bathed	
	14		A.A. guns withdrawn from HEBUTERNE	WWS
	15		12 men interviewed for Special grades by committee. Sector of "yellow line" in Div Area reconnoitred by Section Officers	WWS
	16		CSM proceeded on leave CQMS took over duties of CSM which he performed very satisfactorily. Sgt Wright took over from CQMS	WWS
	17		2nd Lt STILES reported for duty. Issue of Small Box Respirators in lieu of old box respirator + P.H. Helmet. All respirators were carefully fitted + tested under N.C.Os. trained at Gas School 4 OR reinforcements. nothing to record.	WWS
	18		Guns prepared for relief in trenches the following day.	
	19		Company relieved 93rd M.G.C. with 12 guns in the trenches. C.O. accompanied guns into the line; No 3 Section remained behind the CQMS went up with rations every afternoon. Special attention was given to rations + fuel for the trenches during this 12 days in, weather being wet + cold the whole time.	WWS
	20			
	21		Advanced Coy HQ was established just by the first X roads on the W. side of HEBUTERNE.	WWS

WAR DIARY of INTELLIGENCE SUMMARY

VOLUME XII
PAGE 4

No. 92 MACHINE GUN COMPANY.
Date DECEMBER

Army Form C. 2118.

Place	Date	Hour	Summary of Events and Information	Remarks and references to Appendices
	1916 Dec. 21		The M.G. Emplacements occupied were as follows:- No 1 gun K3c 85; No 1A, K3d1040; No 2 gun K9b4489; No 3 K9b4061; No 4 K9b8129; No 5, K10c 6595; No 6, K10d 3662; No 4 gun, K10c 4822; No 8, K10d 5124; No 9 gun, K3c43; No 10, K9a 5432; No 11 gun, K9a 6122; (54 D N.E. 20,000)	
	22		No 1 gun fired during the night on gap in enemy wire at K3c 5548. 1500 rds were expended; No 2 gun fired 1500 rds on a similar gap at K1c94; No 3 gun fired 500 rds on gap at K4d 52 fire being hindered by one of our own working parties in front; No 6 gun fired 500 rds on gap on each side of "Sunken Track" K11a32. Totals rounds expended 3,450.	MNA MNA MNA MNA MNA
	23		No 1 gun fired 1250 rds; No 2 + 3 guns 1450 rds each on gaps on enemy wire; No 6 gun fired 1500 rds during night on gaps in wire arrangements being made with Bath. to withdraw their front line posts whilst we fired	Own Own
	24		No 1 gun fired 1250 rds at gap K12d 54; No 2 + 3 fired on their usual targets; No 6 gun fired on gaps up to 6-40 pm the previous evening only, as arranged with the 11th E.Yorks.R. who raided that night. Total expenditure 2,400 rds.	MNA

WAR DIARY

VOLUME XII
PAGE 5

Army Form C. 2118.

No. 92 MACHINE GUN COMPANY.
DECEMBER

Place	Date	Hour	Summary of Events and Information	Remarks and references to Appendices
	1916 Decr 25		In the afternoon 3½" shells fell on the top of the dug-out at No 8 gun doing no damage. The X roads & vicinity of Advanced Coy HQ were heavily shelled about 4pm. Total rounds expended 47,250. — The Company's Xmas Dinner was postponed until after the relief at the beginning of January. — During the 12 days in the line, socks were changed every day. The fuel allowance enabled us to have a brazier in each gun team dug-out. There were only 4 cases of sickness altogether, but as a large percentage of men were in the trenches for 12 whole days, this was very small.	MMA
	26		Gaps in the enemy wire were fired on throughout the night. When firing on gaps at K.4 & 9/4, shrieks were heard from MMA the enemies lines & it is hoped a working party was caught. Total rounds fired 4000. The night was quiet. OP returned from trenches.	MMA
	29		4 gun teams were relieved from forward positions. Lt ABERNETHY MMA 2nd Lts LAVENDER & STILES conducted the relieving party	MMA

VOLUME XI.
PAGE 6

No. 92
MACHINE GUN COMPANY.
DECEMBER

WAR DIARY

Army Form C. 2118.

Place	Date	Hour	Summary of Events and Information	Remarks and references to Appendices
	1916 Dec 28		Total rounds expended 4400. Certificate of Chief Pay commenced to be received from the Regtl Paymaster.	WWD
	29		Total rounds expended 500.	WWD
	30		500 rds fired.	
	31		Total rounds fired 400. Baths were frequent throughout the month & clean clothes easily obtained from the Divisional Laundry at ORVILLE. During this period all guns were overhauled by the Divisional Armourer. Application for a further issue of watches & for authority for a Company tailor were both disallowed. Number of broken muzzle cups during the latter end of this year was considerably less than at first.	WWD

J. Sm A[?] A/. L. Capt.
Cmdg 92 MGCoy.
1/1/17

Army Form C. 2118.

WAR DIARY
or
INTELLIGENCE SUMMARY.
(Erase heading not required.)

Vol 9

CONFIDENTIAL

WAR DIARY

OF

97nd MACHINE GUN COMPANY

FROM 1st JANY 1919 TO 31st JANY 1919

(VOLUME XIII)

WAR DIARY
INTELLIGENCE SUMMARY

VOLUME XIII
PAGE 1.

No. 12 MACHINE GUN COMPANY
JANUARY

Place	Date	Hour	Summary of Events and Information	Remarks and references to Appendices
	1917			
	Jan 1st		Position of Company's billets & gun positions in the line were as at the end of previous month	Appx
	2nd		Brigade relief. This Company was relieved by 93 M.G.C. in the trenches but retained the same billets	Appx
	3rd		From this day onwards, working party of 4 N.C.Os & 36 men were found every day at the R.E. Park, COIGNEUX	Appx
	4th		Company held concert & Xmas Dinner in the Church hut, COIGNEUX	Appx
	5th		N.C.O. detailed to attend Divl Gas School with a view to his administration of all Gas Duties in the Company	Appx
	7th		Inspection of Company by M.O. for the purpose of finding out if there were any cases of Scabies. There were at the most two or three	Appx
	8th		Careful inspection of all kit, equipment & stores in compliance with Bde. Order instructing that all indents were to be in by 14th of month	Appx
	9th		Preparation for move. Working parties cancelled. N.C.O. rejoined from Gas School	Appx
	10th		Orders had been received the previous day from the C.M.G.O. to assist in an attack made by the 4th Div on MUNICH Trench (just S. of SERRE). 15 guns with teams & carrying parties proceeded via COURCELLES to trenches E. of EUSTON DUMP. Sections were distributed as follows:— No. 1 Section & Coy HQ were in HITTITE Trench. No. 2 & 4 were in SAPPER. No. 3 was in SACKVILLE ST.	Appx

VOLUME XIII
PAGE 2

WAR DIARY
or
INTELLIGENCE SUMMARY
(Erase heading not required.)

Army Form C. 2118.

No 92
MACHINE GUN COMPANY
JANUARY

Place	Date	Hour	Summary of Events and Information	Remarks and references to Appendices
	1917 Jan 10th		Guns were laid for indirect fire on S. slopes of SERRE During the evening. 3 of the carriers were wounded & 1 killed in SOUTHERN AVE, as a result of Shrapnel fire. The remainder of the company with 2 motor lorries, all transport had meanwhile proceeded to AMPLIER (nr DOULLENS nr LENS !!)	(WD)
	11th		The Durham was to move into rest for 6 weeks - this was the first day of the move in line. All guns opened fire at 6.40 am according to programme & fired at varying rates until 4.10am. About 2009 to 2,500 rds were fired per gun. There was very little retaliation on our trenches. A very misty morning favoured us in blinding the flashed of our guns. The company had orders to withdraw at 10am & proceed to COURCELLES. From here they proceeded to join the rest of the Bde. at AMPLIER where they arrived about 4pm. Lt DUNLOP & Cpl WILLIS proceeded on leave.	(Wr)
	12th		Cleaning up all day	(Wr?)
	13th		ditto	(Wr)
	14th		2/Lt LAVENDER & 1 OR proceeded to CAMIERS for Course of Instruction 1 OR proceeded on Signalling Course. Inspection made cleaning up etc. otherwise no work. Secret instructions received for entraining if necessary, as we became an GHQ reserve	(Wr)
	15th		Training Programme was as follows. 9-11am Close Order & Rifle Drill 2 Secs Maxim & 9mm Action. 11am-12M Meet & 9mm Action. Close Order & Rifle Drill. Classes for further instruction were formed for elementary knowledge.	(Wr)

VOLUME XIII
PAGE 3

NO 12 MACHINE GUN COMPANY
Month: JANUARY

WAR DIARY
INTELLIGENCE SUMMARY
(Erase heading not required.)

Army Form C. 2118.

Place	Date	Hour	Summary of Events and Information	Remarks and references to Appendices
	1917 Jan 18		2/Lt LEVY + 6 OR rejoined from CAMIERS. Training programme as follows. 9-11 am Physical training + Close Order Drill 11-1 pm Mech. + 9 mm action. Classes of Instruction as before. Sgt Barker rejoined from leave + 2 OR from hospital. 6 reinforcements from Base.	
	19th		Football match against 92nd + M.B. Instructional Classes as usual. Paths all unworkable owing to 10 days ORs who would a similar rate of new snow were collected + handed in to. The weather continued cold + there was a fall of snow.	
	20th		2/Lt SARGEANT reported from the Base for duty. Programme of work as follows. 9-11 am 2 Sections 9 mm. action + 2 Secs Physical training + Close Order Drill 11-1 pm Sections change over. Classes as usual.	
	21st		1 OR proceeded on leave. Notification rec'd that all animals were to be shod with frost cogs. Route march for whole company. Preparation for move. 1 OR proceeded to Div. Sig School.	
	22nd		Company moved to Longueville. 1 motor lorry was available for the move.	
	23rd		Training as follows. 9-11 am Gun Drill. 11-12 nn 9 mm action 12-1 pm Instruction in Range Duties.	
	24th		Firing on 100 yds range with prepared stoppages. Gas Helmet Drill. Lt DUNLOP Rfl Willis rejoined from leave.	

WAR DIARY or INTELLIGENCE SUMMARY

VOLUME XIII PAGE 4

No 92 MACHINE GUN COMPANY.
Army Form C. 2118.
JANUARY

Place	Date	Hour	Summary of Events and Information	Remarks and references to Appendices
	1917 Jan 25th		Canteen was re-opened in a cellar with considerable success. Supplies were obtained from E.F.C. DOULLENS.	(1M)
	26th		Simple Scheme for attack Route March for Company.	(1M)
	27th		½ Coy on 400 yds range + ½ training	(2M)
	29th		M.G. Training in billets Preparation for range.	(3M)
	30th		2 Sections firing on 400yds range. 2 Sections training in billets	(4M)
	31st		During the latter part of the month, the weather continued extremely cold	(5M)

[signature]
Major MGC

Army Form C. 2118.

WAR DIARY
or
INTELLIGENCE SUMMARY.
(Erase heading not required.)

Vol 10

CONFIDENTIAL

WAR DIARY

OF

92 MACHINE GUN COMPANY

[VOLUME 14]

FROM 1-2-17 TO 28-2-17

WAR DIARY
INTELLIGENCE SUMMARY

Army Form C. 2118.

VOLUME XIV
PAGE 1

No. 92 MACHINE GUN COMPANY.
Date: FEBRUARY

Place	Date	Hour	Summary of Events and Information	Remarks and references to Appendices
	1919 Feb 1		The whole company were in billets at GORGES, about 3 kilos. from BARNAVILLE. The men were in barns, with a plentiful supply of straw for bedding. Frost continued severe, until the middle of the month. All guns were sent to Ordnance for overhauling, throughout the commencement of the month. Training was as follows. am. Route march for Coy. An Sports at	LMS
	2		2/Lt LEVY returned from hospital. Work on range.	LMS
	3		Leave for this Company continued to be postponed, until finally cancelled.	LMS
	4		Another Signaller proceeded on usual Div. Course, which continued whilst the Division was at rest.	LMS
	5		Company fitted out with new Coy. Bde. badges (Coy badge being red size on right shoulder) Training for this day as follows. 2 Sections on range. 2 Sections Gun Drill + attack practice.	LMS
	6		Training as for 5th. 2/Lt LAVENDER returned from Course. 2/Lt APPLETON attended lecture on GAS, at BEAUVAL	LMS
	7		Coy. Route march. Instruction in map reading; use of Protractor for N.C.Os	LMS

VOLUME XIV
PAGE 2

NO. 62 MACHINE GUN COMPANY
Date: FEBRUARY

WAR DIARY
(Erase heading not required.)

INTELLIGENCE SUMMARY

Army Form C. 2118.

Place	Date	Hour	Summary of Events and Information	Remarks and references to Appendices
	1917 Feb. 8		Training as for 5th. Boy bathed.	(M.S)
	9		40 men inoculated with T.A.B. vaccine. Training as for 6th.	(M.S)
	10		Brigade Attack (Practice) New Imprest no. allotted to Company. (M.G.C. 93) Nothing to report.	(M.S)
	11			
	12		2/Lt Ryan won the Semi-Final of the Div. Boxing Competition, but lost Night Operations, marching on a compass.	(M.S)
	13		Tactical Scheme & Instruction in Overhead Fire. 2/Lt LEVY attended Gas lecture at BEAUVAL.	(M.S)
	14		2 Sections on range, 2 Sects advance over rough country.	(M.S)
	15		Tactical Scheme with 10th E.Y.R. & Range Cards & Distance judging.	(M.S)
	16		Advance over rough country, work on range, & Indirect Fire. Coy M.G. Competition for Lieut. M.G. Salton held near BEAUVAL & M.G. Companies Competed. The following were the items of the competition. Horses Saddlery sitting of harness, Limbers & Pack'ing Section, Time, Method, Equipment in Action, & mounting of Guns, Obtaining range, Method of fire and no. of hits. This Company was 2nd with 54 marks, as compared with 56 for the winning Company. (94th M.G.C.)	(M.S)

WAR DIARY
or
INTELLIGENCE SUMMARY

(Erase heading not required.)

Army Form C. 2118.

No 92 MACHINE GUN COMPANY.
Month: FEBRUARY

VOLUME XIV
PAGE 5

Place	Date 1917 Feby	Hour	Summary of Events and Information	Remarks and references to Appendices
	18		Brigade Day. 7 men returned to Base as inefficient.	(m)
	19		Company moved from GORGES to TERRAMESNIL (Ref. map France 57D)	
	20		Company moved to COURIN. 11 guns were moved up to trenches, relieving 58 M.G.C. & occupying positions as follows. CEMETARY (K16c29) CAVONTY (K16a3,5) BRISSOUX (K22b.8,9) JEAN BART (at K22a.9,4, & K22b.4,3) MARIE LOUISE (K22a.3,9½) SERRE Rd. (K19c.2,2¼) NAIRNE (K23c.6,4) FORTBRIGGS (K22d.3¼,6) CHASSEUR HEDGE (K23a.6,6) & ROLAND (K22d 3,1) Trsp. Ref. 57D.N.E. 20.0.0. A gun was also detailed for AA duty at K19a 3,8 but was relieved by a 2 gun next day. The remainder of Coy. moved to SAILLY DELL	(m)
	21		Coy. again moved from the DELL to the "MAIRIE" in SAILLY. Transport lines were at COIGNEUX. No rounds were fired. Operations nil.	(m)
	22		Operations nil.	
	23		SERRE Rd gun at K19c 2,2¼ was withdrawn. 2/Lt APPLETON was Lt ABERNETHY recommended on AFW 3528 for Second in command of a Company	(m)
	24		2 O.R. proceeded to CAMIERS for Course of Instruction.	

VOLUME XIV
PAGE H

No 92
MACHINE GUN COMPANY.
Name ....
Date .... FEBRUARY

Army Form C. 2118.

WAR DIARY
or
INTELLIGENCE SUMMARY.
(Erase heading not required.)

Place	Date	Hour	Summary of Events and Information	Remarks and references to Appendices
	1917 Feb 25		Information received that enemy was evacuating his positions in front of our Sector accordingly. 4 guns in charge of an officer were attached to the 11th E.Y.R. 2 guns in charge of an officer were attached to the 12th E.Y.R. at the same time. 2 of the guns with the 11th E.Y.R. proceeded to the German 3rd line with the infantry & took up positions there & remained mounted until orders came to retire. One gun remained with part of A Coy 11th E.Y.R. in the German 2nd line, while the 4th gun was kept in reserve at Coy H.Q. The 2 guns with the 12th E.Y.R. went as far as our front line & were then ordered to retire & remain in readiness. About this information was received that they were no longer required. Nothing unusual was reported from the other guns in our lines.	1ors
	26		On the afternoon, 2 guns under an officer were placed under orders of O.C. 10th E.Y.R. but did not go forward. 4/Lt Levy proceeded to ETAPLES for dental treatment. Careful inspection of emergency rations. Took Private tradesmen proceeded to BOULOGNE	Guns.

A.5834 Wt. W4973/M687 750,000 8/16 D. D. & L. Ltd. Forms/C.2118/13.

WAR DIARY
or
INTELLIGENCE SUMMARY.

(Erase heading not required.)

Army Form C. 2118.

VOLUME XIV
PAGE 5

No 82 MACHINE GUN COMPANY.
Date: FEBRUARY

Place	Date	Hour	Summary of Events and Information	Remarks and references to Appendices
	Feb 27/28		On the tactical situation remained somewhat indefinite + no targets were presented to the 2 advanced teams, nothing further was done. At this time there were 2 teams forward, 2 in our line and the remainder in reserve. Preparation was made to convey guns, rations etc. to the trenches by means of Pack animals.	

Wingate
O.C. 82 M.G.Coy.

Army Form C. 2118.

WAR DIARY
or
INTELLIGENCE SUMMARY.

(Erase heading not required.)

Vol XI

CONFIDENTIAL

WAR DIARY

OF

No. 92 MACHINE GUN COMPANY

FROM 1st MARCH 1917 TO 31st MARCH 1917

(VOLUME XI.)

VOLUME XV
PAGE 1

Army Form C. 2118.

No 92
MACHINE GUN COMPANY
Date: MARCH

WAR DIARY

INTELLIGENCE SUMMARY

(Erase heading not required.)

Instructions regarding War Diaries and Intelligence Summaries are contained in F.S. Regs., Part II. and the Staff Manual respectively. Title pages will be prepared in manuscript.

Place	Date	Hour	Summary of Events and Information	Remarks and references to Appendices
	1917 Mar. 1st		11 guns were in the line under the immediate control of OC Company. 2 guns were in old German 2nd line firing at ROSSIGNOL WOOD. Ode. Order received to the effect that 2 teams were to accompany each Battn. in the line & 4 teams were to occupy positions in German 2nd line. Lt. ABERNETHY took command of the latter guns. 2/Lt SARGENT with two gun teams proceeded to EUSTON CAMP to join the 11th E.YORKS. R. Rations were sent up by Pack Mules as far as OBSERVATION WOOD	Map Ref 57D NE
	2		Company HQ moved to LA SIGNY FARM, taking over from 58 M.G. Coy. QM Stores were at COURCELLES. 2/Lt SARGENT + 2 teams moved up at 5pm with the 11th E.Y.R. 2/Lt STILES with 2 guns was attached to the 12th E.Y.R. 2 OR wounded at duty.	
	3		2/Lt LAVENDER with 4 guns went up to STAR WOOD in reserve. 2/Lt STILES reported back, being relieved by 2 teams under Sgt. HEMMINGWAY 2/Lt STILES with 4 teams went into line with 13th E.Y.R. Lt. ABERNETHY returned, with 2/Lt SARGENT, to LA SIGNY FARM. 2/Lt THOMSON, being unwell, remained during this time at COURCELLES	
	4			
	5		There were now 8 guns at rest, & 8 guns in line as follows:— L3 o 5.95. L13.b.9.9. L13.b.9.4. L14.a.1k. L13.a.58.(2 guns) L12.d.9.8.(2 guns)	

A5834 Wt. W4973/M687 750,000 8/16 D. D. & L. Ltd. Forms/C.2118/13.

VOLUME XV
PAGE 3

WAR DIARY
or
INTELLIGENCE SUMMARY
(Erase heading not required.)

Army Form C. 2118.

No 92 MACHINE GUN COMPANY
Month: MARCH

Place	Date	Hour	Summary of Events and Information	Remarks and references to Appendices
	1917 March 6		Q.M. Stores moved to LA SIGNY FARM. Canteen was opened in the old M.G. Emplacement in HITTITE trench. Officers Mess accomodation for about 30 men was available in cellars at LA SIGNY FARM. 1 Section & the Orderly Room were in BASIN WOOD in Elephant Dug-outs. There was further accomodation in a large dug out nr. WATERLOO BRIDGE. Nothing of importance.	
	7			
	8		Lt ABERNETHY & 2/Lt STILES, with 4 teams each proceeded to advanced positions in forward line (4 guns, 4 guns remaining in STARWOOD	
	9		Every night whilst boys were at the farm, rations were pushed up by trolley to STARWOOD, where our carrying party distributed the rations	
	10		1 O.R. wounded by shrapnel in the leg	
	11		There were at this time 22 men in hospital, which constituted a record for the company. Sgt Holland returned from hospital. This N.C.O. had been attached 3 months before to the Printing Dept.	
	12		Company relieved in the line by 91 M.G.Coy. This company only took over 2 guns, the others being withdrawn. Company at LA SIGNY FARM. Moved back to COLIN.	

VOLUME XV
PAGE 3

No 92 MACHINE GUN COMPANY
Date: MARCH

WAR DIARY
or
INTELLIGENCE SUMMARY
(Erase heading not required.)

Army Form C. 2118.

Place	Date	Hour	Summary of Events and Information	Remarks and references to Appendices
	1919 Mar 12		Teams coming out of line spent the night at the farm, having breakfast there next morning, joining the rest of the Company afterwards.	
	13		Guns cleaned & preparation for inspection.	
	14		Thorough inspection of small kit, spare parts & all stores. All necessary indents submitted as per instructions from Bde. Whole Company entertained at Div. Cinema, seats being bought by Canteen Profits.	
	15		Issue of new boots to Company. Div. Order received in the afternoon that all units were to be prepared to move Eastward at 4 hrs notice. All preparations made & billet selected as emergency dump. Lieut. MORRISON sent on course at Div. Gas School. All surplus stores sent to Salvage. Limbers thoroughly cleaned; in view of projected move into 1st Army Area preparations were made to cut down all stores & despatch those unnecessary (in excess of mobilisation equipment) to billet in BUS. Their transmission was effected by Company Transport. Owing to condition of roads, motor lorry allotted for the march north, could not come E. of BUS.	

WAR DIARY
INTELLIGENCE SUMMARY

VOLUME XV
PAGE 4

No 92 MACHINE GUN COMPANY
Month: MARCH

Army Form C. 2118.

Place	Date	Hour	Summary of Events and Information	Remarks and references to Appendices
	1917 March			
	19		Preparations for early move on following day	
			Company moved to MARIEUX via AUTHIE & were billeted on the MARIEUX - PUCHEVILLERS Road in wooden huts. [Map Ref. LENS 11. 1/40,000]. All stores dumped at huts were brought on motor lorry, which accompanied us to the end of the move. Each day a mounted officer & orderly were sent to arrange billets for next day	
	20		Company marched via THIEVRES, HALLOY & LUCHEUX to BOUQUEMAISON. Transport lines were in the open & the men in barns. This was the normal accommodation while the march lasted.	
	21		Company moved by FRÉVENT to GUINECOURT. 1 OR suffering from a bad foot fell out at FRÉVENT. This was the only man who fell out during the whole 6 days. Feet were carefully washed & inspected every night.	
	22		Move via OEUF & WAVRANS to MONCHY CAYEUX. Company remained here over following day; time was devoted to cleaning up. All limbers cleaned up & oiled	
	23			
	24		Coy marched to ESTRÉE-BLANCHE (Map Ref HAZEBROUCK 1/40,000.)	
	25		March to ROBECQ. Company were billeted on SE edge of the village	

WAR DIARY

Army Form C. 2118.

VOLUME XV
PAGE 5

No. 92 MACHINE GUN COMPANY
Date: MARCH 1917

Place	Date	Hour	Summary of Events and Information	Remarks and references to Appendices
	1917 Mar.26		Rest, with the exception of inspection & cleaning up.	
	27		C.O. proceeded on leave to U.K. 4 reinforcements joined. 1 O.R. accidentally wounded by discharge of a revolver.	
	28		Company training training as follows. Gas Helmet & Elementary Drill & Stoppages - A.M. Visual & Physical training & gun cleaning - P.M. 8 O.R. attended a Pole Bombing Course which continued to the 31st. 5 O.R. reinforcements	
	29		training as follows 9.30-10 am Inspection & Gas Drill 10-11am Rough Ground Drill. 11.15-12.30/m mechanism. Afternoon. Semaphore. Physical training & Points B. D. & A. firing	
	30		training as before, with the exception of work with limbers & Pack Mules - "coming into action etc."	
	31		training as follows - A.M Stripping, repairs & stoppages etc. P.M. work with limbers & pack mules. Notification received to the effect that all ranks not already inoculated with T.A.B. vaccine, were to be done by 5th troop.	[signature] Lt OC 92 M.G.C.

Army Form C. 2118.

WAR DIARY
or
INTELLIGENCE SUMMARY.
(Erase heading not required.)

CONFIDENTIAL

WAR DIARY

OF

Nº 92 MACHINE GUN COMPANY

FROM 1st APRIL 1917 TO 30th APRIL 1917

[VOLUME XVI]

VOLUME 16
PAGE 1

Army Form C. 2118.

No. 92
MACHINE GUN
COMPANY
Date: APRIL

WAR DIARY
INTELLIGENCE SUMMARY
(Erase heading not required.)

Place	Date	Hour	Summary of Events and Information	Remarks and references to Appendices
	1918 April 1.		All Company & Transport were billeted as at end of previous I.O.R. evacuated in ROBECQ (map. Ref. HAZEBROUCK)	WWS
	2.		G.O.C. Protection. Programme of work as follows:—	
			No 1 Section. Stoppages & Lock Stripping	
			No 2 — Work over rough ground & fire orders	
			No 3 — Action from Limbers & transferring guns from Limbers to Pack Saddles, also Belt filling	
			No 4 — Tests of Elementary Training & Range finding	
			G.O.C. Bde. expressed himself satisfied with the keenness of Officers & men, but drew attention to the fact that a great deal of work was still required on the hacking of Limbers & cleaning of harness and systematisation of duties in handling of guns. During the afternoon the remainder of the Company who had not already been done, were inoculated with T.A.B. vaccine	WWS
	3		I.O.R. rejoined from C.C.S. In accordance with orders received from Bde. to the effect that the Company was to be mobile in view of pending operations by the 5th inst all surplus stores were dumped at ST. VENANT.	WWS

A5834 Wt. W4973/M687 750,000 8/16 D. D. & L. Ltd. Forms/C.2118/13.

VOLUME 16
PAGE 2

WAR DIARY
or
INTELLIGENCE SUMMARY
(Erase heading not required)

Army Form C. 2118.

NO 92 MACHINE GUN COMPANY
APRIL

Place	Date	Hour	Summary of Events and Information	Remarks and references to Appendices
	1917 April 4		All the Company were completed with small kit, & iron rations were carefully inspected & issued where necessary. All men deficient of iron rations were awarded 7 days F.P.No 2. 1 Section under 2/Lt SARGENT & 2/Lt THOMSON took part in a Bde. Field Day in the neighbourhood of BOIS DES DAMES.	(sgd)
	5		1 O.R. evacuated. 1 O.R. to hospital.	(sgd)
	6		1 O.R. evacuated. 2 O.R. reinforcements. All limbers were carefully cleaned & packed. 4 O.R. reinforcements. The majority of the reinforcements received this month were quite satisfactory. All deficiencies were made up under the supervision of Lt KETTLEY, who at this time was Gas N.C.O. for the Company. Temporary Gas Chambers was erected & every Box Respirator in the Company was tested & none were found to be defective.	
	7		Preparations for move on the following day. It was found that the log. was mobile with limbers packed as follows, & fighting limbers packed with guns, tripods etc.	(sgd)

VOLUME 16
PAGE 3

WAR DIARY

INTELLIGENCE SUMMARY

(Erase heading not required.)

No 92 MACHINE GUN COMPANY
Month: APRIL

Army Form C. 2118.

Place	Date	Hour	Summary of Events and Information	Remarks and references to Appendices
B.E.F	1918 April 7		2 Limbers for Officers kit & mess Equipment, 1 Limber for Orderly Room, Signallers, Shoemakers Equipment, 2 Limbers for C.Q.M.S' Stores, Canteen. The G.S. wagon (complete with estab) carried all transport stores, including Drivers packs. The S.A.A was distributed as follows :- 28 filled Belt boxes for fighting Limber & 92 boxes S.A.A distributed equally over 12 Limbers. 1 Blanket per man was carried on a G.S wagon provided by the Bde.	SWD
		8	4 guns were detailed under 1 officer & personnel of 17 OR for A.A. Duty on the ROBECQ - ST. VENANT Rd. on ammunition dumps. The remainder of the Company moved at 10-30am. to billets at ALLOUAGNE (map of HAZEBROUCK) The Coy was now mobile & under 4 hours notice to move anywhere.	SWD
2/Lt THOMSON took over transport Duties from 2/Lt JACKSON.	9.		News received that 1st ARMY had attacked at 5-30am & a further warning was received to be in readiness Lt ABERNETHY & 1 OR rejoined from course at CANIERS. There was also OR reinforcement. Company Drill & gun Drill was done during the day. Cleaning of	SWD

VOLUME 16
PAGE 4

WAR DIARY
or
INTELLIGENCE SUMMARY

Army Form C. 2118.

No B2
MACHINE GUN
COMPANY
Month APRIL
Date

Place	Date	Hour	Summary of Events and Information	Remarks and references to Appendices
	1917 April 10		Some work with Pack mules was done. The Company was rested as far as possible. 1 O.R. to hospital.	SWD
	11		Warning order received in the early morning that the Coy would move a short distance. This was confirmed in detail during the morning & at 1.30 pm. Coy moved to BRUAY [map ref LENS 11.] During our stay here, special attention was given to the cleaning of limbers & harness. 3 O.R. evacuated.	SWD
	12		A.A. guns were withdrawn & all personnel returned to BRUAY. Training continued as before. 5 O.R. evacuated.	SWD
	13			
	14		Company moved to DIEVAL. Both G.O.C. Division & G.O.C. Bde expressed themselves satisfied with the marked improvement of the condition of the limbers and harness. Company training.	SWD
	15		3 O.R. evacuated.	SWD
	16		Warning order received at 1.30 pm that the Company would move almost immediately. This was confirmed in a personal interview with Bde. Information was also received there that Capt FORSTER who had been granted an extension of	SWD

WAR DIARY
or
INTELLIGENCE SUMMARY.

(Erase heading not required.)

Army Form C. 2118.

VOLUME 16
PAGE 5

No 92
MACHINE GUN
COMPANY

Date: APRIL

Place	Date	Hour	Summary of Events and Information	Remarks and references to Appendices
	1917 April 16		leave until 16th inst. on medical grounds, had now been found unfit to return. Official confirmation was received of this on 21st inst. under AGo D/1961 of 18-4-17.	Covers
	17		Company marched with transport to MINGOVAL arriving 8pm. In accordance with orders received the previous evening from XIIIth CORPS. Coy proceeded via AUBIGNY & the ST-POL-ARRAS Rd. to ANZIN-ST-AUBIN. Verbal instructions received that evening from CMGO. to reconnoitre ground N.E. & N.W. of BAILLEUL village [map of ST OMER] with a view to placing 16 m G o. there the following night to co-operate in the attack [to be made on the Canadian Corps. front & by 63rd Div.] with direct overhead fire.	Coys
	18 19 20		Company stood by, awaiting receipt of specific orders. Company Drill, Gun Drill & Stoppages were carried out each day	Coys
			1 O.R. evac. Lt. STEPHENS joined 1 O.R. proceeded to BOULOGNE as skilled tradesman	Coys
			Orders were received on the evening of the 20th that 8 guns were to be sited on P10d and 8 on P233a & that Coy would move into position on the following evening	Coys

WAR DIARY
INTELLIGENCE SUMMARY

VOLUME 16, PAGE 6

No. 92 MACHINE GUN COMPANY
Month: APRIL

Army Form C. 2118.

Place	Date	Hour	Summary of Events and Information	Remarks and references to Appendices
	1917 April 21		Reconnaissance made by Officers. Order of previous night cancelled in the afternoon; new dispositions for attack on 23rd inst. substituted as follows:— 16 guns to be in N. Section of SUNKEN RD. between B28 & B22 c 9.2. These guns were to give overhead fire 300yds in front of artillery barrage, working from W. to E. through northern half of GAVRELLE village [lifting with barrage from zero to zero + 42] 8 of those guns were cancelled later.	SWS
	22		1 O.R. to hospital + 2 O.R. reinforcements. Further reconnaissance made in the morning. Dump for S.A.A. Belts etc. was formed at MAISON de la COTE [B20d 9.0] 8 gun teams with 32 carriers proceeded to trenches via ECURIE, ROCLINCOURT & the ST. NICHOLAS RD. All guns were in position at 3am 23rd.	SWS
	23		Carrying Party under an Officer went back to trenches B26b 1.9. Fire was opened by all guns at the rate of 1 belt per [about 199 rounds were fired in all] 5 minutes, at 4-45am. At 6am all guns with equipment intact, moved back to MAISON de la COTE + from there to billets having had no casualties	SWS

A5834 Wt. W4973/M687 750,000 8/16 D. D. & L. Ltd. Forms/C.2118/13.

Volume 16
PAGE 4

WAR DIARY
or
INTELLIGENCE SUMMARY.

Army Form C. 2118.

No 92 MACHINE GUN COMPANY
Date APRIL

Place	Date	Hour	Summary of Events and Information	Remarks and references to Appendices
	1917 April 24		1 O.R. to hospital. A bance of Physical training was commenced every morning from 9.45 to 10.30, for the whole company. Company training.	JONES
	25		2 O.R. to hospital. Gun Drill, Company Drill - Gun etc. cleaning was done.	JONES
	26		10 O.R. reinforcements. notification received that major V.L.S. COWLEY had been posted to command the company. Since 16th inst: the company had been detached from the Div. under the orders of the 13th C.M.G.O. Details of a further operation in which we were to co-operate were received from him as follows :— Intention was that this day, together with the 93rd, should give barrage & protective fire for an attack to be made by the 2nd. Div. on OPPY-ARLEUX [Trap: ref. 51.B. N.W. town] Our orders were that we should be attached to the 99th Bde from M.N. Y-Z night & that we would be withdrawn at dusk on Z night unless special application was made by 2nd Div. to XIII Corps for our retention in the line Gun Positions & targets were allotted as follows	JONES

VOLUME 16
PAGE 6

WAR DIARY
INTELLIGENCE SUMMARY
(Erase heading not required.)

No. 92 MACHINE GUN COMPANY
APRIL

Place	Date	Hour	Summary of Events and Information	Remarks and references to Appendices
	1917 April 26		8 guns firing from B19d on B12.b.50 to B12.b.45. 4 8 guns about C23.b.08. firing on B12.d.85 to C1a.50. At zero +50' the latter 8 guns were to move forward about the jumping off trenches in order to form a [illegible] protective barrage [in the event of S.O.S. signal] 500 yds beyond "BROWN LINE" in C1c + C9b	KMS
	27		Lt. ABERNETHY, 2/Lt BEST + JACKSON proceeded to the trenches to reconnoitre positions + select headquarters. Company moved up 4.30pm with transport to Maison Rouge + from there to positions. 52 carriers under 2/Lt JACKSON managed all the carrying forward, using some dugouts in B28 c.8. as an intermediate station. Company HQ was established near B28.a.26. Everything was in position by zero hour which was 4.25am. Even with this number of carriers under an officer, which necessitated the cutting down of teams to 1 N.C.O + 3 men. it was not found possible to get forward a really sufficient supply of S.A.A. when guns, equipment, rations etc. had been dealt with.	KMS

VOLUME 16
PAGE 9

WAR DIARY
for
INTELLIGENCE SUMMARY
Army Form C. 2118.

NO 92 MACHINE GUN COMPANY
APRIL

Place	Date	Hour	Summary of Events and Information	Remarks and references to Appendices
	1917 April 28		Barrage fire was opened by all guns at zero, about 25 rounds were fired. Immediately after the barrage, all guns were laid on S.O.S. targets, on this signal being given at 4.30.p.m. all guns opened fire, about 20 rounds being fired in 30 minutes. At 8½pm orders were received from 99th Bde. that we were to remain in our positions until further orders. Later, at a conference at Bde HQ, it was ascertained that we were to co-operate in an attack to be made the following morning by 99th Bde & 63rd Div. Our instructions were to carry out the same programme as before, i.e. to keep barrage fire to bear on enemy trenches 300 yds in front of artillery lifts.	
	29		At 4 am all guns opened fire, expending about 20 rounds. No further rds were fired that day. Major V.H.S. COWLEY reported to take over command of the Coy. 2/Lt PURSER & 1 O.R. reinforcement also arrived. 3 O.R. wounded.	
	30		5 guns under 2/Lts. BEST & JACKSON (Nº 1 & 2 Sections) returned from the line to Gillets; the remainder of the guns under Lt. ABERNETHY were ordered to take over from 99th Bde.	

CONFIDENTIAL.

92nd MACHINE GUN COMPANY.

WAR DIARY.

1st May, 1917 to 31st May 1917.

VOLUME 17.

VOLUME 17
PAGE 1
Title pages France

WAR DIARY

INTELLIGENCE SUMMARY

Army Form C. 2118.

No. 92 MACHINE GUN COMPANY
Date MAY 1

Place	Date	Hour	Summary of Events and Information	Remarks and references to Appendices
B.E.F.	1917 May 1	Map Ref. 51BNW 1/20000	On the night March 31st/May 1st 2 Sections under Lt. ABERNETHY took over from 99th Bde. in B.17d central. advanced by HQ remained as before in B.27a 2.6. 2/Lt STILES was attached from this date to C.M.G.O for duty	Ref. App. I
	2		6 OR wounded. Lt. ABERNETHY wounded in the afternoon by fragment of shell. Orders received from C.O. in the line at ANZIN ST.AUBIN by Lt. DUNLOP who was with the remaining two Sections, to the effect that they would move the same night into positions preparatory for the attack on the following morning. All officers reported to the C.O. as detailed at 4.30p at advanced HQ with the exception of Lt. DUNLOP who remained at near HQ. 2/Lt THOMSON received orders just previous to this, to proceed to the line to take the place of Lt.ABERNETHY, to undertake the duties assigned to that Officer. At midnight advanced HQ were moved to B.17d 4.6. 10 reinforcements received from the Base. 2 OR wounded 1OR to hospital	Ref. App. 2
	3		At 3.00 hour 3.45am. 3 sub-sections as detailed under Lt. STEPHENS. 2/Lt BEST. 2/Lt PURSER moved forward with the Infantry to which they were attached	

WAR DIARY
INTELLIGENCE SUMMARY

Volume 17
Page 2

No. 92 MACHINE GUN COMPANY
Month: MAY

Place	Date	Hour	Summary of Events and Information	Remarks and references to Appendices
Map Ref. Zone 51 B N.W. / 20,000	May 3		In the case of 2/Lt PURSER his teams, they were held up before reaching the place of assembly, owing to the fact that the preliminaries to the assault, were disarranged by unexpected enemy interference. Lt STEPHENS with his teams got as far as the point roughly A18 b central. This officer was wounded by a shell fragment in the face. His sub-section was ultimately compelled to withdraw leaving one gun, which was recovered the same night. 2/Lt REST's teams pushed forward to a point roughly B18 d 15. A report was received from him early in the afternoon, to the effect that the trench in front of him was full of hostile M.G. snipers. This sub-section returned with guns etc. complete, after having fired 15000 rds. The same night 2/Lt. JACKSON-THOMSON moved forwards into a trench B19 d, took over the 2 guns positioned there.	(See para. 3)
		10 p.m	Two teams + a few other details were sent back to what had become our advanced dump at B22c 92. 3 OR. were found to be missing [no further information has been received to date]	
	4			

VOLUME 17
PAGE 3

WAR DIARY
or
INTELLIGENCE SUMMARY.
(Erase heading not required.)

Army Form C. 2118.

No 92 MACHINE GUN COMPANY
MAY

Place	Date	Hour	Summary of Events and Information	Remarks and references to Appendices
Map Ref. 51BNW	1927 May 4	20.00	N° 36299 Pte HUCKLESBY brought back information that he had seen a hostile M.G. firing from an emplacement in a tree in OPPY WOOD at 51B.a.15. It was at once decided to concentrate 4 M.G.on this target. It was reported to Bde. with a request for co-operation from the artillery. Owing to a relief taking place that night the matter was left solely in the hands of the artillery. It is believed with good effect.	a/N.4.
	5		During the day there was nothing of importance. At night the M.G. defence of the Bde. Line was taken over on a re-organised basis from now onwards.	vide a/N.4.
	6		No incident of any note occurred a carrying party of 10.R were sent up from ANZIN consisting chiefly of reinforcements. On inter-section relief was carried out in the line. The company had now 8 guns in the trench running through points under 2/Lts JACKSON - THOMSON & OF Killed. Sections relieved liable	app. 5
	7		A report was received from the Battn in the line that the enemy was massing troops behind OPPY WOOD!!! 4 guns were laid on defensive lines. Line was opened in reply to the "SOS". 5000 rounds were fired. At 11 am the artillery reported large parties of the enemy in front of OPPY the right flank of the Division on our left.	

A5834 Wt. W4973/M687 750,000 8/16 D.D. & L. Ltd. Forms/C.2118/13.

VOLUME 17
PAGE 4

WAR DIARY
or
INTELLIGENCE SUMMARY.

Army Form C. 2118.

Place	Date	Hour	Summary of Events and Information	Remarks and references to Appendices
Map Ref 51ANN 1	May 7	20000	3 guns were laid on so to bring fire to bear on the three sets of roads in B1d. 1,720nds were fired. good effects were observed. At 12.10h two hostile planes meanwhile offensively attacked one of our planes with m.g. fire. One of these planes was successfully engaged by Major V.L.S. CONWEY commanding the company. It was observed to crash in OPPY WOOD at 6pm. Although Section in the line expected to be relieved this day, all arrangements were made this was cancelled at 5pm owing to impending operations on left Div front. At 7pm in reply to the "S.O.S." Signal 12000nds were fired. The Company were relieved in the line at 9.15pm by 94 M.G.Cy. On the way out just near the CRUCIFIX [B16c1.3] Major V.L.S. CONWEY, who was leading the Company out, was gassed. At the time there was a heavy hostile bombardment of gas Shells with this exception there were no other casualties.	a.h. 6
	8		The remainder of the company moved from ANZIN ST. AUBIN to billets in ST. CATHERINE [G15a central] for proceeded on special leave.	

VOLUME. 17.
PAGE 5.

No. 92 MACHINE GUN COMPANY
Date MAY

WAR DIARY
or
INTELLIGENCE SUMMARY.
(Erase heading not required.)

Army Form C. 2118.

Place	Date	Hour	Summary of Events and Information	Remarks and references to Appendices
Up Pol France 51 B NW /20000	1917 May 9		The Sections from the line returned to billets between 6-9am. In the evening orders were received to "stand to" ready to move at 10 minutes notice. All arrangements were made at once but on the order being cancelled, limbers were sent back to transport lines & the men dismissed. 168 knocked on special leave	
	10		Company training in the morning. Bathing in the SCARFE in the afternoon	
	11.		Company training as before	
	12		Instructions received to reconnoitre the RED LINE, running E. of BAILLEUL from P15b to H5c. with a view to placing 6 m.g.s there Report. 9 apparently according to a scheme outlined by the Div 2/Lt Sargent Left hosp. & 2 men took up the MG positions selected in RED LINE	
	13		Gas Drill. CSM Parade. Limber cleaning in the morning Gun Drill. Gas Action in the afternoon.	
	14.		32 Mark II MG barrels with 48 muzzle cups were received from ordnance, old barrels were returned. 2 OR to hospital Gas Drill, CSM Parade, & Inspection Issue of clothing in the morning - Bathing in the afternoon. 7/Lts PLASER & HEANEY relieved the teams in the RED LINE with equivalent personnel.	

VOLUME 17
PAGE 6

Place	Date	Hour	Summary of Events and Information	Remarks and references to Appendices
Map Ref. France 57B NW 1/20000	1917 May 15		Orders received for the relief of a Section of 93 M.G.Coy, holding positions in front of GAVRELLE as follows C25.e.88. C25.e.97. C25.e.93. C25.e.85.	Ref. App. 8
	16		Warning Order received that 8 guns would be required to assist in an attack to be made by the 93rd Bde. the objective of which was to capture & consolidate GAVRELLE trench (roughly C25.6.) It was ascertained by reconnaissance that flanking fire could be given to cover the area between WINDMILL trench & WINDMILL support (coordinates approx. C19.c.95. to C19.a.60. — C19.d.82 to C19.b.32.0.) from positions previously held by this Coy in B17d The duties assigned to this Company were to cover the area shown above & to open fire only in the event of a counter attack. 2/Lt JACKSON with 4 N.C.Os & 12 men relieved the garrison of the RED LINE Orders issued to 2/Lt PATERSON to join 2/Lt JACKSON with 2 m.Gs & four teams. Preparatory to 6 ok killed. moving forward for the operation outlined above 2/Lt JACKSON was instructed to reorganise the	

WAR DIARY or INTELLIGENCE SUMMARY

Army Form C. 2118.

VOLUME 17 PAGE 9

No. 92 MACHINE GUN COMPANY
Date: MAY

Place	Date	Hour	Summary of Events and Information	Remarks and references to Appendices
	1917 May 13		Garrison of the RED LINE into 4 teams, so that with 2/Lt PATERSON'S section there would then be the 8 guns required by the 93rd Bde. in the "left group". 8 guns from 93 M.G.Coy were placed under the O.C. orders to complete the total of 16 for the "left group". Advanced Coy HQ. were established in B2 to 59. During the evening the number of guns in the LEFT GROUP was cut down from 16 to 8. Unfortunately the teams under 2/Lt PATERSON had already reached Bend Coy HQ., but, although it had already been decided to use only 4 guns from 93 M.G.Coy – 4 guns under 2/Lt JACKSON. These were retained for use as carriers to replace casualties their allotted targets by that time were ready to fire but as no occasion arose they were withdrawn according to orders about 7 am. 2/Lt SARGENT with his section relieved 2/Lt BEST. These guns were under the orders of 93 M.G.Coy until the following day. Major V.S. COWLEY returned from Base Hospital to take over command of the company. 114 OR transferred from 2nd/nd MGC to replace casualties	app. 9

WAR DIARY
INTELLIGENCE SUMMARY

VOLUME 17
PAGE 8

Army Form C. 2118.

No 87 MACHINE GUN COMPANY.
Date: MAY

Place	Date	Hour	Summary of Events and Information	Remarks and references to Appendices
Map Ref Zone 51 S NW 1/20000	1917 May 18		All guns & personnel withdrawn from the Oppy Sector & the MG defences of the RED LINE were handed over to 93 M.G.Coy. 4 fresh teams under 2/Lt PURSER & HEANEY proceeded to take over positions in the Support line behind GAVRELLE as follows:— B24.c.90, B30.a.45, B30.c.45, B6a.5.9. Advanced Coy HQ were moved to B29.c.22. 1 OR wounded.	
	19		About 500 rds were fired at hostile aircraft without apparent success. Work on Emplacements was done. 2/Lt JACKSON & 1 OR proceeded on course of Instruction to CAMIERS 2/Lt LAVENDER proceeded on Special leave to UK 2 OR to hospital. 10R rejoined from Cookery Course. 500 rds fired at enemy aircraft, no result was observed No 4526 Pte LALLY sniped two Germans by rifle fire. Both were seen to be hit. 1 OR was to c/s	
	20		The remainder of the Company moved from ST. CATHERINE into a bivouac camp located about A28d 6.4 2 driver reinforcements received.	
	21		The Company in the line was relieved by 224 m.G.Coy. on relief being completed joined the rest of Coy at A28d 6.4	

WAR DIARY or ~~INTELLIGENCE SUMMARY~~

VOLUME 17 PAGE 9

Army Form C. 2118.

No 92 MACHINE GUN COMPANY
Date MAY

Place	Date	Hour	Summary of Events and Information	Remarks and references to Appendices
	1917 May 21		From this date onwards a Section was detailed nightly as the "Duty Section". Duties were to find all fatigues also "Gas Piquet" at night. 1 OR was S/SK REST at OR proceeded on leave	
	22		Company bathed, a given a clean change of underclothing. Cpls Holmes & Ryan rejoined from CAMIERS. 1 OR rejoined from CGS. A return was rendered of M.G. Stores & equipment deficient. The aggregate amount was extremely small. An oven was constructed by the cooks. Owing to rain during the previous night, ground was entrenched & bivouacs rolled up to enable the ground to dry	app. 19.
	23		Notification received No 23320 Bpl. W. KETTLEY had been awarded the Military Medal. Parade under Section arrangements from 9am to 12[noon] keeping in view the forthcoming inter-section competition. Company drill from 2–3pm under O.S.M. A few shots were fired in the evening from the AA M.G. mounted by day in the sunk[en] at some enemy planes which came over from the direction of the FEUCHY S. RIDGE	

VOLUME 17.
PAGE 10

WAR DIARY
or
INTELLIGENCE SUMMARY.
(Erase heading not required.)

Army Form C. 2118.

No 92 MACHINE GUN COMPANY
Month: MAY

Place	Date	Hour	Summary of Events and Information	Remarks and references to Appendices
	1917 May 24		Usual training for Section Competition. Wrestling on mule-back for Officers at 11am.	
	25		2 OR proceeded on leave to U.K. 1 OR to hospital. Thorough cleaning of limbers followed by C.O's inspection of transport. Bathing Parade	
	26		Work on Range under Section Officers from 8.30-10.30am. Anti gas goggles & small kit issued to Coy. No MG established at transport lines. Major W.S. COWLEY appointed DIV. M.G.O.	
	27		Church Parade at 9.30am. All goggles & respirators were tested in Gas Chamber. Only three were found to be unserviceable. 1 OR to hospital.	
	28		60 OR reinforcements 2 OR to hospital 1 OR rejoined from hospital 21 OR from leave 2/Lt. R.S. FAULKES joined from Base vice 2/Lt. H.W. STILES L to be sent to England. 9 — 11am } Training under Section Officers Noon - 2 noon } C'Snig Parade 2 — 4 pm Work with pack mules. G.O.C. Bde visited transport - expressed himself	

Army Form C. 2118.

VOLUME 17
PAGE 11

WAR DIARY
or
INTELLIGENCE SUMMARY.
(Erase heading not required.)

No 92
MACHINE GUN
COMPANY
Month MAY

Place	Date	Hour	Summary of Events and Information	Remarks and references to Appendices
	1917 May 28		Satisfied with its condition.	
	29	9-11 am	Work with Pack mules 11-12 noon C.Smp. Parade. In the afternoon T.O.E.T. under Section Officers. 6/m Revolver practice for 2 Sections	
	30	9-10.30 am	T.O.E.T. firing under Section Officers 10.30-11.15 am Work with Pack Saddles 11.15-12 noon C.Smp. Parade. 2 OR proceeded on leave to UK. 2-4 pm Cleaning Limbers & Pack Saddles under T.O. A Special class of Instruction commenced for backward men under Sgts. BARKER & LAWRANCE. 1 OR rejoined from Sig. Bounce	
	31	9-11 am	C.Smp. Parade 1.15-3 pm examination of Nos 1 & 2 Sections in T.O.E.T. 11.15 am C.Smp. Parade by Bathed.	

W. A. [signature]
Lieut
for OC 92 M.G.Coy

APPENDIX II

Reference Map 1/10,000.

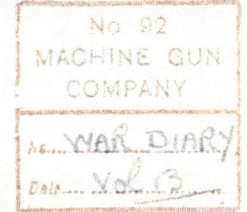

1. An attack is being made by the 1st and 3rd Armies on a date to be notified verbally to Section Officers.

2. The 31st Division is attacking with 2 Brigades, the 92 Brigade on the left and the 93rd Brigade on the right.

3. The objectives of the Brigade is as follows:-
From point C.7.a.7.1. (junction of OPPY support trench and CRUCIFIX Road) thence along the OPPY support trench to C.13.b.5.9. to junction of OPPY support trench and link trench at C.13.b.8.1.

4. BOUNDARIES. Bde
Northern Boundary. From point where embankment crosses ARLEUX LOOP at B.12.d.0.4. crossing ARLEUX-OPPY Road at C.12.d.7.6. through CRUCIFIX LANE at a point C.7.c.46.95 thence to OPPY support trench where it cuts road at C.7.a.8.1
Bde
Southern/Boundary. From B.18.d.4.4. along LINK trench to C.13.d.8.8.

5. The 92nd Brigade will attack with 3 battalions 12th E.Y.R. on left, 11th E.Y.R. in the centre, and the 10th E.Y.R. on the right.

6. The attack will probably be made in one operation, but in order to ensure thorough mopping up, the 1st and 4th waves will only advance to an intermediate line which will run from B.12.d.7.6.S.E. down the road to OPPY CHURCH, thence to junction of roads at C.13.a.5.5., from there Southwards to LINK TRENCH.
This line will be known as the GREEN LINE and the first objective as the RED LINE.

7. Battalions will attack in four waves.
1st and 4th waves objective is GREEN LINE.
2nd and 3rd waves objective is RED LINE.

8. Guns from the 94th M.G. Company will place guns as follows to assist this attack:-

8 guns B.17.c.d.   Target OPPY- NEUVIREUIL Road.
8 guns (not located) Target C.13.c.

9. Guns from the 92nd M.G. Company will be employed as under:-

(a) 2/Lieut. BEST and 2 N.C.O's and 10 men with 2 guns of No. 1 Section will be at the disposal of the O.C., 10th E.Y.R.
He will report to O.C., 10th E.Y.R. at 11.50 p.m. night of Y/Z at point B.21.c.8.5.
The guns will go over with the third waves and will endeavour to find a position nearest C.13.c.2.7. in order to bring fire to bear on enemy in neighbourhood of NEUVIREUIL and to the South-East.

(b) Lieut STEPHENS and 2 N.C.O's and 8 men of No.4 Section with 2 guns already situated in B.17.Central, will be attached to 11th E.Y.R.
He will report to O.C., 11th E.Y.R. at B.23.b.0.8.

at

APPENDIX II (cont.)

at 11.30 p.m.
He will go over in the 4th wave and endeavour to
find positions in the village of OPPY from which
the approaches from the N.E. and S.E. can be swept.

A party of 8 men from the 11th E.Y.R. will carry
up ammunition from point B.23.b.0.8. These 16
belt boxes will be at the point at 11.30 p.m.

(c) 2/Lieut. JACKSON with 2 N.C.O's and 12 men and 2
guns from No.2 Section and Lieut ABERNETHY with 2
N.C.O's, 12 men and 2 guns from No. 2 Section, will
assemble in Northern end of NEW TRENCH which runs
from B.21.b.3.5. to B.15.d.7.3, by midnight on Y/Z
night, under the O.C., 211th Field Coy. R.E. in
order to assist in the consolidation of two strong
posts to be situated as follows:-
  No.1 strong point in CRUCIFIX LANE about
    C.7.c.5.3.
  No. 2 strong point just S. of LINK trench about
    C.13.c.1.3.

(d) 2/Lieut. PURSER with 2 N.C.O's, 10 men, and 2 guns
of No. 1 Section will be attached to the 12th E.Y.R.
He will report to O.C., 12th E.Y.R.
at point B.21.c.8.8. at 9.45 p.m. Y
He will go over with the fourth wave and come
into position in any favourable position to assist
the 12th E.Y.R.

9. 2/Lieut. LAVENDER with 2/Lieut. SARGEANT will remain
in reserve with 4 N.C.O's, 20 men, and 4 guns of Nos.3
Section and one of No. 4 Section, where these guns are
already in position in B.17.c. and d.
They will open fire on any machine gun target that
presents itself.

10. Teams will carry up one petrol tin of water and four
boxes of ammunition per gun.
All spare ammunition will be dumped by the reserve
guns.

11. All ranks will be in possession of an iron ration,
filled water bottles, and one days rations.

12. All spare men will be attached to gun teams as
carriers and orderlies.

13. All gun stores etc will be dumped at B.20.d.7.2.
(MAISON de la COTE) at 8.30 p.m. Y, with the exception of
those of Nos.3 and 4 Sections.

14. Company H.Q. will be with the reserve guns in
B.17.d.

15. A full operation report will be rendered by all
Officers to Company H.Q. together with casualty reports
by 11.30 a.m. and 8 p.m. X

                          Sd. V.L.S. COWLEY Major
                       O.C. 92nd Machine Gun Company.

APPENDIX III
Reference Map:- GAVRELLE. 1/10,000

1.   Our infantry are on the original assembly trench which they hold precariously.

2.   One machine gun is forward at point B.18.a.8.1.

3.   The 6 guns of the 92nd M.G. Company and the 12 guns of the 94th M.G. Company will defend this line.

4.   Fire will be brought to bear on a line running from B.18.b.7.9. to C.13.c.3.4.

5.   Guns will fire at the sector of line relative to their position, and will traverse through 1° on either side of their central line.

6.   The signal to open fire will be when the guns situated by B.17.d.6.7. open fire.

7.   100 rounds will be fired in long bursts and then pause to await further orders to fire.

8.   Guns will be laid on these lines at once.

       Sd. V.L.S. COWLEY Major
       Commanding SHROUD

APPENDIX IV

Reference Map:- GAVRELLE. 1/10,000
----

1.   The machine gun defence of the 92nd Brigade front will be taken over by the 92nd M.G.Company to-night.

2.   The relief will not take place till after ~~dark~~ dark.

3. (a) 2/Lieut. LAVENDER with one sub-section No. 3 Section, and one sub-section No. 4 Section will take over from 2/Lieut THOMSON the positions of No. 2 Section.

   (b) 2/Lieut. THOMSON with 2/Lieut. PURSER and No. 2 Section will remain at Company Headquarters.

   (c) 2/Lieut. JACKSON will take over one gun of No. 3 Section from 2/Lieut. LAVENDER and one Seb-section No.1 Section from 2/Lieut. PURSER, and will proceed to the A dump at point B.22.c.6.2.

   (d) 2/Lieut. BEST with 2/Lieut. SARGEANT and one sub-section No. 1 Section and one gun No. 4 Section will proceed to point B.23.a.5.7. where one gun No. 4 Section will report to him.
   He will take over the positions occupied by one Section No. 94 M.G. Company. A guide from No. 94 Coy. will report to 2/Lieut. BEST at the A dump at 9.30 p.m.

5.   Relieving teams will make certain that they understand the tactical object of each gun.
        Bearings, Q.E's, and Ranges will be explained.

6.   A report will be rendered to Coy. Headquarters immediately the relief is completed.

7.   Guns will be laid on their night line and 2 sentries posted per gun.

8.   All ranks will stand to from 4.15 to 5.15 a.m.

9.   Operation reports, ammunition expenditure state, and casualty return will be rendered to this H.Q. by 7 a.m. 6th inst.

10.   Trenches will be repaird and improved on 6th instant.

                        Sd. V.L.S. COWLEY Major
                             O.C.,92nd Machine Gun Company.

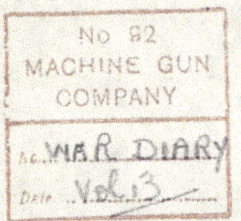

APPENDIX V

Reference 1,10,000
----

1.   One sub-section Nos. 3 and 4 Sections, and No. 1 Section will retain the defence of the support line in position already adopted.
    The remainder of the teams will return to ANZIN to-night.

2.   Gun team commanders will report to 2/Lieut. JACKSON at MAISON de la COTE by 12 m.n. 6th instant, when they will come under his command and be marched back to ANZIN.
    2/Lieut. LAVENDER will arrange that parties from Coy. H.Qrs. will start at 5 minutes intervals, starting at 9. pm.
    A guide will direct the leading team.
    Parties will not be larger than one sub-section.

3.   Gun team of No.4 Section will receive 3 men from the dump.

4.   All stores and equipment will be taken back, including 2 belt boxes of ammunition per gun.

5.   A carrying party of 10 men will report at Coy. H.Q. from the dump by 8.30. p.m.
    These will return to ANZIN for a rest.

6.   Guns, stores, etc., will be dumped at MAISON de la COTE under a guard of one N.C.O, and 4 men of No. 2 Section.

7.   Two runners will remain at Coy. H.Qrs. and 2 at Bde. H.Qrs.
    They will be rationed from the forward dump.

8.   2/Lieut. JACKSON on return to ANZIN will report by wire to Coy. H.Qrs. that all is correct.

                                    Sd. V.L.S. COWLEY Major
                                       Commanding 92nd Machine Gun Company.

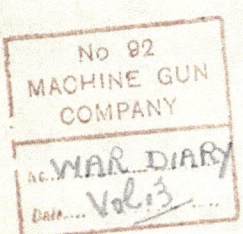

APPENDIX VI

Reference 1.10,000
----

1.   Order No. 5 is hereby cancelled.

2.   The Company will be relieved by No. 94 Company this evening.

3.   All gun teams will stand to at 6 p.m.

4.   There will be 14 boxes handed over per gun team to 94 Coy.

5.   The 4 gun teams under 2/Lieut. BEST will be relieved by 2 gun teams 94 Coy.
     On completion of the relief they will proceed back via the gun pits to MAISON de la COTE.

6.   The remaining gun teams will, on being relieved, proceed to MAISON de la COTE via Bde. H.Qrs. and ARTILLERY AVENUE.

7.   No teams will leave the trench without the order of an Officer.

8.   All guns etc, will be dumped at MAISON de la COTE, and a guard of one N.C.O. and 4 men will be furnished by No. 1 Section.

9.   2/Lieut. BEST and 2/Lieut. THOMSON will report to O.C., Coy at ANZIN that relief is complete.

                         Sd. V.L.S. COWLEY Major
                         O.C., 92 Machine Gun Company.

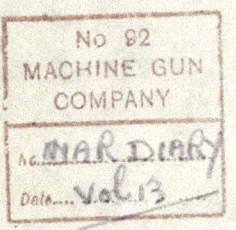

APPENDIX VII

INSTRUCTIONS FOR THE MACHINE GUNS OF THE RESERVE BRIGADE IN THE RED LINE.
(Provisional)
----

1. The Brigade in Divisional Reserve will, until further orders, maintain 6 Vickers guns in the RED LINE, with a view to holding this line pending the arrival of reinforcements.

2. The positions selected are:-

Guns.	Co-ordinates.	Arc of Fire (True)	
R.1	B.16.d.75.55	38°	- 88°
R.2	B.17.c.1.2.	73°	- 120°
R.3	B.23.a.20.85	355°	- 40°
R.4	B.23.c.15.00	90°	- 150°
R.5	B.29.a.1.5.	40°	- 80°
R.6	H.5.a.25.65.	80°	- 120°

3. The personnel required is 1 Officer and sufficient N.C.O's and men to maintain and work the guns.

4. The guns will be kept in temporary emplacements; permanent emplacements for the defence of this line are being made under Corps arrangements.

5. Guns will be dismounted during the day, but will be mounted at dusk and laid on their night lines. The crews are NOT required to keep watch, except as below.

6. Two guns will be mounted during the day, in alternative emplacements, as A.A. guns; one man will be on watch with each of these guns.

7. The work of the Brigade digging the RED LINE is NOT to be interfered with, and on no account are parapets to be undercut.

8. Concealment of these positions from the enemy being of the greatest importance, it must be impressed on the gun crews that they must not wander about near their positions during daylight.

9. 5,000 rounds of ammunition will be maintained at each gun.

10. The Company will arrange its own reliefs, and rations.

11. The above positions will be occupied from the night of the 12/13th May onwards.

General Staff, 31st Divn.

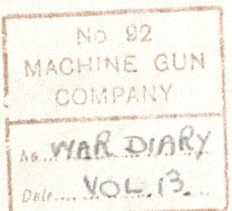

APPENDIX VIII

ORDERS FOR RELIEF. 15/4/17
----

1. You will take up four teams as per attached list to relieve 4 guns of 93rd M.G. Coy. in C.25.c. (in front line)

2. MOVE. You will march via St.NICHOLAS to report 93 Coy. rear H.Q. at H.1.c.5.2. From there you will obtain guides to forward H.Q. near GAVRELLE where you will report to 2/Lieut. AGNEW, in order to obtain further detail about move into forward position.

3. RATIONS AND STORES. Arrangements are being made for guns, rations and water to be brought up to meet you at 93 Coy. Advd. H.Q. They will be under the care of 93 M.G. Coy's T.O.

4. TRIPODS, BELT BOXES, S.A.A. etc., will all be taken over from the teams you are relieving. Please get receipts.

5. REPORTS. You will be temporarily under 93 M.G. Coy. Casualties and operation reports will be communicated as quickly as possible through RIB (93 M.G.Coy) to HULL (93rd Bde.) Casualty reports will always be repeated to CANVAS and SHROUD. This report is due at 12.30 p.m. daily.
T Please keep copies of operation reports sent to JIB for Coy diary.

6. DISPOSITIONS. Please send back as early as possible, co-ordinates of guns and targets. This is essential and will be sent back by carriers (who will return as soon as possible to billets).

7. CARRIERS. 8 carriers will go up with you under Cpl. McDOUGALL as shewn.

8. RATIONS will be sent to 93 Coy. H.Q. (advd) where carriers will be sent nightly.

                                              Sd.   Lieut DUNLOP
                                                  a/O.C. 92 M.G.Coy.

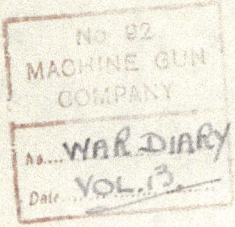

APPENDIX IX

To accompany 93rd INFANTRY BRIGADE OPERATION ORDER No.

ACTION OF MACHINE GUNS.

MACHINE GUNS   1.   44 Vickers machine guns will be available for a co-operation in the attack to be made.

COMMAND   2.   All above guns will be under the command of O.C., No. 93 Machine Gun Company.

OBJECT TO BE ATTAINED.   3.   The object to be arrived at is for these grouped machine guns - firstly, surprise effect in case of counter-attack, and secondly, to deal with any enemy machine guns coming within their zone of fire.

DISTRIBUTION   4.   Guns will be devided into 3 groups as under:-

RIGHT GROUP   Consisting of approximately 20 guns.
    Positions as under:-

    16 in a line running through trench at
       H.6.c.3.2½ to H.6.c.5.8.
    4 in a line from I.1.b.5.3½ to I.1.b.1.7½.
    Targets for this group as follows:-

    16 rear guns. To cover area between I.1.b.8.3
       to C.25.b.2.0 and I.2.a.4.6 to C.25.b.7.3.
    4 front guns. To cover area between I.2.a.4.6
       to C.25.b.7.3 and I.2.a.9.8 to C.25.a.1.6.

CENTRE GROUP   Consisting of 8 guns.

    Positions as under:-

    4 in Support Line (for defensive work only).

    1 at B.24.c.9.0
    1 "   B.30.a.7.6
    1 "   B.30.c.3.9
    1 "   H.6.a.5.8.

    4 in Front Line distributed as follows:-

    1 at C.25.c.9.7½.   )   These guns all have
    1 "   C.25.c.9.6.   )   a good field of fire
    1 "   C.25.c.9.5.   )   direction N.E.
    1 "   C.25.c.9½.3.)

In case of counter-attack these guns will cover WINDMILL MAZE.

LEFT GROUP   Consisting of 16 guns.

    Positions as under:-

    16 guns in a line approximately from B.23.b.6.6
       to B.17.d.6.5.

    Targets.. To cover area between WINDMILL
       TRENCH and WINDMILL SUPPORT. Co-ordinates
       approximately C.19.c.7.5 to C.19.a.6.0 and
       C.19.d.8.2 to C.19.b.3½.0.

                                           Action to be taken.
                                                 (over)

-2-

ACTION TO BE TAKEN.	5. RIGHT GROUP will only open fire if a counter-attack is threatened, or if by observation they can locate any enemy machine guns firing, they will immediately attempt to silence them. No fire is to open before ZERO. CENTRE GROUP. The action of the four forward guns of Centre Group must be left to the discretion of the Section Commanders to decide in accordance with any situation which may arise. The four guns in SUPPORT LINE are purely for defensive purposes, but if necessary one or more of these guns may be required to move forward to FRONT LINE. LEFT GROUP. Same instructions as for Right Group.
COMMUNICATION	6. All orders, messages, etc., will be sent by Brigade Headquarters direct to Captain A.C YORK, O.C., Grouped Machine Guns, at B.29.c.2.2. (R.C.2.) which will be Headquarters of all the grouped machine guns. All messages, etc., from RIGHT, CENTRE, or LEFT GROUPS, are to be sent to above Report Centre addressed O.C., Grouped Machine Guns. Code name --RIB.

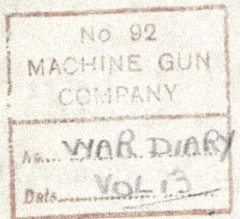

APPENDIX X

RECOMMENDATION FOR AWARD.

(23320 a/Sgt. W. KETTLEY).
Awarded Military Medal 20/5/17.

By his splendid courage and untiring energy under frequent heavy fire, this N.C.O. organised a small carrying party, during the attacks made in the OPPY section on 28/29th April, so as to serve our 16 machine guns, in forward positions, with rations, ammunition and water.

He had to pass through hostile barrage fire more than once, but by his example, he inspired his men with the same spirit of determination to see the work through.

On one occasion, during a bombardment of Gas Shells, when 86769 Pte. E. THORPE had fallen overcome by the gas and was unable to adjust his respirator, Sgt. KETTLEY at considerable personal risk helped him on with it, and carried him into safety.

Sd. Lieut DUNLOP for Major
O.C., 92nd Machine Gun Company

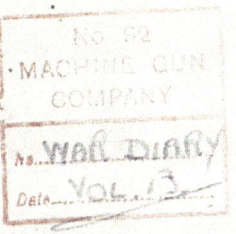

APPENDIX I

Map Reference:- 51.B. N.W.   1/20,000

To:-
Lieut. ABERNETHY.

1. You will take 8 guns from 99th Brigade at once. The two sections as per attached are to be detailed for this duty.

2. Please issue instructions to Lieut. STEPHENS to report to you for duty with these guns.

3. 2/Lieut. JACKSON, if you require him, and as many men from Nos. 1 and 2 Sections as you please, will be available for helping you into position and for providing you with a first supply of S.A.A.

4. Rations and water will arrive at MAISON de la COTE at 9.30 p.m.
   Please find men from Nos. 3 and 4 Sections to carry these and detail 2 men to go in advance to pick up limber.

5. Nos. 1 and 2 Sections are to be clear of trenches and back at billets in ANZIN as soon as possible.

6. An N.C.O. and three men from each of the outgoing Sections will be detailed with their guns and stores near MAISON de la COTE. (preferably in the trench previously used for assembly).
   One dixie, tea and fuel will go up for this party by rations. I have detailed a man to hand these over to the guard.

7. Please decide according to the situation what belts, shovels, etc., you will require to keep.

8. 92nd Brigade is relieving 99th Brigade to-night at 8 p.m. and their Headquarters will be at B.21.a.7.7. Please report completion of relief to Brigade Headquarters repeating this and all messages possible to Coy. H.Qrs. This includes xxxxxxxxxx casualty returns.
   Should you have received instructions about this relief from the C.O. please cancel these.

                              Sd. W. DUNLOP Lieut
                                 for O.C. 92 M.G.Coy.

SECRET AND CONFIDENTIAL

Army Form C. 2118.

WAR DIARY
or
INTELLIGENCE SUMMARY.

(Erase heading not required.)

Instructions regarding War Diaries and Intelligence Summaries are contained in F. S. Regs., Part II. and the Staff Manual respectively. Title pages will be prepared in manuscript.

Place	Date	Hour	Summary of Events and Information	Remarks and references to Appendices

NO. 92
MACHINE GUN
COMPANY

War Diary

for 92nd M. G. Coy.

from June 1st to June 30th 1917

Volume XVIII

WAR DIARY or INTELLIGENCE SUMMARY

Army Form C. 2118.

No. 92 MACHINE GUN COMPANY
WAR DIARY
Date: JUNE

VOLUME 18 PAGE 1

Place	Date	Hour	Summary of Events and Information	Remarks and references to Appendices
Yaona	1917 June 1st	9-11am	1 & 2 Sections under Section Officers. 3 & 4 Sections Exam. in T.O.E.T. [Inter-Section Competition]	
		11-15-12 noon	C.S.M. Janda. 2-4th Transport - Driving Tests at Transport Lines. The whole Company was present. Nº1 Section declared winner. Nº 1 O.R. to hospital. 5-6pm Riding Class for Officers. Nº 2817 Coy.S.Sergt Win left for UK to join a Cadet School. Strength 169.	
	2	9am	Checking of kit & equipment. The usual Deficiency Return was rendered by sections showing an unusually high percentage of items to be charged against the men. This was obviously due to the fact that the return had not been rendered as regularly & carefully this year as last. Inning Guns of all S.A.A. in belts. 11-12 noon Officers Revolver Practice.	
		12 noon	The remainder of the day were employed on filling in shell-holes to improve the site of the camp, this being a point to which considerable attention was paid.	
		1-45pm	Inspection of Clothes. These were found to be in very good condition. No clothes were condemned which could possibly be mended by the men themselves. This was followed by preparations for the move. Strength 169. 1 O.R. evacuated. 100 R reinforcement.	App. I

Army Form C. 2118.

VOLUME 18
PAGE 2

WAR DIARY
or
INTELLIGENCE SUMMARY.
(Erase heading not required.)

No 92 MACHINE GUN COMPANY
WAR DIARY
Date JUNE

Place	Date	Hour	Summary of Events and Information	Remarks and references to Appendices
	June 3rd		Company moved with all transport via ECURIE & MONT ST ELOY & ECOIVRES to Billets, mostly MISSEN huts were particularly clean & comfortable. The lighting limbers were parked here, but the transport lines were at FIS.L 59. 2/Lt LAVENDER rejoined from leave. 1 O.R. to hospital. 1 O.R. rejoined from hospital. Strength 179.	Map Ref. Sheet 51C N.E. F15 A+B
	4		Training programme (as per Appendix 2) began. Particular attention was paid during the week to the improvement of transport & personnel of Section control. 1 O.R. to hospital 2 O.R. rejoined from hospital. 1 O.R. from leave. 1 O.R. proceeded on leave to U.K. Final T.O.E.T. Competition decided in favour of No 1 Section. Strength 179.	App. 2
	5		Consolidated claim for Prof. Pay Class 1 for about 90% of eligible N.C.O's submitted to Paymaster. Ote Holmes appointed Paid L/c. Strength 192 [owing to official notification of transfer 3 O.R. to hospital to C.C.S received.]	
	6		Announcement made by C.O. on bay. Parade, that L/Cpl FORSTER & C.S.M G.A. SMITH had been mentioned in despatches. Strength 192.	
	7		1 O.R. proceeded on leave. We had at this time about 55 men who had not had leave for over 12 months & the vacancies allotted by Bde. were roughly 2 per week.	

WAR DIARY or INTELLIGENCE SUMMARY

Army Form C. 2118.

VOLUME 18 PAGE 3

NO 92 MACHINE GUN COMPANY
WAR DIARY
June

Place	Date	Hour	Summary of Events and Information	Remarks and references to Appendices
	1917 June 7		7 O.R. reinforcements.	
	8		8 limber wheels received from the I.O.M. in return for unserviceable. 2/Lt Jackson returned from course at CAMIERS. Establishment of Petrol Tins fixed at 116 for the company. Fo 28 carried on transport, 24 on Water Carts + 4 per gun team]. Strength 178.	
	9		Sgt LAWRENCE + Cpl MILLS proceeded on Course of Instruction at CAMIERS. Blankets held in possession were new 33⅓% of strength. Strength 178.	
	10		All Officers Surplus Kit sent to Railhead. 4 O.R. returned to Base as inefficient under 1st Army N° 2724/44A d/6-6-17. Warning Order received that the Coy would move to the forward area the following day, as the Div. was relieving the 63rd Div. in the line. The Company attended the Brigade Sports in the afternoon, in which the C.O. won 1st Prize in the "Officers Champion" Event with "Biddy". Strength 169. 10R to hospital. A team was also entered for the "wrestling on mulebank" competition but was not successful.	
	11		1 OR proceeded on leave. Company moved at 5.30.p.m. via MAROUEIL + ST. AMZIN to ST. CATHERINE [S.18.A.N.W.] Hdqrs established at 6.15.69. The transport lines at the same place. Strength 169.	

WAR DIARY
INTELLIGENCE SUMMARY

VOLUME 18 PAGE 4

No 52 MACHINE GUN COMPANY
WAR DIARY June

Date	Hour	Summary of Events and Information	Remarks
1917 June 12	9.10am	Section Drill under Section Officers	
	10-11am	Box Respirator Drill for whole Coy. under C.O.	
	2pm	Bathing Parade. 1 O.R. to hospital. Strength 166. Book showing Stores on charge of Sections [tabulated for showing issues & deficiencies] issued to each Section Officers. Responsibility for maintaining complete establishment was now entirely removed from the hands of the C.S.M. who had hitherto performed this duty.	
13		a/Sgt Reeley promoted Sgt. 2/Cpl Myers promoted Cpl. Pte Doughty & Cochrane appointed paid 2/Cpl. 4 O.R. rejoined from leave. Section Drill. Stoppages of Box Respirator Drill. 2pm Bathing Parade.	
	5.30-4pm	"Auxillary aiming mark & its uses" explained by Section Officers. Strength 166.	
14		2/Lt Jackson proceeded on leave. Signallers commenced to receive instruction in the use of Carrier Pigeons, with a view to their employment in the line. All sections completed to establishment of 56 Belt Boxes & 4 Belts. The CO proceeded to take up his duties as D.M.G.O at Division this day. Strength 161 [5 O.R. evacuated]	

Army Form C. 2118.

WAR DIARY
or
INTELLIGENCE SUMMARY.

(Erase heading not required.)

No. 92 MACHINE GUN COMPANY
WAR DIARY
Date. JUNE

VOLUME 19
PAGE 5

Instructions regarding War Diaries and Intelligence Summaries are contained in F.S. Regs. Part II. and the Staff Manual respectively. Title pages will be prepared in manuscript.

Place	Date	Hour	Summary of Events and Information	Remarks and references to Appendices
	1917 June 15		1 O.R. rejoined from leave. 2 O.R. to hospital. Working Parties, 50 strong under an officer, were found by us morning + evening, for work on range under construction by Bde. in front of ROCLIN COURT. 2/Lt LAVENDER attached Coys HQ to assist C/SG. Box Respirator Drill, cleaning of limbers. Strength 161	
	16		2 O.R. to hospital. 2 O.R. rejoined from hospital. 3 O.R. reinforcements. Stoppage competition fired by all sections on range. Prizes being awarded to winning man of each section. Usual Working Party found for Bde. in the evening + in addition a further working party of 26 O.R. under 2/Lt FAULKS proceeded to report to 1st E.Y.R. at 4 p.m. for the purpose of carrying up duck boards + improving C.T.s in front of OPPY WOOD. Cpls REDMAN + JONES appointed acting Sgts.	
	17		1 O.R. proceeded on leave. 1 O.R. evacuated to C.C.S. Company reached another combing out of officers surplus kit was made. It has been found that this has frequently to be done, just as the C.Q.M.S. has to be carefully watched so that no surplus stores accumulate.	
	18		1 O.R. Reinforcement. 1 O.R. to hospital. 3 O.R. course of tunnelling. Ptes NOBLE and CLAY appointed act P/L Cpls.	

WAR DIARY of INTELLIGENCE SUMMARY

VOLUME 18 PAGE 6.

No 92 MACHINE GUN COMPANY WAR DIARY Date JUNE

Date 1917	Hour	Summary of Events and Information	Remarks and references to Appendices
June 18 (contd).		Two G.S. limbered wagons were entered for the special M.G.C. competition at the Div. Horse Show. Although a great deal of work had been expended on them and they made a really creditable turnout, it is not appreciated that the M.G. limbered wagon (Inventory Board) is quite different from the Infantry G.S. limbered wagon (Inventory Board). 2/Lt Faulks attended a tank demonstration at Wailly (S of ARRAS). Preparation - overhauling of gear preparatory to moving into line.	APP. 4
19		4.O.R. to 1st Army Rest Camp. 2.O.R. admitted to hospital. 1.O.R. evacuated to C.C.S. 1.O.R. accidentally wounded. Sections moved off from billets in the evening in accordance with orders issued by the D.M.G.O. 2/Lt SARGENT acted as O.C. Coy in the line. He is due to see that all the orders and instructions which were received from the D.M.G.O. were carried out. The D.M.G.O. continued to command the Coy, with 2/Lt SARGENT as his Deputy in the line, and the 2nd in Command in charge of all administration at Rear Hqrs. Rear Hqrs. were in ST. CATHERINE. Three nights rations were sent up on pack, but as this entailed the employment of a very great number of mules and drivers it was found more economical to use Coy. limbers.	
20		1.O.R. proceeded on leave. We had at this time in the Coy. 60 men who had not been for 12 mths. the normal Coy. allotment in leave was 1. or 2 vacancies per week.	
21		1.O.R. Returned from leave. 1.O.R. evacuated to C.C.S. 1 Officer admitted to Hospital (2/Lt PATERSON).	

WAR DIARY
or
INTELLIGENCE SUMMARY

Army Form C. 2118.

VOLUME 18 PAGE 7.

No 1. MACHINE GUN COMPANY
WAR DIARY
Date JUNE

Place	Date	Hour	Summary of Events and Information	Remarks and references to Appendices
	JUNE 21 cont.		A new section relief as shown on APP. 5. There were now only 3 Officers available actually to command sections, as Lt SARGENT was at advanced H.QRS	APP 5.
	22		1.C.M.S. Rutherford 2.O.R. Rejoined from Hospital. 1.O.R. admitted to Hospital. Guns opened fire successfully in accordance with D.M.G.O's Orders. 2/Lt FAULKS was now commanding Nos 1 + 4 Sections. 2/Lt HEANEY No 3 Section. 2/Lt PURSER No 2 Section.	APP 6.
	23		Considerable work was done throughout the time we were in the line. Box mountings were fitted in all alternative positions. Range cards and Order Boards were carefully fixed up for every gun. Our two Anti-Aircraft guns frequently acted, but did not succeed in bringing down any planes. No rounds were fired except by A.A. guns.	
	24		2.O.R. evacuated to C.C.S. Guns in rear fired at irregular intervals during the night at given targets. Very great care was taken in maintaining elevation and direction.	
	25		Nothing of interest occurred	
	26		2.O.R. rejoined from Hospital. 1.O.R. rejoined from C.C.S. 1.O.R. evacuated C.C.S. 1.O.R. to Hospital. We were relieved in our positions by 94th M.G. Coy as per APP. 7.	APP. 7.
	27.		The groups known as A.B.+C were successfully established by 4 a.m. June 27th 1917. Ammunition etc. was in position & teams made as comfortable as possible. French chillers were being erected by the Bic's groups. A "position call" for this dug-out was applied for and granted.	

WAR DIARY

VOLUME 18
PAGE 6

Army Form C. 2118.

No. 92 MACHINE GUN COMPANY
WAR DIARY JUNE

Place	Date	Hour	Summary of Events and Information	Remarks and references to Appendices
	JUNE 28.		1.O.R. Reeve to U.K. 1.O.R. Wounded. The sub-section which had returned to billets at ST. CATHERINE for 1 day was used as shown in APP. 8. Rations for this day (on which the 94th BDE. made its attack) were sent up at mid-day. Four men were borrowed from the Infantry, also dug-out accommodation for belt filling, shortly before ZERO 7.10 p.m.)	APP. 8.
	29		1 O.R. Reinforcements from Base. 4 O.R. Wounded. Company was withdrawn from the line as per APP. 9	APP. 9
	30		1.O.R Rejoined from Base. 1.O.R on Detachment to C.C.S. Overhauling & checking of stores. 3 guns were found to be unserviceable, one of the barrel casing of which had been badly damaged by shell fire on the 26th inst, and two others which leaked. No guns lost.	

Stough Lt OC

2/7/17.

SPECIAL ORDERS NO.10. re MOVE TO ECOIVRES

1. No. 92nd M.G. Coy will vacate No 4 Area Billets on 3rd inst & will proceed to ECOIVRES via the Cross Country track from MADAGASCAR CORNER.

2. Stores, Kit etc will be dumped ready for Packing at the following times

   Friday 1st inst
       Blankets in 6 rolls   6.30 p.m.

   Saturday 2nd inst
       Guns, SAA, & Gun Stores   6 p.m.

   Sunday 3rd inst

Signalling Kit Orderly Room, Canteen & Stores	6.30 a.m.
Officers Kits	6.30 a.m.
Officers Mess Kit	6.30 a.m.
Cooks Dixies etc.	6.30 a.m.

3. Transport Time Table.

1st inst	1 limber	H.Q.	6.30 p.m.
2nd inst	8 --	"	6 p.m.
3rd inst	5 --	"	6.30 a.m.
	Cooks Cart		6.30 a.m.
	Officers Chargers		7.15 a.m.

   Parade at Transport Lines in time to position in column MADAGASCAR CORNER at 8.10 a.m.

   The Transport will proceed with the Company.

4. Company Time Table.

   5 a.m.   Reveille
   5.15 a.m.   Strike Tents
   5.45 a.m.   Breakfast
   6.30 a.m.   Latrines filled in & Camp cleaned by Nos 1 & 2 Sections
   6.30 a.m.   Kit loaded by Nos. 3 & 4 Sections

5. Packs will be carried

SHEET II

> No. 92.
> MACHINE GUN
> COMPANY
> APPENDIX I
> WAR DIARY

6. Lt DUNLOP will hand over the camp to a representative from the Area Commandant at 7.30 a.m.

He will go forward and take over the new camp meeting the Company on the road about 1 Kilometre east of ECOIVRES.

Major Commd.
92nd M.G. Coy.

PROGRAMME OF TRAINING   4th to 10th /6/17.

Ref. B.M.4/12.

NO 92 MACHINE GUN COMPANY
WAR DIARY
APPENDIX II
M............
Date...............

DATE 1917.	TIME	PLACE	FORM OF TRAINING
June 4	6.30 - 9am	ECOIVRES	C.S.M's Parade for Transport. Coy. Drill etc.
	9 - 11am	S.I.C to	Work under Section Officers
	11.15 - noon	F.I.S.A.2.G.	Company Drill
	2 - 4pm	—	Cleaning of Limbers
	6pm	—	Inspection of Limbers G/S.
5th	9 - 11am	—	Work with Pack Saddles
	11.15 - noon	—	Cleaning of Pack Saddlery
	2 - 4pm	—	T.O.E.T. + Rough Ground Drill
	2 - 4pm	—	Limber Driving for Transport
	6pm	—	Cleaning of Limbers 6.30pm Inspection of Limbers
6th	All day	—	As for 5th June.
7th	9 - 11am	—	9mm. Action + Firing on Miniature Range. 11.15 - noon. Coy. Drill
	2 - 4pm	—	Drill with Pack Saddles 2-3pm Driving Drill for Transport
	6pm	—	Inspection of fighting Limbers
8th	9 - 10am	—	9mm. Action Competition 10-11am. Pack Saddle Work Competition.
	11.15 - noon	—	Cleaning Limbers, Pack Saddles 3pm. Driving Drill
	2 - 4pm	—	Inspection of Harness etc.
9th	10 - 12 noon	—	Turn-out Competition
	2 - 4pm	—	Driving Competition + Wrestling on Mule Back.
10th		—	Church Parade followed by Company Sports

APPENDIX III

No. 52 MACHINE GUN COMPANY
War Diary
Appendix III

92nd M.G. Coy. SPECIAL ORDER No 11

10.6.17.

MAP. REF. 51B. N.W. 1/50,000

1. The Company will move from the present area during the afternoon of 10th inst. + will take over billets + transport lines of 190th M.G. Coy at G15a 5,2.

2. The following Transport will report to Coy. H.Q. at 3.30 p.m. 10th inst.
   a. 1 Limbd Wagon for Signallers + Office Kit
   b. 2 — — Q.M. Stores + Canteen
   c. 2 — — Officers Mess + Officers kits
   d. 1 G.S. Wagon Stores

3. All stores etc. will be dumped in a convenient place for loading by 3 p.m.

4. No 1 & 2 Sections will load up all Stores

5. No 3 + 4 — do — will clean up camp + fill in latrines etc.

6 a. 2/Lt. JACKSON will proceed to G15a 5.2. to take over billets + will be there at 11.50 a.m. He will meet the Coy. + conduct it to billets
   b. 2/Lt. HEANEY will take over Transport lines

7. Company parade at 5 p.m.

8. Lt DUNLOP will hand over the present billets + will obtain all necessary receipts

9. Lt LAVENDER will inspect billets at 4.30 p.m. + will report to these H.Q. as to their cleanliness

10. Signallers telephone wire will be taken in starting at 1.45 p.m.
    On arrival at new billets a line will be laid out from Coy. H.Q. to Transport lines + to Bde H.Q.

Lt.
for O.C. 92nd M.G. Coy

Appendix 4

SPECIAL ORDERS No. 14 For 19-6-17
For Relief of 94 M.G.Coy by 92 M.G.Coy

1. The 92 M.G Coy will relieve 94 M.G. Coy on night 19th-20th inst. Relief to be complete by daylight June 20th

2. Positions will be taken over by Sections as under

No 2 Sections situated at
- 1. C19c 92 25
- 2. C19c 90 30
- 3. C24d 3.8
- 4. C24d 85 80

No 1 Section's guns situated at [less one subsection]
- B21d 85. 3

No 4 Sections guns situated at
- 1. B19c 75
- 2. B19c 73
- 3. B23a 47
- 4. B23a 85 20

No 3 Section + Subsection of No 1 Section in reserve at Advcd Coy HQ

3. Sections will move off from billets in time to meet guides as under.

No 2 Section at B29d 89 at 11pm.

No's 1. 3 + 4 Sections at Advcd Coy HQ at 11pm.

300 yds distance will be maintained between Sections on the march Pack Animals will accompany Sections.

4. 4 Pack Animals per Section will carry guns, water tins, spare parts boxes etc. as far as Advcd Coy HQ + B29d 8.9. where they will be quickly + quietly unloaded

4. & will return to billets without delay under command of C.S.M. Smith

5. Petrol Tins at the rate of 6 per Section will be taken up

6. Ammunition box mountings at the rate of 2 per gun team will be taken up. They will be erected in the alternative positions as soon as possible. All freshly turned soil to be covered up with sandbags

7. Tripods & ammunition boxes will be taken over from 94 M.G. Coy. Certificates will be given & duplicates sent to Advd Coy HQ

8. Rations for 20th will be carried up by each man.
Daily Rations will be fetched by one man per gun team from Advd Coy. HQ for 1.3 & 4 Sections & from B 29 d 8 9 for No 2 Section. at 11 pm commencing on 20th inst.

9. Signalling communication will be established from Advd Coy HQ to Bde. HQ & No 1 Section at B 17 c 9 4.
No message that gives the situation of guns or any information likely to be of value to the enemy will be sent by telephone except in code.

10. O.C. No 3 Section will detail 2 men to go forward with No 2 & 4 Sections & O.C. No 1 Section will take forward 2 men from his reserve subsection. The men will return to Advd HQ when the relief is complete. They will report their ~~~~~ return & relief complete to O.C. SHROUD in trenches

11. No 4 Section will have 4 guns mounted by day for AA work.
  No 3 Section will send out 2 guns to EAST BAILLEUL POST for AA work.
12. On having taken over + all correct the OC No 2 Section will report to the 13th & 10th E.Y.R.
13. Lt. SARGENT will act as OC SHROUD in trenches
14. Coy. Advd HQ will be established in gun pits in B27d.
15. Completion of relief will be wired to Bde HQ by the code word "BRIDLINGTON"
16. 24 hours after taking over the line, OC SHROUD in trenches will forward to DMGO the co-ordinates + true bearings of centre of line of fire

Lt
for OC SHROUD

Appendix 5.

6MGO/11.

1. (a) On night of 21/22 No 3 Section will relieve No 2 Section in the front line.
    (Nos. 1. 2. 3. & 4 guns).
   (b) ½ Sub Section No 1 Section will relieve ½ Sub. Section No 1 Section.

2. All arrangements of guides &c. will be made by Section Commanders concerned.

3. Tripods ammunition boxes, ammunition, will be handed over & receipt given.

4. All work in progress will be continued

20.6.17.

Major
Cmdg 92 MGCoy.

No 92
MACHINE GUN
COMPANY
WAR DIARY
APPENDIX 5

No. 92
MACHINE GUN
COMPANY
WAR DIARY
APPENDIX VI

APPENDIX VI

1. On the night of 22nd June at a time to be notified later (about 10.30 p.m.) the following guns will open fire on targets indicated

2. (a) 1 Sub Sect. No.1 Sect. near B23d 7.7. to fire on B18 b 8.2.
   (b) 1 Sub Sect. No.4 Sect. near B23a 4.6 to fire on C13 c 7.6.
   (c) 1 Sub Sect. No.4 Sect. near B17c 7.5 to fire on C13 b 8.1.

3. Guns will not be fired from their battle positions

4. 14. Boxes of ammunition will be available at each gun position, + 3 boxes S.A.A. to replete expended belts.

5. Guns will be masked from the front by sand bags which will be kept wet.

6. Guns will be refilled with water after every 2,000 rds

7. 2 Petrol tins of water will be by each gun

8. Duration of fire. Fire will die down at 40 mins past ZERO

9. No 2 Section guns will NOT open fire unless ordered to by the O.C. Infantry in case of emergency.

10. All belts will be filled immediately they are empty

11. Great care will be taken to maintain elevation + direction
    Guns will be clamped as tightly as possible.

12. Guns will be mounted at 9.45 pm care being taken to avoid exposure.

13. Q.E. + bearings of targets will be forwarded to Adv. Coy H.Q. by 9 a.m. on the 22nd. They will be checked by O.C. SHROUD in TRENCHES.

14. Section officers will check the laying of the gun before + during firing. He is responsible for the safety of the troops over whose heads we are firing.

15. O.C. SHROUD in TRENCHES will arrange to replenish ammunition supply as soon as possible.

Cmdt 92 MG Coy.

APPENDIX VII

> No 92 MACHINE GUN COMPANY
> No. Appendix VII
> War Diary
> Date

The following redistribution of guns of 92nd M.G. Coy will be carried out on night 26/27 June.

1. No 2 Section and 1 Sub Section No 4 Section will occupy positions at B17c7.3.
   2 Tripods and existing ammunition belonging to 94 M.G. Coy will be taken over.
   This group will be known as A group and will be under the command of 2/Lt FAULKES.

2. No 1 Section will occupy positions at B23a3668.
   One tripod and ammunition belonging to 94 M.G. Coy will be taken over from No 4 Section.
   This group will be known as B group and will be under the command of 2/Lt. PURSER.

3. No 3 Section will be relieved by one section of 94 M.G. Coy. Guides to conduct incoming teams will be at advanced Coy HQRS at 10.15 p.m.
   Ammunition + tripods will be handed over and receipt obtained.
   Section will proceed to new positions in EAST BAILLEUIL POST at B23a7.2.
   This group will be known as C group and will be under the command of 2/Lt. HEANEY.

4. No 4 Section (less 1 sub section vide para.1.) will return to billets.

5. Sites for guns will be previously reconnoitred and selected by Section Officers.

6. One emplacement per gun will be constructed immediately.

7. 14 Belt boxes and 10 S.A.A. Boxes will be in each position by each gun.

8. Tripods and ammunition boxes of at 7 & 8 gun positions (B23a) will be dumped outside the trench at junction of TYNE and TYNE ALLEY with one man as guard.
   These will be handed over to party from 94 M.G. Coy + receipt obtained.

9. All groups will be in their new positions by 11 p.m.

10. Advanced Coy HQRS will be established at B17c7.3.

11. Telephone communication will be obtained to 94 BDE HQRS through Battn H.Q. at B17c6.1.

12. Groups will report by runner to Advanced Coy H.Q. that change has been carried out.

13. O.C. SHROUD in TRENCHES will report by wire completion of change to D.M.G.O. by the code word "HOME".

14. Targets & firing instructions will be issued later.

23.6.17

Major
Cmdg 92 MGCoy.

APPENDIX VIII

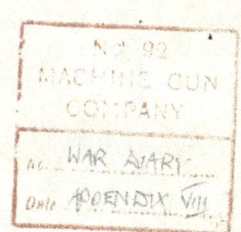

1. The sub section of No 1. Section which will return to billets on night 26/27 will be used as under for operations in near future.

2. Supposed strength* = 2 N.C.O's 8 men.

3.   1. N.C.O. + 2 men to group A at B17c 6.4.
       1. N.C.O. + 2 men to group B at B23a 3.6.
           2 men to group C. at B23a 7.2.
     2 men to Bde H.Q. at B27a 8.8. (vide D.M.G.O. 30(ii))

4. As many men as you can gather together will help sections with belt filling.

5. Sub section with spare men will go up with rations as per D.M.G.O. 30" of to days date.

26.6.17.

     * This was the actual strength.

Major
Cmdg 92 MGC.

Army Form C. 2118.

WAR DIARY
or
INTELLIGENCE SUMMARY.
(Erase heading not required.)

Vol 15

CONFIDENTIAL

WAR DIARY

of

92nd MACHINE GUN COMPANY.

From 1st July 1917 To 31st July 1917.

[VOLUME 19]

VOLUME 19
PAG. 1

WAR DIARY
INTELLIGENCE SUMMARY

Army Form C. 2118.

No 92 MACHINE GUN COMPANY
Date July

Place	Date	Hour	Summary of Events and Information	Remarks and references to Appendices
B.E.F.	1917 July 1st		Company was billeted in ST CATHERINE, day was spent overhauling kit & equipment. 1 OR proceeded on course at CAMIERS. Coy strength 170 OR	O.S.K.
	2.		Company relieved 9th M.G. Coy in the line in accordance with orders issued by DMGO 96 as before. Lt SARGENT acted as OC Coy in the line. Coy HQ remaining at ST CATHERINE. 2 OR rejoined from course. 1 OR from hospital. 2 OR from CCS 3 OR admitted to hospital.	App I
	3		1 OR killed. 3 OR sent to Rest Camp. Lt JACKSON rejoined from leave.	O.S.K.
	4		2 OR killed & 9 OR wounded.	O.S.K.
	5		2/Lt BEST was ordered a medical board in UK found unfit to return to the B.E.F. 1 OR rejoined from leave. Throughout the time company was in the line, considerable work was done in the trenches. Company suffered severe casualties & on night 5/6 was relieved by 195th M.G.C. in accordance with orders issued by Br 60. 3 OR to hospital. 3 OR on tunnelling course & 4 OR rejoined from Rest Camp.	O.S.K. App 2
	6 4-20am		2/Lt BALL + 5 OR reinforcements joined. 1 OR to hospital, 1 OR rejoined from hospital. The relief was successfully completed. The whole Coy proceeded to ECURIE	O.S.K. O.S.K.

WAR DIARY

INTELLIGENCE SUMMARY

VOLUME 19 PAGE 2

Army Form C. 2118.

No 92 MACHINE GUN COMPANY
Date July

Place	Date	Hour	Summary of Events and Information	Remarks and references to Appendices
	6/7/16		Company proceeded to ECOIVRES in motor lorries, arriving at 4am. Day spent in checking kit & equipment.	ASK
	7th		Training programme attached. 2 OR to hospital + 1 OR sent on Sanitary Course.	App. 3 ASK
	8th		Coy. Strength 168 OR. Coy Training. 1 OR inoculated on leave.	ASK
	9th		Coy. Training. 5 OR sent on tunnelling course.	ASK
	10th		Coy. Training. 1 OR rejoined from leave. 1 OR to hospital	ASK
	11th		Orders were received that the company would move into line to relieve the 76 C.M.G.C. on night Dec 13th. 2/Lt W. THOMSON was admitted to hospital sick & evac. to C.C.S.	
			1 OR to CCS. 2/Lt TEMPERLEY joined from Base Depot. No 11249 C/L DAWSON was awarded the Military Medal for gallantry in the field	ASK
	12th		Company moved with all transport to new transport lines at FRD 58. [51 et 20.00]	
			Company less No 1 Section moved up to line to relieve No 1 Section in accordance with orders received from D.M.G.O. No 2 Section remaining at Transport Lines. Lt DUNLOP commanded the Company in the line. advanced HQ being at S23 C 1/4.+2 [Rollecourt map] Coen HQ remaining with Transport lines under 2/Lt FAULKS.	App 4
			2 OR to hospital. 2 OR evac. to CCS. 1 OR rejoined from hospital. 2/Lt FAULKS was recalled from Rel.Course.	ASK

WAR DIARY or INTELLIGENCE SUMMARY

Army Form C. 2118.

No. 92 MACHINE GUN COMPANY

VOLUME 19 PAGE 3

Month: JULY

Place	Date	Hour	Summary of Events and Information	Remarks and references to Appendices
	9/7/17		1 Sub Section of No 2 Section under 2/Lt PURSER moved into line & relieved 1 Sub. Section 13th C.M.G.C. in accordance with orders issued by D.A.G.O. 3 OR rejoined coy from on course.	App. H.
			1 OR wounded. Lt SARGENT + 1 OR proceeded on leave.	
	14		2/Lt TEMPERLEY took over command of No 1 Section. 1 OR rejoined from leave. Company Strength 164.	
	15		1 OR was wounded & died the same day. 2 OR to hospital. 1 OR rejoined from ECS.	
	16		Sub-Section of No 2 Section under Lt KING relieved the Sub Section in the line according to orders issued by D.A.60.	
	17		2/Lt CLEAVER joined from Base Depot. 3 OR to Rest Camp. BOULOGNE. 1 OR was evac. to ECS. 2 OR rejoined from Tunnelling Course.	
	18		2/Lt HEARNEY was admitted to hospital + evac. to ECS next day. Lt LAVENDER returned from leave & took over command of No 4 Sec. 3 OR rejoined from Rest Camp. Coy Strength 163 OR. During night 17/18th a sub-sec. of No 2 Section were slightly gassed by hostile gas shells — no serious consequences ensued.	
	19		10 OR reinforcements joined. 2 OR rejoined from leave. 1 OR from ECS. 1 OR from hospital. 1 OR proceeded on	
	20		leave. 1 OR admitted to hospital.	
			1 Officer, 1 or Section, + 4 NCO 2 men per gun from 243 M.C. were posted for instruction in the line	

WAR DIARY
or
INTELLIGENCE SUMMARY

Army Form C. 2118.

VOLUME 19 PAGE 4

No. 92 MACHINE GUN COMPANY   JULY

Place	Date	Hour	Summary of Events and Information	Remarks and references to Appendices
	19th July 20		Gun teams being reduced to 1 NCO & 5 men. Surplus men were sent back to transport	app 5 9sh
	21st		Orders received for the Company to cooperate in an operation carried out on the night of 22/23rd by Canadians on our left. Section Officers reconnoitred positions to be occupied on the following night. WoL Strength 13 OR. 2 OR rejoined from hospital	9sh 9sh
	22nd		Strength of the Coy mustered	9sh
			In accordance with instructions sent down to near HQ, gun team remaining in the line	9sh 9sh 31st 6 9sh
	23rd		Report of the operation by the Dn 60 is attached nothing to report	
	24th		During this time Company was in the line, with the exception of the operation on night 22/23 no guns fired at all, and nothing of importance occurred. Considerable work was done improving the trenches & making alternative positions etc.	9sh
			On the night 24/25 Company was relieved by 2.5 MGCoy in accordance with orders received from Dn 60. During the day 2/Lt PURSER proceeded to MONT ST ELOY to reconnoitre the billets	9/7 7 9sh
	25th		Company moved with all transport to billets in MONT ST ELOY Lt WOOD (attd from Base) Syllabus of training attached	9sh app 8

WAR DIARY
INTELLIGENCE SUMMARY.

(Erase heading not required.)

VOLUME 19   PAGE 5

Army Form C. 2118.

Place	Date	Hour	Summary of Events and Information	Remarks and references to Appendices
	July 25		Checking of kit equipment, usual deficiency returns were required by section officers. Gun stores were checked. Copies - overhauled + usual deficiency returns rendered. 2/Lt HARDY proceeded to us for admission to a Cadet School. Lt. R. on leave. L/SARGENT + 10 R. rejoined from leave.	65k 63k
	26		DRIVERS proceeded on fees Course. Company training as per Programme. 6 OR reinforcements. L/Training + 7 OR proceeded on leave. Yr. allotment of leave at this time was about 8 per week. We had about 50 men who had been without leave for over 12 months. Strength 197 OR	74k
	29		A Church Parade was held in the Billet. Owing to inclement weather, sports for the same reason, sports which had been arranged had to be postponed.	83k
	30		Company training. Lt. DUNLOP was admitted to Corps/ Post. Station 2 Amt. 2 OR proceeded on leave.	83k
	31		Bombing training. 2/Lt PURSER was attached to 84 Siege Battery. 3 OR went sent to 1st Army Rest Camp. All the arms of the Coy. were inspected by a Divisional armourer.	98k

DMGO/S/6.   Appendix I

Orders for relief of 94th M.G.Coy by 92nd M.G.Coy

1. 92nd M.G.Coy will relieve the 94th M.G.Coy in the line on night of 2nd/3rd July.

2.

	Gun	Position	Direction	
No 1 Sect.	No 1 gun at	C.19c.75.25	direction 165°	QE
	2	C.19c.8.9	135°	
	3	C.19a.48.00	0°	
	4	C.19a.1.6	127°	
No 2 Sec.	5	B.24.b.67.88	59°	
	6	C.19c.18.50	0°	
	7	B.24.d.1.7	30°	
	8	B.24.b.28.63	130°	
No 3 Sec.	9	B.17c.66.30	94°	6° 20'
	10	B.17c.70.38	96°	6° 20'
	11	B.23a.36.68	91°	8° 10'
	12	B.23a.38.64	93°	8° 10'

No 4 Sec. in reserve under OC SHROUD in trenches in dug-out at B.17c.7.3. Guns to be mounted at night near dug-out on bearing of 105. QE 7°.   No sentry need be posted. In event of SOS signal guns will be manned & will fire on lines given above.   All bearings true.

3. Nos. 3 & 4 Sections will relieve 3 & 4 Sections 94 Coy. by daylight on 2nd inst. They will be at Cross Roads ROCLINCOURT [A.29.c.55] at 3 pm.
   OUSE trench will be used.
   Sub-sections will advance at 200x intervals. Guns will not be carried on the shoulder, but will be carried by 2 men by the straps. Great care will be taken to avoid exposure from view.

4. Nos 1 & 2 Sections will meet guides from 94 Coy at the Concrete Emplacements at 10.30 pm. whence they will be led into position.

5. Tripods, 14 Belt Boxes & 10 boxes SAA also 12 Sights will be handed over to 94 Coy. Receipts will be given.

6. 2 guns from No 2 Section & 2 guns from No 3 Section will be used for AA work by day. Battle positions will not be used.

7. Every effort will be made to improve trenches near emplacements & the strictest trench discipline will be maintained at all times.

8. The greatest vigilance will be maintained at all times.

9. Lt SARGENT will be OC SHROUD IN TRENCHES.

10. Telephonic communication will be obtained with Bde.

11. On completion of relief the code word "DOVE" will be wired to DMGO 31st.

[signed] V.L.S. COWLEY Major
DMGO 31st Div

1/7/17

Appendix 2

SITUATION REPORT

July 3rd 8am — The front line was heavily shelled, No.1 Sec. having 1 killed & 1 wounded. Throughout the day hostile shelling rendered communication very difficult.

No.4 Section was withdrawn from the RED LINE to reinforce No.3 Section in front & support lines.

July 4th — The support lines were heavily shelled & No.2 Sec. had 1 N.C.O. & 3 men wounded.

No.1 Sec. had 1 man killed & an N.C.O. & 3 men wounded, the N.C.O. remaining at duty. During the afternoon one gun position occupied by No.2 Sec. was completely destroyed & the tripod & quantity of SAA blown up. The gun was therefore withdrawn to Section HQ ready to be used on its aux/mounting in case of attack.

During the night an inter-section relief was carried out, the two guns in the front line being relieved.

July 5th — No further casualties occured in spite of intense hostile shelling.

No. 92 MACHINE GUN COMPANY
WAR DIARY
JULY

App III
O.C. 92 M.G. Co. Appendix 9.

TRAINING PROGRAMME.

92nd M.G. Company.

JULY.

SATURDAY 7th.
- 9 - 11 a.m.   Pack Drill from Limbers.
- 11.15 - 12 a.m.   Infantry Drill under Section Officers
- 2 - 3 p.m.   Immediate Action.
- 3 - 4 p.m.   Mount gun.

SUNDAY 8th.
- 9 - 11 a.m.   Pack Drill from Limbers.
- 2 - 3 p.m.   Baths.

MONDAY 9th.
- 7 - 8 a.m.   Officers Riding.
- 9 - 11 a.m.   Practice M.G.Competition without Firing.
- 11.15 - 12 noon.   Immediate action.
- 2 - 3 p.m.   Packing Limbers against time.
- 3 - 4 p.m.   Mount gun.

TUESDAY 10th.
- 7 - 8 a.m.   Officers Riding.
- 9 - 12 noon.   Practice M.G.Competition on Range. (4 targets to be applied for).
- 2 - 2.30 p.m.   Rifle Inspection.
- 2.30 - 3.30 p.m.   Immediate action.
- 3.30 - 4 p.m.   Mount gun.

WEDNESDAY 11th.
- 7 - 8 a.m.   Officers Riding.
- 9 - 11 a.m.   Practice M.G.Competition.
- 11.15 - 12 noon. (Sergt.Majors' Parade.
- (B.A.B.Code class for Officers.
- 2 - 3 p.m.   Immediate action Competition.
- 3 - 4 p.m.   Auxiliary Aiming Mark instruction.

THURSDAY 12th.
- 7 - 8 a.m.   Officers Riding.
- 9 - 12 noon.   Practice M.G.Competition on Range.
- 2 - 3 p.m.   Relief of sentries.
- 3 - 4 p.m.   Trench Drill.

FRIDAY 13th.
- 7 - 8 a.m.   Officers Riding.
- 9 - 11 a.m.   Practice M.G.Competition.
- 11.15 - 12 noon.   Building up of Sandbags and emplacement making.
- 2 - 3 p.m. (Sergt.Majors Parade.
- (B.A.B.Code instruction.
- 3 - 4 p.m.   T. O. E. T.

SATURDAY 14th.
- 7 - 8 a.m.   Officers Riding.
- 9 - 12 noon.   Emplacement Making.
- 2 - 4 p.m.   Methods of putting on Q.E.4, direction and maintaining same.

SUNDAY. 15th.
- Morning -   Divine Service.
- 2 - 4 p.m.   Baths.

MONDAY 16th.
- 7 - 8 a.m.   Officers Riding.
- 9 - 12 noon.   Competition to decide team for Rifle Meeting.
- 2 - 3 p.m. (Sergt.Majors' Parade.
- (Officers Revolver Shooting.
- 3 - 4 p.m.   Lecture - "Methods of M.G.Defence."

TUESDAY. 17th.
- 7 - 8 a.m.   Officers Riding.
- 9 - 11 a.m. (Team for Competition practice under Lieut.Thompson.
- Building up of Sandbags and making of emplacements.

-2-

(Contd.)

TUESDAY, 17th.	11.15- 12 noon.	Section Drill.
	2 - 3 p.m.	Packing Limbers.
	3 - 4 p.m.	Relief of Gun teams.
WEDNESDAY, 18th.	7 - 8 a.m.	Officers Riding.
	9 - 11 a.m.	(Team for Competition Practice.
		(Emplacement making Competition.
	11.15 - 12noon.	(Sergt.Majors' Parade.
		(Officers B.A.B.Code Competition.
	2 - 3 p.m.	Officers Revolver Shooting. Gas Drill.
	3 - 4 p.m.	Immediate action.
THURSDAY, 19th.	7 - 8 a.m.	Officers Riding.
	9 - 12 a.m.	Open Fighting Exercise.
	2 - 3 p.m	Trench Drill.
	3 - 4 p.m.	T. O. E. T.
FRIDAY 20th.	7 - 8 a.m.	Officers Riding.
	9 - 10 a.m.	T. O. E. T.
	10 - 11 a.m.	Gas Drill.
	11.15- 12 noon.	Use of Auxiliary Aiming Marks and methods of maintaining. Q.E. & direction.
	2 - 3 p.m.	(Sergt.Majors' Parade.
		(Officers Revolver Shooting.
SATURDAY 21st.	7 - 8 a.m.	Officers' Riding.
	9 - 12 noon.	Range Work.
	2 - 3 p.m.	Cleaning Guns.
	3 - 4 p.m.	Belt Filling Competition.

V.L.S.Cowley.

Major,
O.C. 92nd M.G.Company.

D.H.Q.
7.7.17

Copies to:-
92nd Inf.Bde.
C.M.G.O.

Appendix 4.

92nd M.G. Coy ORDER No. 20.

1. The 92nd Bde. will relieve the 1st Canadian Bde in the line on night 12/13th July

2. The front line extends from T.17.d.5.4 to T.9.c.3.3 & is held by two Battns.

3. The 92nd M.G.C. will relieve the 1st C.M.G.C. on night of 12/13th July & one sub-section 13th C.M.G.C. on night 13/14th

4. The following are positions of HQs
   - Bde HQ   S.24.c.3.9   Rt Battn.   T.22.a.6½.3
   - Lt Battn   T.19.b.8.9   Support Bn   S.18.d.6½.2
   - Reserve Bn. M.G Coy   M.G Coy   S.22.b.4½.4½
   - T.M.B.   S.29.c.4.4   HQ. of R.E.   S.24.c.5.9.

5. There will be no communication by day between any HQs by runner, except in very special cases. All HQs are in exposed positions & under direct observation & it is therefore necessary to keep them as quiet as possible.

6. Company less No 2 Section will parade at 7.45 P.M. 12th July & will follow the transport of the 1st C.M.G.C. to the forward dump at T.21.d.3.9

7. Guides will meet the transport at T.21.d.3.9 & will conduct gun teams to their positions

8. The Coy. will be distributed as under —

Front Line

Section	Guns	Co-ordinates	Sec. Cmdr.	Sub-Sec Cmdr.	Section HQ
3	BERWICK	T.21.b.83.28.	Lt JACKSON	2/Lt BALBI	T.22.a.6.9
	ABERDEEN	T.22.b.37.80			
	ARGYLL	T.16.d.21.36.			
	ANTELOPE	T.16.b.48.17			

Support Line

1	BEDFORD	T.21.d.10.63	Lt SARGENT		T.21.d.10.63
	BANGOR	T.21.a.85.05			
	BIRKENHEAD	T.21.a.42.24			
	BLACKPOOL	T.20.b.65.40			
4	BLACKBIRD [2 guns]	T.14.c.40.54	2/Lt HEANEY		T.14.d.10.84
	BUFFALO [2 guns]	T.14.d.10.05.			

In reserve

S-Section
No 2 — Transport lines at F.11.d.58 L.E.KING
                                      2/Lt PURSER
will relieve 1 S-Section 13th C.M.G.C. on night 13/14th July at BADGER T.20.c.2.0

9. 1 Tripod, 8 Belt boxes & S.A.A. will be taken over at each gun position & receipts given

10. There will be as little movement by day as possible at gun positions. Sections will be in possession of periscopes where MG allows.

Appendix 4 contd.

11. Telephonic communication will be obtained between Coy HQ. & HQs. Nº 1 & 3 Sections. No conversation or message will be sent by telephone which may be of use to the enemy. Messages will be sent in RAB code.

12. 2 men from each Section will be sent to Coy HQ where they will live. They will be used as runners. They will go up to Section HQs with the relieving teams returning to Coy HQ with reliefs from side.

13. Section Officers will render a return to Coy HQ on night 11/12th July, shewing:—
    a. Position of guns   b. Amount of SAA taken over
    c. Work in progress   d. Work proposed
    e. Material required   f. Accomodation available
    g. Nº of box mountings required

14. It is proposed to move 1 gun from BUFFALO to T.15.b 15.59
    1 gun from BLACKBIRD to T.15.b 15.95.
    O.C. Nº 4 Sec. will reconnoitre these positions on night 13/14 & report on their progress.

15. BUFFALO, BEDFORD & BANGOR Guns will be mounted by day for A.A. firing. A.A. sights will be used.

16. Rations for 13th July will be issued on 12th. One man from each gun team will be sent to ration dump at T.21.d.39. at 10-30pm daily for rations.
    One petrol tin per gun team will be taken up

[Signed] V.L.S. COWLEY Major
OC 92 M.G. Coy

11/7/17.

SECRET   Appendix 5.

92 M.G. Coy Order No 2

1. The Canadian Division on our left is carrying out an operation on night of 22nd/23rd July. The machine guns of the 92nd M.G.Coy will co-operate by bringing fire to bear on the trenches SW. of & on the houses of HÉRICOURT.

2. The following guns will be employed on lines of fire indicated —

	Guns	Position	Off. i/c	Direction True Bearing	Q.E.
Group "A"	2 from BLACKBIRD	T.9.c.0.5	2/Lt CLEAVER	51° 54°	
	2 — BUFFALO	T.15.a.6.9	Lt. LAVENDER	55° 56°	4° 16'
	2 — BADGER	T.15.a.8.8	2/Lt PURSER	56° 60°	
Group "B"	ANTELOPE	T.16.b.48.17	2/Lt BALBI	18°	2° 15'
	ARGYLL	T.16.d.21.36	} Lt. KING	23°	3° 47'
	ABERDEEN	T.22.b.37.60		27°	4°

3. On 21st July Lts LAVENDER & CLEAVER will meet D.M.G.O. at 8pm. at BADGER & will reconnoitre positions to be taken up.

4. On 21st July, 3 men per gun team carrying 2 belt boxes each will be at BADGER at 10pm. They will proceed under 2/Lt. TEMPERLEY up PEGGY trench to its junction with TEDDIE GERRARD where they will be met & conducted to gun positions. One shovel per team will be carried.

5. On night of 22nd July gun teams will be conducted to their new positions by officer in command immediately it is dark enough to move.

6. Gun teams of Group "A" will consist of 1 N.C.O. & 5 men, two of whom should be from 243 Coy. If gun teams are not up to this strength they should be made up from BIRKENHEAD & BEDFORD teams.

7. 6 additional belt boxes will be taken, also oil, guns, tripods, spare parts & 1 petrol tin of water per gun.

8. All guns of both groups will be in position ready laid on lines of fire as above by 10.45 pm.

9. Zero hour will be notified later.

10. OPERATION   At zero hour all guns will open rapid fire traversing through 4° to right of original line of fire. When one belt has been fired all guns will elevate by 1° and continue firing with 4° traverse till another belt is expended. This will be continued for 3 subsequent lifts, i.e. 5 belts will be fired on elevation differing each lift by 1°. Traverse each time to be 4° to right of original line. Relaying & oiling up after each belt will be done as rapidly as possible.

11. After 5 belts have been fired, barrel casing will be refilled. Guns will then fire another 5 belts depressing by 1° after each belt. Stops will be used to avoid depressing lower than the original elevation.

Opn. 5 contd.

10 Contd.
On completion of operation, guns of group "A" will be withdrawn by order of the DMGO who will be at the junction of PEGGY & TEDDY GERRARD.

Guns of "B" Coy. will fire an additional 4 belts & will then relay on their SOS. lines.

11. On return to normal positions, guns will be cleaned & amount of S.A.A. expended noted. This will be reported by to DMGO. by wire on 23rd July.

[signed] V.L. SCOWLEY Major
OC gun Coy.

20/4/17

Appendix 6

Report on Action of MGs of 31st Div. in Conjunction with Operation by 3rd Canadian Division night of 22/23rd July 1917

21st July — Section Officers reconnoitred positions as per 92 MG Coy. Order No 2. Lines of fire laid out and luminous sticks placed for direction. SAA carried forward & dumped behind gun positions.

22nd July 8pm — "A" group guns moved forward along PEGGY trench, remaining in TEDDY GERRARD trench till dusk when they were mounted in front of trench on lines laid out. All QE's & lines of direction checked by DMGO & gun teams sent back to trench.

23rd July 12-45am — Gun teams stood to & Section Officers finally checked depression & traversing stops.

ZERO – 1am — All guns opened fire simultaneously. One belt was fired on the original line & at each of 4 subsequent lifts of 1° traversing through 4°. On completion of 5th belt of SAA, guns fired a further five belts depressing by 1° after each belt, finishing at the original QE. All guns had fired their 10 belts by Zero + 20 mins. 2 more belts per gun were fired at intervals of 3 minutes. "B" group guns fired 3 extra belts.

ZERO + 33 mins — Guns cleaned & withdrawn.

NOTES ON OPERATION

1. "A" group guns were sited behind a slight rise, so as to hide the flash. Canvas screens were erected on left of guns where observation was possible.

2. There was no enemy shelling on gun positions except a few 5.9" or 4.5" shells at ANTELOPE gun which was not masked by a screen. It was thought that the ground sufficiently masked the flash, but it is suggested that an order be issued that a screen should always be erected at night to hide all possibility of guns being seen.

3. Direction & elevation were excellently maintained throughout, being checked after each belt by an officer or NCO. The necessity for an extensive issue of clinometers, ie at least one per 2 guns, was emphasised. Luminous posts were not satisfactory. An electric torch throwing a beam of light on a screen, similar to an apparatus invented by Major DENNY, MGTC would have been invaluable. A large amount of time was taken in checking QE's with existing appliances.

Appendix 6 Contd

4. Guns fired with very few avoidable stoppages owing to the previous careful tuning up of guns & checking of S.A.A. boxes.
Two metal boxes were taken up, but these proved useless & had to be replaced by web belts refilled on the spot. These refilled belts caused the only stoppages that there were, owing to the impossibility of checking them in the dark. It is suggested that a proportion of spare belts be issued which can be filled beforehand & carefully checked. Additional boxes are not required as these take up a large amount of room in the limbers & add extra weight.
Number of Spare Belts suggested —
4 per gun ie 64 per Company

5. The unavoidable stoppages were —
   a. a broken roller
   b. a piece of metal from burst cartridge case stuck in feed block
   c. several No 4 stoppages owing to faulty ammunition
   d. one broken tumbler

6. Casualties — nil.
7. S.A.A. expended — 28,650 rounds.
8. Results — observation impossible.

23/7/17

No. 92 MACHINE GUN COMPANY
WAR DIARY
JULY

[signed] V.L.S. COWLEY
Major
D.M.G.O.
1st Div

DMGO/SO/6.   Appendix 7

Orders For Relief of 92 Coy by 243 Coy

1. 243 Coy. will relieve 92 Coy. on night of 24/25th July
2. The following guns positions are being taken over — ANTELOPE. ABERDEEN. ARGYLL BERWICK. BEDFORD. BLACKPOOL. BIRKENHEAD. BADGER [2] BUFFALO [2] BULLDOG [2] Rear HQ [3]
3. 10 boxes SAA. 12 Belt boxes, 1 Tripod. 2 Petrol Tins & other Trench Stores will be handed over
4. Guns will be mounted at dusk & gun teams standing by their guns. SAA will be dumped in dug-out. Belt boxes will be in recess near gun positions
5. SAA from BANGOR will be fetched to complete to 10 boxes per Gun by No 4 Section. Remaining boxes to be sent with team to BADGER on night 23/24th
6. A list of Stores ammunition etc at each gun position will be made out & handed to incoming teams. A receipt will be obtained.
7. A guide from each of the gun positions as per (2) will be at RATION DUMP at 10-45 p.m. 24th to guide incoming teams to their new positions.
8. BLACKBIRD & BANGOR positions will be vacated on 23rd/24th Gun teams going to BULLDOG & rear Coy HQ respectively
9. On completion of relief gun teams will file out carrying Spare Parts, extra Petrol Tins etc to Ration Dump where Transport will be waiting.

Appendix "Y" Contd.

9. Contd

They will return to Transport Lines under Lt. LAVENDER.

The gun team at Rear Coy. HQ. will go out under Lt. JACKSON. — Transport for this team & Coy. Stores will meet them at Adv. Coy. HQ.

10. Completion of relief will be wired to 92nd Bde HQ & DMGO. by code word "SUCCESS".

[signed] V.L.S. COWLEY Major
O.C. SHROUD.

23/7/17

92 M.G.Coy

PROPOSED PROGRAMME OF WORK OF 92nd M.G.COY Appendix 8.
whilst out of the line at MONT. ST. ELOY.

Wednesday
25.7.17.   9.10 a.m. Sergt. Majors Parade.
           10.- 11.15. Inspection of guns and stores by section officer.
           11.30-12.30. Cleaning Limbers.
           2.-4.   Clothing inspection & lecture on economy.

Thursday
26.7.17.   6.15-7.15. Officers Riding.
                       Sergt. Majors Parade.
           8.45-9.45. Immediate Action.
           9.45-10.45. Trench drill & relief of sentries.
                       Transport driving.
           11.0-12.30. Pack drill.

Friday
27.7.17.   6.15- 7.15. Officers Riding.
                       Sergt. Majors Parade.
           8.45- 9.45. Immediate Action.
           9.45-10.45. Trench drill & relief of sentries.
                       Transport driving.
           11.0-12.30. Pack drill.
           6.0 p.m.   Boxing.

Saturday
28.7.17.   6.15-7.15. Officers Riding.
                       Sergt. Majors Parade.
           9.0-12.30. No.1. Section. Firing on LA MOTTE Range.
           2.0- 4.30. No.2. Section. Firing on LA MOTTE Range.

Sunday
29.7.17.   A.M.   Divine Service.
           2.0-4.0.   Company Sports.

Monday
30.7.17.   6.15- 7.15. Officers Riding.
                       Sergt. Majors Parade.
           8.45-9.45. Pack Drill.
           9.45-10.45. Methods of putting on and maintaining
                       elevation and direction.
           11.0-12.30. Tactical Section Exercise.
           2.0- 3.0.   Officers B.A.B. Code.

Tuesday
31.7.17.   6.15- 7.15. Officers Riding.
                       Sergt. Majors Parade.
           8.45- 9.45. Immediate Action.
                       Transport Driving.
           9.45-10.45. Cleaning Limbers.
           11.0-12.30. Map reading and reconnaissance.
           2.0- 3.0.   Officers B.A.B. Code.
           6.0- 7.0.   Boxing.

Wednesday
1.8.17.   6.15- 7.15. Officers Riding.
                       Sergt. Majors Parade.
           9.0-12.30. No.3. Section. Firing on LA MOTTE Range.
           2.0- 4.30. No.4. Section. Firing on LA MOTTE Range.
           10.0-11.0. Transport driving.

Thursday
2.8.17.   6.15- 7.15. Officers Riding.
                       Sergt. Majors Parade.
           9.45-12.30. Tactical Section Exercise and study of ground.
           2.0- 3.0.   Cleaning limbers.

-2-

Friday
3.8.17.   6.15 - 7.15.   Officers Riding.
                            Sergt Majors Parade.
            8.45 - 9.45.   Immediate action.
            9.45 -10.45.   Indirect Fire Drill.
            11.0 -12.30.   Limber and Pack Drill.

D.H.Q.   V.H.A. Cowley   Major.
25.7.17.   D.M.G.O.
                                               31st Division.

Volume 1917.

Vol 16

Confidential

War Diary.

202nd Machine Gun Company   31st Division

August 1917.

VOLUME 20 PAGE

WAR DIARY

Army Form C. 2118.

No 91 MACHINE GUN COMPANY
Date August

Place	Date	Hour	Summary of Events and Information	Remarks and references to Appendices
B.E.F.	Aug 1st		Company was in billets in MONT-ST-ELOY. 2 Officers to Camouflage Demonstration. Lts KING & TEMPERLEY with two N.C.O. to Yukon Pack Demonstration at ROCLINCOURT. Company training – see App. I	App. I
	2		Weather wet however range work not done but substituted by lectures. Shoots also postponed, arranged for afternoon. Dispositions, instructions for, were received, in event of hostile attack on own & Right Div. front. 3 O.R's returned from Rest Camp & 1 from leave. Leave allocation received today allow two per day up to 19th inst.	
	2		Weather wet – training programme carried out as possible – men lectured. G.O.C. 91st inspected Company billets, training & transport – quite satisfactory. Shoots again postponed. 2 O.R's proceeded on leave, 2 O.R. returned from leave, 2 O.R. evacuated (notice rec'd) & 1 O.R. to hospital.	App.
	3		Company Training – Nos 3 & 4 Sects. fired stoppages on range. Nos 1 & 2 Sects lectured on Indirect Fire. Weather wet. Div. Orders concerning relief – night 4/5th by Coys of 2 & 3 Coy. Instructions received to send an officer – transport house at Alberville on 10th. Lt FAULKS detailed. Transport house at Shoots abandoned. 2 O.R. for leave & 2 returned leave.	App.

WAR DIARY

VOLUME 20
PAGE 2.

Army Form C. 2118.

MACHINE GUN COMPANY
Date: AUGUST

Place	Date	Hour	Summary of Events and Information	Remarks and references to Appendices
	1914 4th Aug		Company preparing for trenches & moved to 2 & 3 Coy. horse lines – Bde. Orders No 5 re Relief received. Church Service held. 2 OR on leave – 1 OR to hospital.	A.
	5th		Company moved into line at 9pm & relief completed by 2am 5th = Coy. in line – no casualties during relief on this day – 3 guns in position, 1 for A.A. duties at Rehn HQ. "Hostile shelling "BADGER" & "ANTELOPE" only, no damage – no rounds fired. Lt. EKINS from 2/3 Coy. reported & took over command. 2 OR on leave, 1 OR reported on transfer from 2/3 Coy.	App. 2. B.
	6th		Coy. in line, hostile M.G. reported from M.A. firing intermittently at "ANTELOPE" position, front otherwise quiet. Coy. HQ "BADGER". Work done on trenches, in many parts waterlogged condition other teams improving emplacements & altering locations. casualties nil – rds fired – nil. 1 OR Sanitary Course. 1 OR Lewis gun Course at A.S.C. 2 OR on leave. 1 OR reinforcements joined – 1 OR returned from tunnelly Course. Available men employed assisting Transp. lines construction	B.
	7th		Shelling reported near "BERWICK" & R.SC.HQ – hostile M.G. fire continued "ANTELOPE" – no damage done & casualties. Work by teams – trenches revetted & emplacements improved. Lt EKINS arrived Coy HQ with DMGO – reported Adv. Pde & proceeded to "BADGER" & assumed command from Lt. LAVENDER acting G.	B.

WAR DIARY

Army Form C. 2118.

VOLUME 20
PAGE 3

No. 92
MACHINE GUN COMPANY

month AUGUST

Place	Date	Hour	Summary of Events and Information	Remarks and references to Appendices
	1918 Aug 8		ANTELOPE team again reports harassing fire by same hostile M.G. trench improvement. Work. No casualties - no rounds fired. Lt. DUNLOP from hospital. Remaining at Tharsphet. 2 O.R. on leave. 1 O.R. returned from leave. Gas Bombardment notification [proposed] circ. 13/M.G. received & officers notified.	
	9th		"Front quiet" - work on trenches & empl. continued - casualties nil - no rounds fired. 2 O.R. on leave. 1 O.R. returned from hospital.	
	10		"Front quiet". Position [new] at 'AUK' completed - taken over with 3 OR from hospital & 2 OR on leave. AINTREE'& ASCOT' - by 2/R.BRALM - no casualties & no guns fired.	
	11th		Hostile activity normal. Casualties nil. Rounds fired - nil. Work as before Sgt. reinforcement. 1 O.R. to hospital & 1 O.R. from hospital 2 O.R. on leave & 2 O.R. returned	
	12th		1000 rounds expended on hostile aircraft - 3 being driven off. Tharsphet. casualties - nil. 2 O.R. went on & 2 O.R. returned from leave.	
	13th		"Front normal, no casualties. 3000 rds A.A. expended - result unknown. 1 OR from leave. 1 OR evacuated. 2/Lt. CLEAVER with gun team from reserve. to operation position in TEDDY GERRARD.	
	14th		Hostile aircraft activity. 8000 rds fired, results satisfactory. 1 OR wounded - AA shrapnel. to hosp. 1/4 OR to Rest Camp. 2 OR from leave + 1 from ECS. Lt. DUNLOP proceeded on leave to U.K.	

VOLUME 10.
PAGE 4

WAR DIARY

Army Form C. 2118.

No. 99
MACHINE GUN
COMPANY
August

Place	Date	Hour	Summary of Events and Information	Remarks and references to Appendices
	1917 Aug 15		7/Lt CLEAVER returned to Coy HQ - team remaining until operation.	
	16th		Hostile aircraft active - 300 rds fired during these back. 2 OR from leave. Hostile M. fire again carried out - 1000 rds expended. 1 OR from leave. 1 Sgt. reinforcement reported.	
	17th		Company relieved in line by 243 Coy. without incident. Relief complete at 2am. Company returned to billets at MONT ST-ELOY[5] A without casualties. 3 OR from leave.	att/A3 att/4
	18th		Coy in Rest Billets. Programme of training carried out. 3 OR from leave - 2 OR on leave.	
	19th		Coy. training. 1 OR on leave, 1 OR on Turnelly Course, 1 OR on Signally Course. 2 OR returned from leave.	
	20th		Coy. training. 1 OR on leave - from leave from Turnelly Course.	
	21st		Coy training. Coy Arms inspected by Armourer Sergt. 1 OR rejoined from ECS - 1 OR from hospital + 2 OR from leave.	
	22nd		Training — 1 OR on leave + 3 OR rejoined from leave.	
	23rd		— do — Lt. LAVENDER + 2 OR to hospital. 1 OR from leave. Notification recd - leave extension Lt DUNLOP Coy 9-9-17.	
	24th		— do — 3 OR from leave.	
	25th		— do — 1 OR from leave. ESM from course at CAMIERS	
	26th		— do — 2 OR from leave - 1 OR on Sig. Course.	

WAR DIARY or INTELLIGENCE SUMMARY

Army Form C. 2118.

VOLUME 20. PAGE 5

No. 92 MACHINE GUN COMPANY

Month: August

Date	Hour	Summary of Events and Information	Remarks and references to Appendices
1917 Aug 27th 28th		Coy. training as per programme. 3 Off. from leave.	
		do	
		28th m.G.C. 2 Officers attended Bde. en. lecture. 1 Off. on leave. 89 G. Barker & Ball transfd. to Orders received for relief - 243 Coy. 2 Off. to Rest Camp.	
29		Coy. moved to 243 Coy. lines. Preparation for trenches 3.30 p.m. Cooks sent in advance to prepare necessary meal. OC Coy. & 2/Lt CLEAVER proceeded in advance of the Coy. & moved by Sections 8.30 p.m. to meet guides 10.15 p. 4 Off. from Rest Camp.	App. 5
30		Relief complete. Wire was wired cple "Delighted" direct DH.Q.&Div. Casualties nil - no rounds fired.	
31		1 Off. on course at CAMIERS. 1 O.R. to hospital. 1 Off. on veterinary course. Casualties & operations - nil. Front normal.	

Jackson
Lt
For O.C. 92 M.G. COY.

Appendix I.

92 M.G. Coy.

PROPOSED PROGRAMME OF WORK OF 92nd M.G.COY

whilst out of the line at MONT.ST.ELOY.

Wednesday
25.7.17.
- 9.10 a.m. Sergt. Majors Parade.
- 10.- 11.15. Inspection of guns and stores by section officer.
- 11.30-12.30. Cleaning Limbers.
- 2.-4. Clothing inspection & lecture on economy.

Thursday
26.7.17.
- 6.15-7.15. Officers Riding.
- Sergt. Majors Parade.
- 8.45-9.45. Immediate action.
- 9.45-10.45. Trench drill & relief of sentries.
- Transport driving.
- 11.0.-12.30. Pack drill.

Friday
27.7.17.
- 6.15- 7.15. Officers Riding.
- Sergt. Majors Parade.
- 8.45- 9.45. Immediate action.
- 9.45-10.45. Trench drill & relief of sentries.
- Transport driving.
- 11.0.-12.30. Pack drill.
- 6.0.p.m. Boxing.

Saturday
28.7.17.
- 6.15.-7.15. Officers Riding.
- Sergt. Majors Parade.
- 9.0.-12.30. No.1. Section. Firing on LA MOTTE Range.
- 2.0.- 4.30. No.2. Section. Firing on LA MOTTE Range.

Sunday
29.7.17.
- A.M. Divine Service.
- 2.0.-.4.0. Company Sports.

Monday
30.7.17.
- 6.15- 7.15. Officers Riding.
- Sergt. Majors Parade.
- 8.45-9.45. Pack drill.
- 9.45-10.45. Methods of putting on and maintaining elevation and direction.
- 11.0-12.30. Tactical Section Exercise.
- 2.0.- 3.0. Officers B.A.B. Code.

Tuesday
31.7.17.
- 6.15- 7.15. Officers Riding.
- Sergt. Majors Parade.
- 8.45- 9.45. Immediate action.
- Transport driving.
- 9.45-10.45. Cleaning limbers.
- 11.0.-12.30. Map reading and reconnaissance.
- 2.0.- 3.0 . Officers B.A.B. Code.
- 6.0.- 7.0 . Boxing.

Wednesday
1.8.17.
- 6.15- 7.15. Officers Riding.
- Sergt. Majors Parade.
- 9. 0-12.30. No.3.Section. Firing on LA MOTTE Range.
- 2. 0- 4.30. No.4.Section. Firing on LA MOTTE Range.
- 10. 0-11. 0. Transport driving.

Thursday
2.8.17.
- 6.15- 7.15. Officers Riding.
- Sergt. Majors Parade.
- 9.45-12.30. Tactical Section Exercise and study of ground.
- 2. 0- 3. 0. Cleaning limbers.

Friday
3.8.17.   6.15 - 7.15.   Officers Riding.
                              Sergt Majors Parade.
              8.45 - 9.45.   Immediate action.
              9.45 -10.45.   Indirect Fire Drill.
              11. 0 -12.30.   Limber and Pack Drill.

D.H.Q.   Major.
25.7.17.   D.M.G.O.
                                                    31st Division.

For O.C. 92 M.G.COY.

Appendix 2

ORDERS FOR RELIEF OF 243 M.G.Coy. BY
92 M.G.Coy. NIGHT 4/5 Aug '17

1. The Company will relieve 243 Coy.
by Sections in the following order —
   FORWARD GUNS —
   ABERDEEN ⎫
   ARGYLL   ⎬ No 4 Section under
   ANTELOPE ⎬ 2/Lt CLEAVER.
   BERWICK ⎭

   BEDFORD   ⎫ No 1 Section &
   BIRKENHEAD ⎬ No 1 team of No 3 Sec.
   BLACKPOOL ⎬ under Lt. SARGENT
   BADGER   ⎭

   BUFFALO [2 guns] ⎫ No 2 Section
   BULLDOG [2 guns] ⎬ under Lt. KING

   REAR HQ — 1 gun team No 3 Section

MOVE
2. Company will parade with
Section Limbers [gun stores] re packed
in empty No 3 Limbers & proceed
via NEUVILLE ST-VAAST, where gun
teams will look out for guides of
243 Coy at York Rd.
   HQ Limber & party will proceed via
the TWINS to Rear Coy HQ
Section Gun Limbers under Lt SARGENT

2. Contd.
will proceed with guides via LES TILLEULS to Ration Dump at WILLOW - NEW BRUNSWICK Rd T21d 2.7 - where guides of 243 Coy. will be met.

3. Gun teams will take in with them the following stores per gun — Gun, Spare Parts - AA Sights - Condenser Bag & tube.
Nº 4 Section — 1 Periscope per gun.
→ will also take over 2 guns from Nº 3 Sec. —
Following will be taken over from 243 Coy. ——— Trench Stores Belt Boxes - Tripods - Water Tins + SAA —— + all possible informatⁿ

Section Officers nearest will get into touch immediately with Battn. & Coy. HQs. & report nightly.

4. On completion of relief respective gun teams to notify Coy. HQ. through Sec. Officers

5. Two runners per Section will be returned to Coy. HQ with Relief Reports & lists of Stores urgently required. These runners

5 Cont'd

...will be stationed at Coy. HQ for communication with their Sections.

6. Gun positions for which AA positions have been provided, will arrange for AA protective measures at an early date.

7. All ranks are reminded that all unecessary movement, smoke etc. & anything likely to give away existing gun positions, are strictly forbidden by Bde & will incur severe disciplinary action.

Jackson.
Lt
for OC 92 M.G.Co

3/8/17
10.30pm

No 92
MACHINE GUN
COMPANY
WAR DIARY
AUG 17

Copy No 8   Appendix 3

ORDERS FOR RELIEF OF 91 MG Coy BY 246 Coy
By Capt E.R. NEKINS Comdg 91 MG Coy

1. RELIEF   The 91 MG Coy will be relieved
   by 246 Coy on night 16/17 Aug 1917.

2. TRANSPORT REQUIRED. A. One half
   limber for Lt SARGENT Section to be
   Ration Dump at 11·30 pm.
   B. One half limber for 2/Lt TEMPERLEY at
   12·15 am at Ration Dump.
   C. Full limber to be at Dump at 1·15 am
   for Lts. KING & BALBI.
   D. One full limber to be at Hd.qrs Coy HQ
   at 10·45 pm.
   ~~E.~~ Above to withdraw relieved
   teams.
   E. HORSES 2 Horses for Lts SARGENT & TEMPERLEY
   to be at Div Canteen, NEUVILLE ST. VAAST
   at 12·50 am.
   2 Horses, Lts. KING & BALBI at Div.
   Canteen at 2·15 am.
   3 Horses, o/c. Lts JACKSON & LAVENDER
   to be at TWINS at 4·0 am.

3. HANDING OVER   Section officers will
   hand over all Trench Stores, Tripods
   & all Belt Boxes, obtaining receipts
   for same.

SHEET 2.   C/4/1.

4. 2/Lt CLEAVER & team will provide guide to proceed with Advd guides & on relief will march out with No 2 Section. No horse will be available.

5. MOVE on completion of relief Sections will move independently to billets & Transport lines at MONT ST. ELOY.

6. GUIDES. Section Officers will send guides from respective gun teams to meet relieving Coy. at Ration Dump at 10.30pm.

7. RELIEF COMPLETE will be reported in writing by Sec. Officers to OC Coy at BADGER, enclosing receipts for Trench Stores etc.

8. Acknowledge.

G Jackson
Lt.
for OC 97 MG Coy.

AAG
15-8-17

Copies to -
No 1 - OC 24 D Coy.
2 - T.O. 97 Coy.
3-7 - all Sec. Officers
8 & 9 - Retained.

Copy No 4.　　　　　　　　　　Appendix 1
ORDERS FOR RELIEF OF 243 M.G.Coy. BY 92 Coy.
　　　　　　NIGHT 29th/30th AUG.

1. The 92nd M.G.Coy will relieve 243 M.G.Coy on night of 29th/30th inst.

2. The following positions will be occupied by O.C. Coy —
　BADGER　——　Forward HQ
　Transport　——　Rear HQ [F11a]
　Bde. HQ　as before.

3. Distribution of Sections
　　　　　　　　　— 2 guns — ABERDEEN
　No 1 Section　— 1　——　ANTELOPE
　　　　　　　　　— 1　——　ARGYLL

　No 2 Section　— 1　——　AUK
　　　　　　　　　— 1　——　ASCOT
　　　　　　　　　— 1　——　AINTREE
　　　　　　　　　— 1　——　BUFFALO

　No 3 Section　— 1　——　BERWICK
　　　　　　　　　— 1　——　BIRKENHEAD
　　　　　　　　　— 1　——　BEDFORD
　　　　　　　　　— 1　——　BLACKPOOL

　No 4 Section　— 1　——　BADGER
　　　　　　　　　— 1　——　BULLDOG

1 Sub Sec. in reserve in Sunken Rd.
S23b 7½ 4½ under 2/Lt TEMPERLEY

2.

3 Cont'd
The Officer i/c Reserve Sub-Sec. will report on arrival to Adv. Bde H.Q. & afterwards once daily. —
One gun of Reserve Sub-Sec. will be mounted daily for A.A. duties, & a GAS picquet mounted nightly. —

4 RUNNER. — A runner from above Sec. will be detailed & continually on duty in reliefs, for communication with Adv Bde H.Q. [A.A.I] —

5 GUN TEAMS — A list of gun teams & runners is being handed to Sec. officers, with their respective gun positions —

6 MOVE — The Company will parade at Transport Lines with limbers packed. Rations will be taken & 2 tins of water per gun team arranged. Sections will march off independently to former Ration Dump T.21.d.29 where guides will be met —

7 TRENCH STORES — All belt boxes, tripods & trench stores will be taken over & a return rendered to Coy. HQ by 9 am on 30th.

3.

8. <u>RANGE CARDS</u> will be checked on relief & belts taken over inspected —

9. <u>RUNNERS</u> will move with their respective Sections & on completion of relief — report to Coy. HQ BADGER with taking over certificates

10. <u>CODE</u> word for "Relief Complete" "Delighted"

Jackson
Lt. for Capt.
O.C. 92 M.G. Coy.

29/8/17

<u>Copies</u> —
No 1 — retained
  — 2 — DMGO
  3 – 6 — Sec. Officers
  7 + 8 — War Diary

Appendix 4.

Programme of Training
Period 18th to 29th Aug.

Date	Time	Form of Training
1917 Aug 18	9 am	Inspection Parade.
	9-30–11-30 am	Cleaning & Checking of Gun Stores & Spare Parts
	11-45–12-30 am	Inspection of Kit & Equipment.
	2-30–5 pm	Duty Section, work on Transport. 2-30 pm Bathing.
19		Divine Service.
20	8-30–9 am	CSM's Parade. 9-30 am Inspection Parade
	9-45–11 am	Gas Drill & Inspection of appliances.
	11-10–12-30 p	Cleaning of Limbers.
	2-30–3-30 p	Officers Riding Class.
21	8-30–9 am	CSM's Parade. 9-30 am Inspection Parade.
	9-45–11 am	Rangefinding & construction of Range Cards.
	11-10–12-30 p	T.O.E.T. for Backward Men. Driving for Transpt. Use of Gound Rover.
22	7-30–8-15 am	Officers – Riding. 8-30–9 am CSM's Parade.
	9-45–11 am	Indirect Fire methods
	11-10–12-30 p	T.O.E.T.
23	8-30–9 am	CSM's Parade. 9-30 am Inspection Parade.
	9-45–10-15 a	Gas Drill. 10-30–12-30 pm Tactical Section – Exercise with Pack Mules.
	2–4 pm	Inter-Section Competition.
24	8-30–9 am	CSM's Parade. 9-30–12-30 p On Range.
	2-30–4-30 p	On Range. Transport — Driving
	2–3 pm	B.A.B. Code for Officers
25	7-30–8-15 am	Officers Riding. 8-30–9 am CSM's Parade.
	9-30 am	Inspection Parade. 9-45–10-15 am Gas Drill.
	10-30–11 am	T.O.E.T. Compass work for N.C.Os.
	11-10–12-30 p	Limber cleaning
26	—	Divine Service A.M. Coy. Sports P.M.
27	8-30–9 am	CSM's Parade.
	9-30–12-30 p	On Range. 2-30–4-30 pm On Range.
28	8-30–9 am	CSM's Parade.
	9-45–11 am	Indirect Fire methods.
	11-10–12-10 p	Lecture on Trench Routine
	2–4 pm	Baths.
29	—	Preparation for Line. Inspection of Guns, Gun Stores etc. Packing of Limbers.

No 92 MACHINE GUN COMPANY
WAR DIARY
AUG 17

B. Jackson.
Lt. for Capt.
OC 92 M.G. Coy

Army Form C. 2118.

WAR DIARY
or
INTELLIGENCE SUMMARY.

(Erase heading not required.)

No. 92 MACHINE GUN COMPANY

Vol 17

CONFIDENTIAL

WAR DIARY

OF

No 92 MACHINE GUN COY.

From 1st Sept. 1917 To 30th Sept. 1917

[Volume 21]

Instructions regarding War Diaries and Intelligence Summaries are contained in F. S. Regs., Part II. and the Staff Manual respectively. Title pages will be prepared in manuscript.

WAR DIARY

VOLUME 21
PAGE 1

Army Form C. 2118.

No. 82 MACHINE GUN COMPANY
SEPTEMBER

Place	Date	Hour	Summary of Events and Information	Remarks and references to Appendices
BEF	(1917) Sept 1		Company had relieved 243 Coy on 29th ult. & were still in the line. Situation normal - casualties nil. Coy strength was 186.	
	2		Nothing to report.	
	3		Notification received from Div. to relief of Coy on 4th/5th	
	4		Coy. relieved by 98 & 165 C.M.G. Coys. Company marching out of line were caught in a hostile Gas shell bombardment. Cases of the men's skin being blistered were very prominent - the gas having penetrated the clothing. In some cases the eyes were also effected. There appeared to be few cases of internal injuries owing to respirators.	
Being in position near ECURIE			Relief was complete about 11pm. Coy. marching to ROBERTS CAMP near ECURIE. 10R on leave. 10R evac. to CCS.	
	5		19 OR admitted to hospital & evac to CCS. suffering from effects of Gas. Transport lines moved from F.11a. to ECURIE. 3 OR evac[uated].	
	6		Coy bathed & given clean change. Checking of Gun Stores kits etc. 2/Lts B.R.BALBI & W.B.CLEAVER and 14 OR to hospital & evac - gas.	
			Preparation for line on following day - the Coy was taking over a new sector on the night of 7/8 new one.	
	7		Coy relieved 205 Coy in the line, one party leaving at 1.30pm one at 4h 30 m Transport lines moved to manchos camp remaining at ECURIE. Notification received

WAR DIARY

VOLUME 21 PAGE 2

No. 92 MACHINE GUN COMPANY
September

Place	Date	Hour	Summary of Events and Information	Remarks and references to Appendices
	1917 Sept 8		Capt. EKINS to hospital-Gas. Capt. G.S. KING took over command of Coy. Lt. DUNLOP rejoined from leave.	A.
	9		Lt. SARGENT to hospital - evac.-Gas. Total Gas casualties were now Officers = 3, OR = 33 - 5 OR were admitted late in the month making a total of 38 OR.	A.
	10		1 OR reinforcement. 1 OR to wed. 1 OR from hospital. Capt. KING attended Bde Conference on Defence Scheme for Sector. Guns got ready for Gun Operation which was however postponed. Guns did night firing on selected targets.	#
	11		2 OR rejoined from Rest Camp. Gun Operation again postponed. Guns co-operated in bursts of fire on enemy lines.	A.
			Capt. KING attended Bde Conference & Liaison with Artillery and subsequently D.M.G.O's Conference 1st June. Coy died night firing. Instructions received to Co-operate with Infantry raid on 11/12. 1 OR evac. Lt. JACKSON to Corps Rest Station. 2/Lt HENLEY posted to Coy. Strength = 152	App. 5 App. A
	12		3 OR accidentally injured. AFW 3428 rendered. 1 OR from leave. Notification received that Lt. JOHNS was posted to command Coy. Guns co-operated with Barrage fire in raid on enemy lines 9/10 = 5 P.R. off 6	B.

WAR DIARY

INTELLIGENCE SUMMARY

VOLUME 24 PAGES

Army Form C. 2118.

Place	Date	Hour	Summary of Events and Information	Remarks and references to Appendices
	12.		and also in the Inspection by knots of fire.	app. 6.
	13.		Instrn order for the Operation issued to Guns fired in connection with this.	app. 7.
	14.		2r.-or reinforcements joined. 1 OR. rose to CQS [Gn. an S.S.] 4 OR. rose to CSS [Gn. an S.S.] 1 OR. returned from hospital. 2 guns fired on selected angle during night. Guns fired co-operating in a Tun Shoot with Barrage Line. 1 OR. evacuated on leave. 1 OR. from hospital.	app. 8 app 9
	15.		2/Lt. G.F. HEARNEY - G.H. ARROWSMITH joined from Proceeded from Line relieved. 2 guns fired at night.	
	16.		1 OR. reinforcements joined. 1 OR. 6 + 1 OR from Tunnelling Coys. 1 gun field shoots during nights.	app. 10.
	17.		Coy relieved in line by 93 A.G. Coy, relief being complete by 6.30 a.m. marching out to WELLINGTON Camp, N. of ROCLINCOURT.	app. 11
	18.		1 OR. rejoined from hospital. No casualties had occurred during this tour of duty in the early trenches. Company training as per programme.	
	19.		C.S.M. G.A. SMITH appointed to permanent commission posted to m.G.C. Base Depot as 2/Lieut. under authority of A.G. 1st to hosp.	app. 12

WAR DIARY

VOLUME 21 PAGE 4

No. 92 MACHINE GUN COMPANY
SEPTEMBER

Army Form C. 2118.

Place	Date	Hour	Summary of Events and Information	Remarks and references to Appendices
	1917 Sep 20		Lt. H.A. JOHNS joined & took over command of Coy. 3 OR reinforcements joined. 2 OR returned from leave to U.K. Coy. training	
	21		4 OR proceeded to Rest Camp. Training	
	22		Lt. JACKSON reported from hospital. 2/Lt. TENPERLEY + 2 N.C.O. proceeded to Div. Gas School for a three days course. 2/Lt. FAULKS proceeded on leave to U.K. Coy. training	
	23		3 N.C.O. to A.A. Course at Le Crepe School. Training as per programme	
	24		Coy. less Transport moved to DURHAM Camp. nr. ST. ELOI	
	25		1 O.R. reinforcement. Coy. training	
	26		Training. Orders for relief on 30th received from Bde. Under Div. arrangements a 'bus was available for 2 Officers	
	27		7 OR to proceed to BETHUNE for the day. 2 O.R. reinforcements. 1 OR to hospital	
	28		Training as per programme	
	29		1 OR from leave. 3 OR from Sig. Course. Information for line.	
	30		Company relieved 93 Coy in the line, relief being complete 5.30 p.m. Foot-Hq., details remained at Transport lines WARDRECQUE. 1 OR proceeded to a N.C.O. course from HQ. Course at CASSEL	

SECRET.   APPENDIX. 1.

OPERATION ORDER FOR RELIEF OF 92 M.G. Coy BY 9th & 15th
CANADIAN M.G. COYS ON NIGHT 4/5 SEPT 1917.

                                                    BADGER
                                                    3/9/17

1. (a) 92 M.G. Coy will be relieved by the 9th & 15th Canadian
       M.G. Coys on night of 4/5. Sept. 1917.
   (b) The 9th M.G. Coy will take over the following positions:–
       AINTREE, ASCOT, AUK, ANTELOPE, BUFFALO, BADGER & BULLDOG,
       also RESERVE H.Qrs in SUNKEN ROAD.
   (c) The 15th C.M.G. Coy will take over positions:– ARGYLE
       ABERDEEN (2 guns) BLACKPOOL, BIRKENHEAD, BEDFORD BERWICK

2. (a) A Section of 9th C.M.G.C. will relieve No 2 Section of 92 MGC
       at AINTREE, ASCOT, AUK, & BUFFALO.
   (b) C. Section of 9th C.M.G.C. will relieve the two guns of No 4
       Section of 92 M.G. Coy at BADGER, BULLDOG.
   (c) One gun of B Sec 9th C.M.G.C will relieve one gun of No.1
       Sec 92. M.G.C. at ANTELOPE.
   (d) Two guns of B Sec 9th C.M.G.C will relieve the two guns
       of No 4 Sec 92 M.G.C. at Reserve H.Qrs in SUNKEN ROAD.

3. (a) 3 guns of B Sec. 15. C.M.G.C will relieve 3 Guns of No.1 Sec
       92. M.G.C. at ABERDEEN & ARGYLE.
   (b) Four guns of C. Sec 15 C.M.G.C. will relieve No 3 Sec 92 M.G.C
       at BERWICK, BEDFORD, BIRKENHEAD, & BLACKPOOL.

4. (a) 2/Lt Temperley will detail 1. N.C.O. & 4 men to proceed to
       Rear H.Qrs on the morning of 4th inst. This party will
       report to Lieut Jackson and will act as guides for relieving
       Sections of 9 & 15 C.M.G.C. as far as Ration Dump.
   (b) Section officers will arrange for one guide from each
       gun team to be at Ration Dump at 9.0 pm on night 4th inst.
   (c) 2/Lt Balbi will detail an N.C.O to take charge of these
       guides and meet the relieving teams.

5. (a) Tripods and belt boxes will be handed over except in the
       case of the guns being relieved by the 9th C.M.G.C. At these
       positions belt boxes only will be handed over and the tripods
       are to be brought away.
   (b) All trench stores, maps, etc will be handed over and
       receipts obtained. Receipts to be sent to BADGER immediately
       on completion of relief.
       (NB. W.P. RATION BAGS are Trench Stores. Clinometres will
       not be handed over.)
   (c) Full complement of Petrol Tins. S.A.A etc must be at each
       gun position ready for handing over.

6. Transport Arrangements:–
   (a) One full limber for No 3 Section & two guns of No 4 Sec
       to be at Ration Dump at 10.45 p.m.
       2/Lt Balbi will be in charge of this party.

– 2 –

(b) One half limber for No. 1 Section to be at Ration Dump at 11-15 p.m.

(c) One half limber for No. 2 Section to be at Ration Dump at 12.0 mid.

(d) One half limber for Reserve Sub. Section in SUNKEN RD at – (Time to be arranged by Transport Officer.

(e) One horse for O.C. and one horse for 2/Lt Cleaver to be at the TWINS at 3 a.m.

(f) Transport Officer will arrange times and rendezvous for remaining horses and notify OC as soon as possible.

7. On completion of relief Sections will move independently to ROBERT'S CAMP.

N.B. ROBERT'S CAMP is situated on the right of LENS-ARRAS ROAD about 3000' SOUTH of the CROSS ROADS at LES TILLEULS. A guide will meet Sections on the road near the Camp.

When acknowledging receipt of Operation Order please inform me whether you fully understand the above instructions. If not clear please report at BADGER and I will show you position on map.

8. Completion of relief will be reported to BADGER. CODE WORD "PEACE".

9. <u>ACKNOWLEDGE</u>

(Signed) Ronald N. Ekins
Capt
OC GARNER.

3/9/17.

Jackson.
Lt
For O.C. 92 M.G. Coy

"OPERATION ORDER N°29" BY CAPT. F. MEKINS COMDG. 92 M.G.Cy

6 Sept. 1917

Appendix 2

1. The 92 M.G.Cy. will relieve the 205th M.G.Coy. on night 7th/8th Sept. 1917 — on the R. Battn. Front L.I.

2. Following is position of respective HQ.

   Brigade HQ. — T.20.b.05.40   M.G. Coy HQ — B.10.b.70.
   R. Battn. — B.12.A.14.75   L. Battn.   — T.27.d.3.8.
   T.M.B   — B.11.d.   A.T. R.E.   — B.10.b.9.5.

3. There will be no communication by day between Coy. HQ. & Sections by runner — except in cases of emergency.
   Coy. HQ. being in a very exposed position, will be kept as quiet as possible. NO MOVEMENT BY DAY IS TO BE ALLOWED

4.
A. N°4 Section, 92 M.G.Cy. will relieve N°1 Sec. 205 Coy. at positions "C" & "E"
   & N°4 Sec. 205 Coy at positions "20" & "22"
B. N°3 Section, 92 M.G.Cy. will relieve N°2 Sec. 205 Coy at positions — "4", "5", "14", "15"
C. N°1 Section, 92 M.G.Cy. will relieve N°4 Sec. 205 Coy at positions "4"&"6" & will take over 2 positions at "9" & "9A" [Both RED LINE]
D. One Sub-Section of N°2 Sec. 92 M.G.Cy. will relieve one Sub-Sec. of N°3 Sec. 205 Coy at positions "6" & "7" [The Willows]
E. One Sub-Section of N°2 Sec. will be in reserve at Rear HQ. provisionally, until accomodation is selected in RED LINE

5. A. GUIDES
   Guides for the following positions — "C","E","20","22","4","5","14","15" will meet the relieving teams at "Skyline Post" at 3pm
   A guide to "Skyline Post" will be obtained from 205 Coy Rear HQ
B. Guides for Nos. "6" & "7" (the "Willows") will meet the teams at Coy. HQ in the line, & guides for Nos. "4","6","7" & "9A" (RED LINE) will meet the teams at N°6 position (on Road) at B.10.c.25.25.
   These teams will move into the line with 205 Coy's. relieving limbers — Time of departure will be notified later.

6. Tripods & 8 belt boxes per gun will be taken over at each gun position, with the exception of "7" & "9A" — teams of which will go in with them, tripods and 10 belt boxes per gun & 2 filled water tins per gun.
   Their relieving teams will take in 2 boxes per gun.

7. All Trench Stores, maps &c. including 2 full tins per gun team will be taken over — and receipts given — one of

7. Corres
   ~ of receipt for each gun position to be sent to Coy HQ
   immediately on completion of relief.

8. Runners
   One man per section will be sent to Coy. H.Q. on completion
   of relief & will remain for duty as runners

9. Section officers will render an early report to HQ showing
   exact location of guns, accomodatn. available, work to be
   done & material required

10. Details of marching in will be issued seperately

11. Code Word for completion of relief — "EXACT"

12. Dispositions.

Section	Gun Position	Co-ordinates	Section HQ
No 1 Sec.	No 4	B.10.A.60.60	Dug-out at No 7 Gun
	No 6	B.10.C.25.25	
	No 7	B.16.a.85.80	
	No 9A	B.16.d.45.90	
No 2 Sec.	No 6	B.11.A.75.80	Coy. HQ
	No 7	B.11.A.80.85	
No 3 Sec.	No 4	B.11.D.52.72	Z Trench
	No 5	B.11.B.38.80	
	No 14	B.11.A.82.75	
	No 15	B.11.B.63.35	
No 4 Sec.	'C'	B.12.A.95.10	Dug-out at No 20
	'E'	B.6.D.35.40	
	No 20	B.12.A.43.25	
	No 22	B.5.D.73.23	

13. Section Officers will render a roll of gun teams
    proposed for each position to Orderly Room by 10am. 9th inst.

14. ACKNOWLEDGE

Ronald N Elkins.
Capt.
OC 92 M.G. Coy.

6/9/17

Copy No 1 to DMGO
   "   2 OC Coy
   " 3-7 Sec. officers
   " 8-9 War Diary
   " 10 retained.

S. Jackson.
Lt.

Appendix 1 — to Order No 2.3.

Move into line. 7th Sept 17.

1/. The Company will parade for moving into the line as follows.

1. Nos 3 & 4 Sections will parade at 1.30 pm to pack limbers. Move off at 2.0 pm, under Capt King.
Lts Lavender & Woods.—

Note — One team of No 2 Section will move with the above party —.

2. The remainder of the Coy will parade at 7.15 pm,— under Lts Sargent and Timperley.

3. Dress — Battle order — all waterbottles to be filled

4. Rangefinder Instruments will be taken into the line by Nos 1 and 3 Sections

5. Please initial when read.

Jackson/y

O.C. 92 M.G. Coy.

APPENDIX 4.

Operation Report on Night Firing 10/11.9.17.
Refee 92 Bde. O. 152

Number of Guns   10.
Rounds fired.   7500
Targets engaged:-

    Enemy Front line trenches & wire
    between following points:-
    C1C 656   -   C1C 60.61.
    C1a 1242   -   C1a 4808
    C7c 33   -   C7c 1018

(Signed). G Stuart King Capt
O/C GARNER.

12-9-17.

Jackson.
Lt.
For O.C. 92 M.G. COY.

APPENDIX 5.

OPERATION REPORT NIGHT FIRING 11/12 9/17

Number of Guns   4.
Number of Rounds Fired 5000.
Targets engaged:-

   1. Brigouts Switch Trench
      C7c and C8a

   2. Railway C2b 1078

   3. Trench Foot alley from
      C1b 53 . C1b 64

(Signed) G Stuart King
                     Capt
    O/C GARNER.
      12/9/17.

No 92 MACHINE GUN COMPANY
War Diary
September

Jackson.
Lt.
For O.C. 92 M.G. COY.

APPENDIX 6.

REPORT ON MACHINE GUN OPERATIONS ON NIGHT OF 12/13 Sept. 1917

1. RAID BY 92nd INFANTRY BRIGADE

10 Guns 92. M.G. Coy were placed into previously prepared night firing positions as soon as it was dark on 12th instant.

Lines of fire, and 14 Belt Boxes of ammunition were prepared by daylight.

Flash screen and depression stops were used by each gun.

OPERATION

Targets:—
- C.1.a.4.6 — C.1.a.7.4.
- C.1.c.63.63.
- C.1.c.7.5.
- C.1.c.60.14 — C.7.a.6.9.
- C.7.a.08.86.
- C.7.a.34.67.
- C.7.a.37.50.

These were selected as positions from which machine guns had been seen firing, and which were expected to cause trouble.

The time of Zero was obtained by sending an Officer to the Raiding Battalion, and was not received in writing.

Fire was opened by all guns at Zero hour (11.35 p.m.) and maintained at 'Rapid' Rate until Zero plus 25 minutes.

Guns searched and traversed round targets.

Guns were organised into Batteries which rendered the actual control of the guns by Officers most simple and efficient.

Central belt filling depots, under the charge of an N.C.O, were used with advantage at each Battery.

Rounds expended — 23,750

Result. The raid was a success.
- No hostile fire came from areas swept by our M.G. fire.
- Very few stoppages.
- Retaliation — very slight.
- Casualties — Nil.

2. COMBINED GAS, ARTILLERY + M.G. BOMBARDMENT

Guns used 10.

The guns were grouped into Batteries prior to the operation.

Q.E. and Direction of all guns checked by an Officer.

OPERATION
- U.19.c.10.72 to U.25.c.20.13.
- T.30.b.70.72 to T.30.d.60.76.
- C.1.c.6.0 to T.1.c.6.6.
- U.5.d.12.20

Fire was opened by all guns at Zero plus 5 minutes (3.35 a.m.) and maintained as 'Rapid' fire for 5 minutes, after which it was reduced in rate till Zero plus 60.

At Zero plus 90 and till Zero plus 95 Rapid fire was again opened and was continued at rate of 50 rounds a minute till Zero plus 120.

Guns searched and traversed according to orders.

Elevation and direction constantly checked by Gun Commanders.

- 2 -

Ammunition expended
            38,000 Rounds.

RESULT
    Unobserved.
    Retaliation - very slight
    Casualties - Nil
    Guns fired well; only stoppages being 1 bulged barrel (cause unknown), 1 seized extractor, 1 broken firing pin, and several No. 3 caused by the difficulty of filling belts in the open.

LESSONS FROM THE TWO OPERATIONS

1. Owing to the large number of rounds fired during the night, the number of belts allowed with each gun (14) was insufficient 39 being used by each gun. It was necessary to refill belts continuously. It is suggested that an additional 5 belts per gun be added to the establishment.

2. The positions taken up were consolidated shell-holes in the open. In consequence no lights could be used, and the belt filling had to be done in darkness, which caused unnecessary stoppages.
    Belt filling depots were found very satisfactory where the guns were grouped together in Batteries.
    Belt filling should be done in a dry place and with floor boarded, otherwise belts and ammunition get dirty and wet, causing stoppages.
    Unless the gun numbers have a feeling of safety, the accuracy of their filling suffers. This points to a dug-out rather than a shelter only.

3. Owing to the time it takes for a message to reach the widely distributed batteries, it would be of advantage if Zero hour and final instructions could be issued earlier.

4. Where possible Battery Commanders should be connected to Group Commanders by telephone.

14/9/17.   Copy.

                                            Jackson Lt.

Appendix. 7.

OPERATION REPORT – GAS PROJECTION – 13th·9·17

1. The following programme was carried out in connection with above.

2. Number of guns used – 10.
   Targets engaged were the same as those of the previous night, with the exception of Group 8.

   Number of rounds fired – 16,000 rds.

   Fire was opened at Zero + 5 minutes & maintained rapid until Zero + 10 minutes. From Z.+10 to Z+20 fire was maintained at rate of 100 rnds per minute.

   Casualties – nil.
   Retaliation – nil
   Stoppages – one gun out of action as its inside plate springs broke.
   Broken extractor &
   Lock Spring.
   2 Broken Gib Springs
   Broken Collar Roller.
   A few slight No. 3 Stoppages.

   Night firing screens were used, also traversing & depression stops.

Copy.

A. Jackson.
Lt.
For O.C. 92 M.G. Coy.

No 92 MACHINE GUN COMPANY
WAR DIARY
SEPTEMBER

APPENDIX. 8.

OPERATION REPORT Night 14/15. 9. 17.

The following targets were engaged at irregular intervals through the night.

No. of Guns.   2.
Targets   No 6   C1d 3604
            No 7   C8 c 58

Rounds   4000
Casualties   Nil
Retaliation Nil

(Signed) G Stuart King Capt.
for O.C GARNER.
15. 9. 17.

Copy.

G Jackson
Lt
For O.C. 92 M.G. COY.

No 92 MACHINE GUN COMPANY
War Diary
Date September

Appendix 9.

OPERATION REPORT 24 HOURS ENDING 9 a.m. 17.9.17

AA Work. On three occasions during the day our A.A. guns engaged E.A. but without visible result. Rounds Expended 2,500.

1. Ref. G4GE. 8/36 In connection with operation by T.M.B. and Artillery, the following programme was carried out with the object of keeping Enemies heads down as far as possible and preventing them from observing the positions of the T.M.B's

   Number of Guns   8.
   Rounds fired.   7,500.

2. Targets engaged
   - C1a 3560   ⎫
   - U.25.C1529   ⎬ A. Battery
   - U.25 C4055   ⎟
   - T30 d6085   ⎭

   - C1 d 47   ⎫
   - C1 C 64   ⎬ B. Battery.
   - C1. c 6060 ⎟
   - C1 d.6080   ⎭

   Guns traversed and searched round their targets according to orders.
   Casualties Nil
   Retaliation Nil
   Stoppages a few slight cross feeds.

3. Guns were in position and ready laid at Dawn 16.9.17 And in the case of A. Battery (B11 a 98) 2 men per gun were in the emplacements by that time and remained all day.

4. Guns were carefully camouflaged and no movement was allowed near their positions during the day.

5. Depression Stops and A A M's were used.

6. Guns opened fire at Z–1. and maintained rapid fire until Z+5.

7. **NIGHT FIRING** During the night 2 guns carried out harassing fire at selected targets.
   4000 rounds were fired
   (1 fusee spring broken).

Copy

J. Jackson Lt.
For O.C. 92 M.G. COY.

No 92 MACHINE GUN COMPANY
War Diary
September

APPENDIX 9

OPERATION ORDER 3/4 1/4

1. In connection with an operation by the T.M.B. and Artillery tomorrow 16.9.17. You will carry out the following programme:-
2. Guns from 45 46 14 15 7 9a Red line positions will be used.
3. Guns will be in position and laid by Dawn on 16.9.17.
4. Gun Emplacements will be carefully camouflaged and no movement will be allowed near them by day.
5. In the case of A Group of Guns Nos 1 + 2 will be in the emplacement at dawn and will remain there until dusk - rations will be taken but no movement or cooking is to be permitted.
6. Guns will be withdrawn at dusk to their Battle positions.
7. Depression Stops will be used and A.A.M's put out - these latter must be kept very low - it would be preferable if a natural object could be chosen for this purpose.
8. Special precautions will be taken to avoid Steam and Smoke from the guns as far as possible.
9. Eight belt boxes per gun will be in the Emplacement with it.
10. Zero hour will be approximately 5.pm tomorrow but instructions as to this and as to rate of firing will be issued later.
11. Reports will be rendered to Coy H.Q as soon as possible.

Particulars of Targets &c

A GROUP.

No	Gun Position	Target	Grid Bears	Tray Used	QE	Search	Remarks
1	B11 a 9.8	C.1a 3560	63°	3°L	246	Up 30'	
2		V.25c 1509	56°	3°R	222	Up 30'	
3		V.25 C 4055	55°	1.EW	308	Up 30' Down 30	
4		T.30 d 6085	45°	2.EW	241	Up 30	

B. GROUP.

1	B.11 6 78 9	C1 d 47	68	1EW	233	Up 30 Down 30	
2		C1 c 64	66½	2°L	120	Up 30	
3	B.11 6 75 25	C1 c b 66	66	3°EW	129	Up 1°	
4		O1 b 5340	61	1°EW	305	Up 30° Down 30°	

(Signed) G. Stuart King Capt
for O.C. GANNER
15-9-17.

APPENDIX 10.

OPERATION REPORT Night 16/17 Sept.

Number of Guns   6
Rounds fired   4000.

Targets engaged:—

Enemy wire and Front line at following points.
from   C 1 c 62 63
to   C 7 a 6 8.

Fire was opened at

    8-15 pm
    1-15 am.
    3-50 pm

One belt per gun being fired at each burst

Casualties Nil.

Retaliation None affecting M G's.

           (Signed) G. Stuart King
                        Capt
               O/c GARNER.
              16/9/17.

Copy.

Jackson.
For O.C. 92 M.G. COY.

Appendix II.

SECRET

OPERATION ORDER for relief of 92nd
M.G. Coy by 93rd M.G. Coy on afternoon
18. Sept 1917.

(1) The Company will be relieved by the
93rd M.G. Coy on the 18th Sept 1917.

(2) All positions at present occupied by the
Company will be handed over

(3) Section Officers will arrange for one guide per
gun team to be at THE TUNNEL B15c64
at 2.30 pm on 18.9.17 — They will
report to Sergt Jones who will take charge
there and meet the incoming teams.

(4) All details for the forward guns (ie)
except THE WILLOWS & RED LINE
will move via TOMMY ALLEY.

(5) The following will be handed over at
each position.
   1 Tripod.
   14 Belt Boxes
   10 Boxes SAA (minimum)
   2 Petrol Tins FULL of WATER
   all additional petrol Tins

"All trench stores" Maps &c
T bases will be handed over where
in possession.

Receipts will be obtained.

(6) Dugouts Emplacements Latrines &c
will be left in scrupulously clean
and sanitary condition and a
certificate to this effect obtained
from the incoming team in each case

(7) All receipts and certificates will be
handed in to Coy H Q adv immediately
on completion of relief.

(8) Transport Arrangements.
Three full limbers will be at
the top of TOMMY ALLEY near SKYLINE
POST at 5.15 pm.

Three horses will be at the same place
at that hour.

One horse for the acting OC will be
at the same place at 6.15 pm

(9) On completion of relief Sections
will move independently to WELLINGTON
CAMP — RHQ will arrange for guides to
meet them if necessary

Completion of relief will be reported to Coy HQ by code words "QUIETLY AWAY".

ACKNOWLEDGE.

G Stuart Kay Capt

for OC GARNER
17.9.17.
10 a.m.

Copy 1 Lt Lavender
      2 Lt Woods
      3 2nd Lt Temperley
      4 RHQ
      5 War Diary
      6 93rd MG Coy.

Copy

Jackson
For O.C. 92 M.G. Coy.

Appendix "12"

No. 92
MACHINE GUN
COMPANY
G.5/11
Date 19-9-17

Programme of Training
19th Sept. to 1st Octr. '17.

Date	Time	Nature
Sept. 19	11 am.	Inspection Parade
	11-30 am	Pay Parade.
	2-30 pm.	Baths.
20th	9 am	Inspection Parade
	9-15-11-30.	Inspection & checking of Gun Stores, kit & equipments.
	11-30-12-30	Cleaning Limbers
	2-30-3-30 p	Officer's Riding
21st	9-10 am	Inspection Parade & Coy. Drill
	10-15-11 am	Gas Drill & Inspection of Gas Appliances.
	10-11 am	Transport – Driving
	11-15-12-30	Barrage Drill.
	2-30-3-30 p.	Officers Riding
22.	9-10 am.	Inspection Parade & Coy. Drill
	10-11 am	Transport Driving
	10-15-11 p.	Map reading & Sectioning
	11-15-12-30 pm	Advancing over open country.
	2-30-3-30 p.	Officers – B.A.B. Code.

Date	Time	Nature	2
Sept 23rd	am	Church Parade	
	pm	Football	

24th 9-10am Inspection Parade & Coy Drill
10-15-11-30a Revolver Practice
11-45-12-30p Compass Work
10-11am Transport Driving
pm Firing on Range

25th 9-10am Inspection Parade & Coy Drill
10-15-11-30 Revolver Practice
11-45-12-30p Compass Work
pm Firing on Range

26th 9-10am Inspection Parade & Coy Drill
10-15-11-30 Bombing Practice
11-45-12-30p Gas Drill
2-30-3-30p Officers Riding

27th 9-10am Inspection Parade & Coy Drill
10-15-11-30 Methods of Putting on
Elevation & Direction
11-30-12-30p T.O.E.T.

28. 9-10am Inspection & Coy Drill
10-15-11-30 Tactical Exercise with
Pack Mules
2-4pm Inter Section Competitions

Date	Time	Nature
Sept 29	9-10 am	Inspection & Coy. Drill
	10.15-11.15	Map reading & Compass work
		Barrage Drill
	11.30-12.30p	Barrage Drill
	2.30-3.30	Officers B.AB Code.
30	9-10 am	Inspection & Coy. Drill
	10.15-11.15a	Map reading & Compass work
	11.30-12.30p	Advancing over open ground.
Oct. 1st	9-10 am	Inspection & Coy. Drill
	10.15-11.15a	Methods of Indirect Fire
	11.30-12.30p	Cleaning Limbers

G Stuart King
Capt.
OC 92 M G Coy.

Jackson
Lt.
For O.C. 92 M.G. COY.

No 92 MACHINE GUN COMPANY
War Diary
September

OPERATION ORDERS No 20 BY CAPT HA JOHNS. COMMdg 92 M.G.COY.
29th SEPT. 1917.
                                                    Appendix. 13.

1. The 92nd M.G. Coy will relieve the 98th M.G. Coy on the 30th Sept 1917.
2. Following is position of respective H.Q.
   Bde. H.Q.   B.20.b.05.40   M.G.Coy H.Q.   B.14.a.90.81
   R. Batt.   B.12.a.10.75   L. Batt.   T.29.a.38
   T.M.B.   B.14.d.   H.Q. R.E.   B.10.b.95

3. Disposition in line. The following positions will be taken over.
   No. 3 Section plus one gun team from No. 2 Section will take over
   ALTON, BICTOR, ANNESLEY, ASHFIELD, AMBLESIDE.
   No. 2 Section less one gun team will take over BACUP, BLACKBURN,
   BURNLEY.
   No. 1 Section will take over BOLTON, BROMLEY, BATLEY, BEDALE.
   No. 4 Section will take over CROSSLEY, CLAYTON, CAMBERLEY,
   CAMBRIDGE.
   OFFICERS. 2/Lt. Heaney will be attached for duty in the line
   to No. 3 Section.

4. GUIDES. Guides from these positions will meet the relieving
   teams at TUNNEL DUMP at 1 pm. 30-9-17.

5. TRENCH STORES. Tripods and 14 Belt Boxes will be taken over
   at each position.
   All Maps, Trench Stores &c including 2 full tins of water
   per gun team will be taken over and receipts given. Copy
   of such receipts to be sent to Coy. H.Q. immediately on
   completion of relief.

6. RUNNERS. Each section will detail one man to report to H.Q.
   immediately on completion of relief to remain for duty as a
   runner.
   No. 4 Section will in addition detail one man to report to
   Bde H.Q. for duty as a runner.
   Sergt. Raymond will detail 2 Signallers for duty at Coy H.Q.

7. GREAT COATS. Great Coats but not packs will be taken into the line.
   They will be rolled and carried strapped underneath the haversack.

8. FIGHTING LIMBERS. 2 limbers will be packed with Guns
   and stores for the line by 12-30 pm on 29th.

9. CODEWORD for completion of relief CLEAR.

   ORDERS FOR 30th SEPT 1917

10. PARADE. The Company as detailed will parade at 11. a.m.
    Full marching order less packs, and proceed by Light Rly to
    DAYLIGHT SIDING by train leaving MT. ST ELOY at 11-30 a.m.

11. TRANSPORT ARRANGEMENTS. 1 limber will be packed with
    Rations for Company in the line.
    Lieut Woods will arrange for this limber and the 2 Fighting
    limbers referred to in para. 8, to be at SKY LINE POST by 12.30 pm.
    The rest of the limbers, the G.S. Waggon and additional G.S. Waggon
    will be packed with remainder of Stores and Kit by 10. a.m.
    The Limbers and G.S. Waggons now in the Transport lines will
    report at DURHAM CAMP at 8. a.m.

12. ACKNOWLEDGE. Copy 1. to D.M.G.O.
                      2.   O.C. Coy
                      3/7   Section Officers
                      8/9   War Diary
                      10   O.S. 92 Coy H.Q.
                      11   Retained

                                                    Capt
                                                    OC 92 M.G.COY

                                              S. Jackson. Lt
                                              For O.C. 92 M.G.COY.

Army Form C. 2118.

WAR DIARY
or
INTELLIGENCE SUMMARY.
(Erase heading not required.)

No 92 MACHINE GUN COMPANY

Vol 18

CONFIDENTIAL.

WAR DIARY.

OF

92 MACHINE GUN COMPANY.

FROM 1st OCT. 1917. TO. 31st OCT. 1917.

VOLUME XXII

WAR DIARY or INTELLIGENCE SUMMARY

(Erase heading not required.)

VOLUME 22 PAGE 1

No. 92 MACHINE GUN COMPANY

OCTOBER

Army Form C. 2118.

Place	Date	Hour	Summary of Events and Information	Remarks and references to Appendices
	1917 Oct. 1.		As at the end of previous month. Coy. were in the line with near Hdqrs. at transport lines. Capt. King took charge of Army M.G. School. 1 O.R. proceeding on Armilling Course. Guns in line fired 3,000 rds.	Ref. App. 1. App.1. & 1a. Ref.
	2.		No. 790 was fired. Guns cooperating in a gas projection by smoke of fire.	Ref.
	3.		Instructions received that one section would be proceeding overseas from Marseilles about 14th inst. (GHQ letter OB121 d. 30-9-17.) No. 3 Section under Lt. Jackson & 28 men was detailed for this. 34,000 was fired. 4 O.R. proceeded to Rest Camp. 1 O.R. from Course.	Ref.
	4.		No. 3 Section returned from the line, positions being occupied by redistribution of remainder of Coy. T guns of 94 M.G. Coy. Guns fired 3,500 rd.	App. 2.
	5.		No. 3 Section preparing for move, stores, kit, equipment etc. being checked. Reference vaccination. 4 O.R. rejoined from Rest Camp & 2 O.R. families from Leave. 1 O.R. to Hosp. T.50 rds was fired. 1 O.R. slightly wounded. No. 3 Section own men set across etc. 1 O.R. to Hospital.	Ref. Ref.
	6.		Coy strength 150. No. 3 Section fully equipped with transport entrained at ARRAS at 16.30 hrs for MARSEILLES cooperating in a raid by 94 Bde. 15,250 rds fired.	Ref. App. 3.

WAR DIARY
INTELLIGENCE SUMMARY

VOLUME 22 PAGE 2

No. 92 MACHINE GUN COMPANY

OCTOBER

Army Form C. 2118.

Place	Date 1917	Hour	Summary of Events and Information	Remarks and references to Appendices
	Oct. 7		3. OR on Lewis Gun Course. Winter that were received at 1 a.m. 4,300 rds fired.	Ref.
	8		5,560 rds fired. 1. OR rejoined from course & 2 OR from hospital.	Ref. Ref.
	9		5,560 rds fired. 1 OR from hospital.	Ref.
	10		Notification of relief by 93 M.G. Coy. on 12th inst was received. 11,050 rds fired. 1. OR to hospital. 1. OR evac. to C.C.S.	Ref. Ref.
	11		1. OR to hospital. 7,500 rds fired.	Ref.
	12		Coy was relieved in the line by 93 M.G. Coy. returning to DURHAM CAMP. WENT BY ROY by light railway arriving about 8.30 p.m. 1. OR evac. to C.C.S. 1 OR to hospital.	App 4 Ref. Ref.
	13		1 OR from course. Cleaning of Guns + Stores etc. Coy Strength 150.	Ref.
	14		L WOODS. proceeded on leave. 1. OR on tunnelling course. 2 OR to Rest Camp.	Ref.
	15		Training as per programme attached. 4 OR adjoined from Rest Camp.	App. 5 Ref.
	16		Coy training. 14. OR who had received some M.G. training under Capt. KING were attached from the Infantry.	Ref.

WAR DIARY

Army Form C. 2118.

VOLUME 22. PAGE 3.

No. 92 MACHINE GUN COMPANY

OCTOBER

Place	Date 1917	Hour	Summary of Events and Information	Remarks and references to Appendices
	Oct 17		Training as per programme. 1 OR proceeded on leave.	Ref.
	18		Coy training.	Ref.
	19		1 OR from Hospital. 1 OR from leave.	Ref.
			Coy training.	Ref.
	20		1 OR on leave.	Ref.
	21		1 OR from leave.	Ref.
	22		} Training as per programme.	Ref.
	23		Training & preparation for line.	Ref.
	24		Coy relieved 93 MG Coy in the line leaving ECOIVRES by light railway at 11-30 a.m. Relief was completed by 6-0 p.m.	App. 6. Ref.
			1 OR to hospital.	
	25		On the night 24/25 2/Lt J.H.TEMPERLEY was accidentally killed by being suffocated by fumes from a brazier in his dug-out. 2 OR were also affected, one of that was admitted to hospital & one remained at duty. A Court of Enquiry was held into the proceedings followed through the usual channels.	App. 67. Appendices 24/31 Oct. Ref.
	26		2/Lt TEMPERLEY was buried in ROCLINCOURT Cemetery at 2 p.m. on 26 inst. 2 guns fired 1600 rds during night.	
	27		Guns fired co-operating with 9th projector 6000 rds. Lt WOODS returned from leave. Coy strength 149. 4,250 rds fired	

Army Form C. 2118.

WAR DIARY

VOLUME 22. PAGE 4.

Instructions regarding War Diaries and Intelligence Summaries are contained in F. S. Regs., Part II. and the Staff Manual respectively. Title pages will be prepared in manuscript.

(Erase heading not required.)

NO 92 MACHINE GUN COMPANY
October

Place	Date	Hour	Summary of Events and Information	Remarks and references to Appendices
	28.		Lt. Woods proceeded to the line. 2 OR rejoined from Rest Camp. 6,750 rds fired.	Ref app. 6
	29		Lt Dunlop rejoined from Camiers. 1 OR from leave. 1 OR from Course. 1 OR proceeded on Lewis Gun Course. 6,500 rds fired.	Ref.
	30.		1 OR on leave. 8,500 rds fired.	Ref.
	31.		Lt. Dunlop proceeded to line. 4,750 rds fired.	Ref.
			The only Batt casualty that occurred during the month was 1 OR slightly wounded.	

A.S. [signature]
2/Lieut.
For O.C. 92 M.G. Coy.

Appendix 1

OPERATIONS. FROM. 1-10-17 TO. 12-10-17.

2-10-17. In addition to night firing and the carrying of the necessary S.A.A. the following work is in progress:—
Fresh latrines for teams are being constructed at several positions. Work being done to improve deepen or revet the trenches in the neighbourhood of certain positions.
An A.A. position is being rebuilt. Gun position at BACUP is being improved and completed.
Last night our guns fired as under:—

    2,000 Rds on tracks & centre of activity in C.7.b.
    1,000 " " " " " " " C.8.a
* 2,000 " " track running E from U.25.a.30.b.
        * in conjunction with R.F.A.

3-10-17. S.A.A. to replace carried to firing positions. Work on new latrines & improvement of trenches.
2 new A.A. positions under construction and existing positions being improved.
Last night our guns fired as under:—

Rounds fired	Target
2000.	C.1.c.55.80. & neighbourhood
2000.	C.1.d.6.7.
3,250	C.1.d.72.98.
3,500	C.1.d.9.6.
3,500	C.1.d.8.3.
2,500	C.1.d (generally)
40.	E.A.

Total fired 16,790.

4-10-17. S.A.A. to replace carried to firing positions. Work continued on building new & improving old A.A. positions. Preparations made for handing over ALTON & BURNLEY positions to 94 M.G.Coy and for general re-shuffle of other gun teams on relief of No.3 Section. Work continued on improving & completing BACUP position.

Firing last night in connection with the Gas Projection:—

Target	Rds fired	Remarks
T.30.d.9.5	5,000	Gun searched & traversed slightly.
U.25.c.20.76.	5,000	do do
U.25.c.5.9.	5,000	do do
U.25.a.80.05	4,000	do do
T.30.d.9.2	5,000	do do
U.25.c.90.65.	5,000	do do
General traverse over gassed area.	5,000	2 guns.
	34,000 rds	

6-10-17. An elephant dug out is being put in at ANNESLEY position to provide additional accommodation required by team.
Last night we fired C & D. shoots as under:—

1 gun fired 1,250 rounds on C.1.d.46.75 to C.1.d.95.72.
1 " " 1,500 " " C.1.d.92.78 to C.1.d.77.28
1 " " 1,250 " " C.1.d.97.70 &
1 " " 1,000 " " C.1.d.73.73
1 " " 1,500 " " { C.1.c.55.80.
                                                          { C.1.c.8.2
                                                          { C.1.c.97.30.

SHEET II

Firing was kept up in short bursts throughout the night.
Cooperation with the Artillery was arranged.
In addition later about 500 rounds were fired yesterday
evening at E.A's.
    Total rounds fired - 7,000.

7-10-16. On the night of 5/6 we fired 7,000 rds and S.A.A. was
carried yesterday to replace expenditure.
Owing to the rain little work in the trenches could be done
yesterday. A fresh night firing position was made at
Ambleside position. Tunnel dug outs in our occupation
were thoroughly cleaned out and some gas blankets fixed.
Considerable attention was given to practising speedy & accurate
belt filling by hand; times were taken and comparatively few
failed to pass the standard laid down, but there is still room
for much improvement.

  Firing on night 6/7.
4 guns fired 10,750 rds on trench from T.30.a.65.25 to U.25.a.20.10.
1 gun fired 2,000 rds on FRESNOY PARK area.
2 guns fired on tracks behind the point where operations were
    taking place.
2500 rds. were fired at intervals throughout the night.
  Total rds fired 15,250.

8-10-17. Yesterday some S.A.A. was carried to replace expenditure.
In the morning some work was done on the trenches and in
preparing fresh positions for night firing. Later in the day
it was too wet for this work to be continued and teams were
put through some more belt filling practice; guns & all gear
were also thoroughly overhauled & cleaned.
  Night firing last night.
Last night 4 guns fired on the following tracks, firing being
kept up in short bursts at intervals throughout the night.

      Target.   Rds fired
1 gun. C.1.d.46.75 to C.1.d.95.72 1000
1 gun   C.8.c.35.80   800
1 gun   C.1.b.62.54   1000
1 gun   C.2.c.10.25   1500
       Total rds fired   4,300

The Artillery were informed of our targets & co-operated.

9-10-17. Between 25 & 30 boxes of S.A.A. have been carried to night
firing positions. Teams were given additional practice in
belt filling. A new night firing position was worked upon
and the existing night firing positions in KENT ROAD were
improved - the gun platforms being lowered and rebuilt.
Drainage at BACUP position was improved.
  Firing last night.
1 gun fired 1000 rds on C.1.d.5.0. firing in short bursts at
                              intervals throughout night.
3 guns " 3000 " traversing from C.8.a.0.0. to C.14.a.0.0.
                         These guns fired from dusk to 9.30 pm
                         & from 4 am. to daylight.
1 gun " 1500 " on U.26.a.0.5.
Total rds fired 5,500.
The Artillery were given list of targets.

SHEET III

10-10-17. S.A.A. was carried to replace expenditure. Belts which had become wet during the firing were emptied, dried & refilled. A working party was collected & a hole was commenced for a new dug out to give additional accommodation at Headquarters. The trench at Headquarters was also widened and a new latrine made & roofed in. KENT ROAD trench was cleared at a point where it had fallen in owing to the rain. Work was also done on the trenches in the neighbourhood of gun positions.
Firing last night.
At the request of the Artillery we searched ROAD running N.E. from U.25.c.5.4. and HENIN LIETARD RD. from U.25.a.20.45. (2 guns fired 3000 rds in all)
1 gun kept Hdqrs. at C.1.a.50 under fire at intervals throughout the night - 1000 rds fired.
1 gun fired 500 rds into FRESNOY PARK.
We cooperated in the two minute bursts of fire - firing 1000 rds in addition to above. Total fired 5,500 rds.

11-10-17 S.A.A. was carried to replace that fired. Work upon the hole for the new dug out was continued at Hdqrs by a working party of spare men collected from the various positions. Duckboards were also laid in the trench.
At the gun position teams were given some practice in belt filling by hand. Dug outs were cleaned & sprinkled with Cresol. Work was also done on trenches in neighbourhood of gun emplacements.
Firing last night.
  Target   Rds fired
1 gun Cross rds at U.26.d.05 1500
2 guns " " " C.1.b.6.5. 4000
2 guns traversed from C.8.a.0.0 } 5,500
    to C.14.a.0.0 }
    Total rds. 11,000 rds
This morning some firing has been done on E.A? without success up to the present.
The Artillery were informed of our targets. We are now connected by wire with 165th R.F.A. Bde. Hdqrs.

12-10-17. S.A.A. was carried to replace that fired. The hole of the new dug out was completed by a working party collected from the various gun positions, & the trench at Hdqrs was further improved. Trenches in the neighbourhood of gun positions were worked upon & improved.
Empty cases were carried to Hdqrs for return to salvage.
Night firing last night. Rounds fired
1 gun C.8.3.45.80   1750
1 " C.2.c.12.22   1000
2 guns HENIN LIETARD RD. &
 RD running through U.25.c & d. 3,000
 (at request of 165 Bde RFA)
About 1000 rds were fired at 9.20 & 10.10 p.m. to-day
750 " " " " E.A's yesterday morning
  Total rds fired 7500 rds

Copy

R.P. Faults. 2/Lt.
for O.C. 92 M.G. Coy.

No 92
MACHINE GUN
COMPANY
War Diary
October

App. 2

In consequence of the withdrawal of No 3 Section from the line the following moves will take place:-

3 guns under Lt. ARROWSMITH will move as follows.

BURNLEY on relief by 94 M.G. Coy (taking place at dawn on 4-10-17 will move to AMBLESIDE.

BLACKBURN on relief by Lt. LAVENDER, No 4 Section, will move to ALTCAR.

BACUP on relief by Lt. LAVENDER No 4 Section, will move to ANNESLEY.

2/Lt. ARROWSMITH will take up his headquarters at AMBLESIDE & be in charge of the 4 guns AMBLESIDE, ASHFIELD, ANNESLEY & ALTCAR.

BURNLEY will stack belt boxes & tripod on the road from SUGAR FACTORY to ARLEUX at point where ARLEUX LOOP cuts the road. Lt. LAVENDER will detail 2 men to take charge of these until collected by the transport tomorrow night. Trench stores will be handed over at BURNLEY to 94 M.G. Coy, & receipt obtained.

BLACKBURN & BACUP will hand over all stores which they took over from 93 M.G. Coy to Lt. LAVENDER. This will include belt boxes & tripods.

2/Lt ARROWSMITH will take over from 2/Lt HEANEY tripods, belt boxes & all trench stores which 2/Lt HEANEY took over from 93 M.G. Coy. No 2 Section will bring their own guns, spare parts etc to their new positions.

LT LAVENDER will move guns from CLAYTON & CAMBERLEY to BLACKBURN & BACUP. Belt boxes & tripods at CLAYTON & CAMBERLEY will be stacked on the SUGAR FACTORY - ARLEUX RD conveniently for the transport & a guard left in charge. Ration limber will collect these tomorrow night. LT LAVENDER will take over belt boxes & tripods at BLACKBURN & BACUP & all stores handed over by 93 M.G. Coy to 2/Lt ARROWSMITH. LT LAVENDER'S teams will move from CLAYTON & CAMBERLEY by 6 AM on morning of Oct 4th.

The whole of No 3 Section will be relieved (4 gun teams ALTON, ALTCAR, ANNESLEY & AMBLESIDE.)

ALTON gun will be relieved by 94 M.G. Coy at dawn on Oct 4. Tripod & belt boxes will not be handed over but brought down with the gun & gun stores to Coy Hdqrs. Trench stores will be handed over.

No 3 Section on relief will move back to transport lines. Guns, spare parts & all gear being taken out will be dumped at Coy Hdqrs, where A/C.S.M. Webb will arrange to take charge of it, and at night load it on ration limber.

No 3 Section will proceed to the transport via TOMMY TRENCH & not over the open. Teams may proceed independently, & not more men will be sent across the open from TOMMY TRENCH to Coy Hdqrs than necessary. A/C.S.M. Webb will detail guides to show teams where to leave TOMMY & the way to Coy Hdqrs.

The unconsumed portion of tomorrow's ration will be taken out by No 3 Section.

Copy

R S Faulks 2/Lt
for O.C. 92 M.G. Coy.

No. 92
MACHINE GUN
COMPANY

October

App. 3

1. Information – A Coy of 12 Y. & L. Regt will raid the enemy's posts at T.24.d.40.35 & T.24.d.40.55 on the night of 6/7. Oct.

2. In co-operation with above 4 guns of 92 M.G. Coy under 2/Lt TEMPERLEY will barrage on trench running along N. edge of FRESNOY PARK from T.30.d.65.85 to U.25.a.20.10.
   Rate of fire.

ZERO to Z + 4 mins	Intense	(350 rds per min. per gun)
Z+4 – Z+10 ,	Normal	(125 , , , , ,)
Z+10 – Z+15 ,	Rapid	(250 , , , , ,)
Z+15 – Z+20 ,	Intense	
Z+20 – Z+30	Normal	
Z+30	Cease fire.	

3. Guns of 94 M.G. Coy are barraging as under.

2 guns from	T.24.b.2.1	to	T.24.b.35.23.
2 , ,	T.24.b.40.28	,	T.24.b.40.40.
6 , ,	U.19.c.10.62	,	U.25.a.12.95.
2 , ,	T.24.d.60.60	,	T.24.d.85.20.

4. In addition the following guns of 92 M.G. Coy will fire
   1 gun (2/Lt ARROWSMITH) will traverse & search the area of FRESNOY PARK.
   2 guns (Lt. LAVENDER) will fire on tracks etc to catch possible movement by the enemy in connection with the operations.

5. ZERO.
   The following arrangements are being made for ZERO. The approximate time will be 9.30 pm. The actual time will be fixed by O.C. 170 Bde R.F.A. on his receiving the message in code from the front line that all is ready. The artillery will fire a salvo at ZERO, and this will be the signal for the M.G's & T.M's to open fire.

Copy

R S Faulks 2/Lt
for O.C. 92 M.G. Coy.

No. 92
MACHINE GUN
COMPANY

War Diary
October.

App 4

RELIEF ORDERS

1. The Coy will be relieved by 93 M.G. Coy on Oct 13/17

2. Section Officers will detail 1 guide from each of their gun positions to be at TUNNEL DUMP at 1 pm to guide in incoming teams. Reliefs will be brought in. Teams will go out by TOMMY ALLEY & will not use the light railway on the ARLEUX–SUGAR FACTORY ROAD.

3. Lists of stores to be handed over at each position will be prepared. One copy will be sent to these Hdqrs by 11 a.m tomorrow. Another copy signed by the incoming & outgoing gun team commanders will be handed in at these Hdqrs when relief is reported complete.

4. Section Officers will arrange that relief complete is reported at these Hdqrs.

5. When relief is complete, gun teams will move with stores & gear which is being taken out to SKY LINE POST under arrangements to be made by section Officers.

6. Two limbers will be at SKY LINE POST at 5.30 pm. Each section will pack its gun stores in a separate half limber. Brakesmen will be detailed by Nos 1 & 4 Sections.

7. Four lorries will be at the DIVISIONAL CANTEEN, ROCLINCOURT at 6 pm. One lorry will be taken by each section. The remaining lorry is for Coy Hdqrs. Lorries may move independently to ST ELOY under Section Officers.

8. SGT WEBB will prepare lists of stores at Hdqrs as directed in para 3. SGT RAYMOND will arrange for the removal of all telephone instruments. These will not be disconnected at KENT ROAD Hdqrs until relief there is complete.

Copy
J Faulks ?/Lt

PROGRAMME OF TRAINING. 15/10/17 To. 23/10/17   App. 5.

Monday 15th Oct.
- 9-10 a.m. Coy Drill.
- 10-12.30. Checking of Gun Stores
  Inspection of Box Respirators
  Cleaning of Guns & Stores.
- Afternoon Football.

Tuesday 16th Oct.
- 9-10 a.m. Revolver Practice
- 10-11 Belt Filling
- 11-11.45 Physical Training
- 11.45-12.30 Lecture
- Afternoon Football & 1 Section on Range.

Wednesday 17th Oct.
- 9-10 a.m. Coy Drill
- 10-10.30 Use of Clinometre
- 10.30-11.30 Gas Drill.
- 11.30-12.30 Care & cleaning of Guns & Stores
- Afternoon Football & 1 Section on Range.

Thursday 18th Oct.
- 9-10 a.m. Barrage Drill
- 10-11 a.m. Belt Filling.
- 11-11.45 Physical Training
- 11.45-12.30 Stoppages
- Afternoon Football & 1 Section on Range.

Friday 19th Oct.
- 9-10 a.m. Coy Drill
- 10-11 a.m. Fitting of Spare Parts & use of Spare Parts Box.
- 11-11.45 Gas Drill.
- 11.45-12.30 Care & cleaning of Guns & Stores
- Afternoon Football & 1 Section on Range.

Saturday 20th Oct.
- 9-10 a.m. Revolver Practice
- 10-11 a.m. Barrage Drill
- 11-11.45 Physical Training
- 11.45-12.30 Stoppages
- Afternoon Football.

Sunday 21st Oct. Divine Service.

Monday. 22nd Oct.
- 9-10 a.m. Immediate Action
- 10-11 a.m. Barrage Drill.
- 11-11.45 Physical Training.
- 11.45-12.30 Stripping
- Afternoon Football.

Tuesday 23rd Oct.
- 9-10 a.m. Physical Training
- 10-12.30 Preparing Guns & Stores for line.

Copy

For O.C. 92 M.G. Coy.

Appendix 6

OPERATION ORDERS. NO 26 BY CAPT N A JOHNS COMMD'G 92 MG COY

1. 92 MG Coy will relieve 93 MG Coy in the line on the 24th inst.
2. No 1 Section (less one gun team) will take over ALTON, ASHFIELD & ANNESLEY (this gun is now at AMBLESIDE) positions
   No 4 Section will take over BOLTON, BROMLEY, BEDALE & BLACKBURN
   No 2 Section (plus one gun team from No 6 Section) will take over CARDIFF, CAMBRIDGE, CLAYTON, CROSSLEY & CANT
3. Guide for all positions except CARDIFF & CAMBRIDGE will be at TUNNEL DUMP at 1 p.m. Guides for CARDIFF & CAMBRIDGE will be at the cross trenches in TOMMY ALLEY between SKYLINE POST & TUNNEL DUMP at 1 p.m.
4. Tripods and belt boxes will be taken over at the above positions from 93 MG Coy. 10 Tripods and all belt boxes in DURHAM CAMP together with 7 Yukon packs, will be stacked under cover and handed over to 93 MG Coy by 2/Lt Arrow Smith who will obtain a receipt. 2/Lt Arrow Smith will also hand over the Camp to 93 MG Coy.
   Two limbers will proceed to SKYLINE POST with guns etc & rations.
5. Each section will pack guns & gun stores for the line in a separate half limber. Section Officers will make the necessary arrangements between themselves as to these half limbers. Remaining half limber will take rations for Coy in line.
6. Reveille tomorrow will be at 6-45 a.m. Blankets will be rolled in bundles of ten & packs packed by 7 a.m. Breakfast 7-15 a.m. 8 a.m. all stores will be packed and Camp cleaned.
   The Orderly officer will inspect the Camp at 10 a.m.
   Company will parade in full marching order (less packs) on football field at 11-10 a.m. Train at ECOIVRES at 11-30 a.m.
7. Section officers will arrange to send list of names of their teams at each position to the C.M.S, and also a copy to Coy Hdqrs
8. Officers Kits will be ready for loading by 9-30 a.m.
9. Sergt. Raymond will arrange to take over from Signallers of 93 MG Coy
10. After relief is complete No 1 & No 4 Sections will send 1 orderly to Company Headquarters with list of stores taken over. This orderly will be retained at Hdqrs as Section Runner, and should therefore bring all his Kit with him. Code word for reporting relief complete will be CALIFORNIA.
11. No 2 Section will detail 1 Bde Runner who will proceed to Coy Hdqrs with CLAYTON gun team.
12. Great Coats but no packs will be taken up the line. They will be rolled & carried strapped underneath the haversack.
    Attention is drawn to orders for Dress. If wet waterproof sheets will be worn.
13. TRANSPORT 2/Lt Faulks will arrange for the 2 limbers referred to in para 5 to be at SKY LINE POST by 12-30 p.m.
    The limbers now at the Transport lines will report at DURHAM CAMP at 8 a.m.
    All stores will be packed by 10 a.m.

Copy
R S Faulks 2/Lt.
For O.C. 92 M.G. Coy

N A Johns Capt.
Commg 92 M.G. Coy.

Appendix Y

OPERATIONS REPORT FROM 25-10-17 to 31-10-17.
SHEET. 1

25-10-17. Firing Night Oct 24/25.
2 Guns last night fired 1,000 rds at intervals from 11.0pm onwards throughout the night, traversing from C.8.a.0.0. to C.14.a.0.0.

26-10-17. Attention was given to guns, stores & ammunition which were thoroughly cleaned. Dug-outs & shelters were cleaned & cresol sprinkled in them. Work was also done on trenches in the neighbourhood of gun positions. A working party was collected & worked at fitting the new deep dug-out in Kent Road. Wood was carried from Pepper Dump and stairs were fitted down one of the shaft entrances.
Night Firing Oct 25/26.
In conjunction with the gas projection last night 3 of our guns fired 6000 rds on C.7.a & C.7.c. Fire was kept up on this area in short bursts throughout the night.

27-10-17. Firing last night Oct 26/27.
Tracks & dug-outs in C.1.d. were kept under fire at irregular intervals throughout the night by 2 guns — 2000 rds were fired.
Three guns only co-operated in the minute bursts of fire scheme last night firing a belt at the three times stated in the programme. 2250 rds were fired.
Total fired 4,250.
Yesterday work was continued on the new deep dug-out at BOLTON position — work being done on the entrances & in the interior. Some work was done in clearing trenches where they had fallen in, but a good deal remains to be done.

28-10-17. Work was done on clearing trenches in the neighbourhood of gun positions which had fallen in owing to the wet weather, especially at the Kent Rd. positions, CANT & CROSSLEY & AMBLESIDE positions. Work was continued on the new deep dug-out at BOLTON position. Gun & stores were moved from ANNESLEY position (B.6.d.0.2) to AMBLESIDE (B.12.a.45.25).
Firing night Oct. 27/28.
(At E.R. morning Oct 27 about 250 rds.)
Two guns fired three bursts each under Burst of Fire programme. Rds fired 4,000.
1 gun fired at intervals through the night on U.19.c.78.20 searching up 400. Rds fired 1250.
1 gun fired on C.1.d. 40.05 (Hdqrs & track centre) Rds fired 500.
1 gun fired on road running from C.1.b.0.5 to Foot Alley covering a number of tracks in this neighbourhood, running at right angles to the road. Rds. 750.
Fire on the last two targets seemed to draw retaliation from enemy M.G's. Total fired 6750.

App 6
SHEET II

29-10-17. Work was done in clearing & repairing trenches in the neighbourhood of gun positions. Guns & spare parts were cleaned & ammunition taken from belts in positions where no firing is done, cleaned & replaced. A party was collected to work on BOLTON new dug out. Wood was carried & work was continued at finishing the boarding at the sides of the dugout, putting up beds, etc.

Firing night 28/29
5 guns co-operated in the minute burst of fire scheme at 11.40 pm & 3.5 am. Rds fired 2500.
1 gun fired on U.19.c.78.20 & neighbourhood. Rds fired 1250.
2 guns fired on C.2.a.00.43 to C.2.a.40.30. (Suspected dump & centre of movement. Rds fired 500.
At E.A's during morning 28 Oct. 1250 rds.
Total fired 6,500 rds.

30-10-17. Work on the new dug out at BOLTON position was continued. Work was also recommenced on the new dugout at Coy Hdqrs, and material collected & carried. Trenches in the neighbourhood of gun positions were cleaned & repaired. At ASHFIELD position the emplacement was repaired & strengthened & a T Base put in.

Firing night Oct 29/30.   Rds fired
1 gun fired on CHAPEL CROSS ROADS
   C.7.b.1.1. at intervals during the night }   3000
1 gun fired on C.1.d.47.73   1,000
1 gun   "   " C.1.b.6.5.   2,500
1 gun   "   " C.1.d.33.05.   2,000
                                  Total fired   8,500

31-10-17. A covered place for S.A.A. was constructed at AMBLESIDE position, where the trench has also been cleaned and renovated.
Work has been done on the latrine at ALTON & the gun emplacement considerably strengthened at ASHFIELD. A new latrine has been constructed at BLACKBURN. 30000 rds of S.A.A. have been brought up to the KENT ROAD positions.
The dugout being made at Coy Hdqrs is almost completed.

Night Firing Oct 30/31.
1 gun fired on C.1.d.47.73 - 500 rds.
1 gun   "   " C.1.b.60.50. 250   "
1 gun   "   " C.1.d.33.05   500   " (this gun traversed 2° right & left.)
1 gun   "   " U.26.d.0.5. 2500   "
1 gun   "   " C.7.a.40.90. 750   "
1 gun   "   " C.7.a.25.50. 250   "
                Total fired 4750
All guns co-operated in the set bursts of fire as arranged

[stamp: No 82 MACHINE GUN COMPANY War Diary October]

Copy
R.S. Faults 2/Lt.

Army Form C. 2118.

WAR DIARY
or
INTELLIGENCE SUMMARY.
(Erase heading not required.)

WAR DIARY.

of

92. M.G. Coy.

For Month of

NOVEMBER. 1917.

VOLUME XXIII

Vol 19

CONFIDENTIAL

Army Form C. 2118.

WAR DIARY
or
~~INTELLIGENCE SUMMARY~~
(Erase heading not required.)

No. 92 MACHINE GUN COMPANY
Date: NOVEMBER 1917

VOLUME 23.
PAGE 1.

Place	Date	Hour	Summary of Events and Information	Remarks and references to Appendices
	1-11-17		Company in line. 1. O.R. proceeded on Course. 1. O.R. from Hospital.	app. 1.
	2-11-17		10,000 rds. were fired.	
	3-11-17		9,250 rds. fired. 1. O.R. rejoined from leave.	
	4-11-17		3,500 rds fired. 1. O.R. proceeded to Cadet Unit (U.K.)	
	5-11-17		1. O.R. on leave.	
			10,750 rds fired. 1. O.R. from Course.	
	6-11-17		6,000 rds fired. Strength of Coy. 148.	
	7-11-17		2,500 rds. fired. 1. O.R. to Hospital.	
	8-11-17		Guns co-operated in daylight Raid by 11. E. Yorks Regt. 37,000 rds were fired. Company were relieved in the line by 93. M.G. Coy. and proceeded to DURHAM CAMP MONT ST. ELOY arriving about 7. p.m.	app. 2. + 3.
	9-11-17		One Officer (2/Lt. W.H. ALLEN) and 1. O.R. reinforcements joined from Base Depot. CAPT. N.A. JOHNS proceeded on Course to CAMIERS. CAPT. G.S. KING took over Command of Company.	app. 4.
	10-11-17		Cleaning of guns + stores etc. Company training as per programme.	app. 5.

WAR DIARY

Army Form C. 2118.

VOLUME 23. PAGE. 2.

No 92 MACHINE GUN COMPANY
NOVEMBER 1917

Place	Date	Hour	Summary of Events and Information	Remarks and references to Appendices
	11-11-17		Coy. Training. 1. O.R. from leave. 1. O.R. on leave. 2.O.R. on Course.	
	12-11-17		Coy. Training. 1. O.R. on Course. 1. O.R. from Course.	
	13-11-17		Coy. Training. 1. O.R. from Hospital. Strength of Coy. 148.	
	14-11-17		Coy. Training.	
	15-11-17		Coy. Training. 1. O.R. to Hospital.	
	16-11-17		Coy. Training. Preparation of Guns & Stores etc for line. 1. O.R. to Hospital. 1.O.R. is U.R. special course of instruction.	
	17-11-17			
	18-11-17		No. 2 + 4. Sections relieved two Sections of 140. M.G. Coy in line. The remainder of Company proceeded to Coy. H.Q. in RAILWAY CUTTING.	app. 6. app F.
	19-11-17		No. was fired. 2.O.R. from Course. 1. O.R. to Base Depot.	
	20-11-17		No. was fired. Strength of Coy. 147. 1.O.R. to Hospital.	
	21-11-17		No. was fired. No. 4. Section on being relieved by a section of 94. M.G. Coy. took over 4 positions held by 243 M.G. Coy. No. 1 Section proceeded from RAILWAY CUTTING to ROBERTS CAMP.	app. 7

Army Form C. 2118.

WAR DIARY
or
INTELLIGENCE SUMMARY

(Erase heading not required.)

No 92 MACHINE GUN COMPANY
NOVEMBER 1917.

VOLUME 13.
PAGE 3.

Place	Date	Hour	Summary of Events and Information	Remarks and references to Appendices
	22.11.17.		No rds. fired. 1. OR on leave.	App 8.
	23.11.17.		No rds fired. 1. OR on leave.	"
	24.11.17.		No rds fired. 1. OR on leave.	"
	25.11.17.		3000 rds fired. Interaction relief. No. 4. Section proceeded to ROBERTS CAMP.	App. 9.
	26.11.17.		1,000 rds fired. 1. O.R to convac.	
	27.11.17.		1250. rds fired. Strength of Coy. 147.	
	28.11.17.		2250. rds fired. Guns cooperated in Chinese attack - 7,500 rds were fired. 1. OR on leave. 1. OR on Convac.	App. 10.
	29.11.17.		3,000 rds fired. 1. OR to hospital. 1. OR evac to C.C.S.	
	30.11.17.		1,000 rds fired. 1. OR from leave. 1. OR to hospital.	

For O.C. 92 M.G. COY.

OPERATIONS FROM 2-11-17 to 7-11-17 (INCLUSIVE) 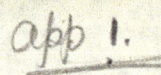App 1.

Date	
2-11-17.	Dug out completed at H.Q. Work was continued on trenches. Firing done:-

    1 Gun fired 1500 rds. at C.8.b.9505.
    * 1 " " 2000 " " T.30.d.6535 to T.30.d.5585. and
                                  T.30.d.59. to T.30.b.51.
    1 " " 1000 " " U.26.d.05. (10 m r l traverse)
    1 " " 2500 " " C.2.a.1025.
    1 " " 1500 " " C.7.a.3055.
    Total rds. 8500
usual co-operation in burst of fire last night.
  * Gaps in wire fired on after midnight.

3-11-17. Improvement of trenches + latrines continued.
Firing.
    1 Gun fired 1500 rds at C.1.C.50. (4.15 pm)
    1 " " 1500 " " C.7.a.45. (4.15 pm)
    1 " " 2000 " " C.2.a.04
    1 " " 2500 " " C.7.b.11.
    1 " " 1750 " " T.30.d.6555 to T.30.d.5585. and
    Total rds 9250   T.30.d.59 " T.30.b.51.
                            (at intervals after midnight)
usual bursts of fire during night.

4-11-17. Officers latrine constructed at BOLTON position.
Firing Report.
    1 Gun fired 2000 rds. at. C.1.d.
    1 " " 1500 " " C.1.a.50. To FOOT ALLEY.
minute burst of fire from usual M.G's at 2.45 this morning.

5-11-17. Work was chiefly confined to construction of battery positions in view of forthcoming operation.
    1 Gun fired 1500 rounds at FOOT ALLEY + to left.
    1 " " 5000 " " C.7.d. + C.7.a.
    1 " " 1500 " " C.1.C
    1 " " 2750 " " U.26.C.1025. and at C.7.a.
    Total rds 10,750   (afternoon firing is included in this)
There was the usual bursts.
Owing to patrols being out, the only gap in the wire engaged by us was at C.7.a.3055.

6-11-17. New Battery positions completed
    1 Gun fired 1500 rds. at C.2.d.0565
    1 " " 1500 " " C.1.d.5005.
    1 " " 1500 " " C.8.c.4576.
    1 " " 1500 " " C.7.a.2050.
The usual bursts of fire during the night with the artillery. Owing to the fact that patrols were out last night gaps in wire could not be engaged with the exception of the last target shown.

7-11-17. Firing report.
    1 gun fired 2500 rds. at H.Q. in C.1.d

APP 2.

REPORT ON OPERATION OF THE TWO BATTERIES OF 92 MG Coy. on 8.XI.17

Fire was opened by the 2 Batteries belonging to 92 MG Coy. at 12 Mid-day. Zero aiming posts and T shaped aiming marks having been placed in position at dawn.

Each Gun Commander was supplied with a Gun Chart & considering that this was the first time these had been used, the thing was a very big success. 17,000 rounds were fired. With the battery on the left of the road leading to ARLEUX from SUGAR FACTORY - there were only a few stoppages (on the same gun) during the 50 minutes that fire was maintained. These stoppages were due to the fact that the roller kept coming off & having to be replaced.

As the positions had been carefully camouflaged & escaped all observation, even during the morning when two or three hostile planes came quite low over them. There was no retaliation to speak of, and as soon as the action was finished, everyone was withdrawn under cover. Shortly after 2 pm. a message was received from Group H.Q. that we were no longer required. On receipt of this - the battery in KENT ROAD under LT. WOODS at once withdrew, having fired 20,000 rds & drawn practically no retaliation.

The other Battery under LT. DUNLOP remained where it was until dusk, in case the position might have to be used again. (being under direct enemy observation)

No casualties were sustained & as information was received from the raiders that we had afforded them invaluable protection & inflicted heavy casualties on enemy reserves brought up hastily to counter attack; the result of this operation was very satisfactory.

Group Orders No 1 Group.   app 3.

1. The following orders are supplementary to Machine Gun instructions D.M.G.O./R dated 1.11.17 and 4.11.17.

2. Group Hdqrs will be at Right Bn Hdqrs in ARLEUX LOOP.

3. The positions of the batteries will be as follows:—
   "A" Battery Sunken Road near BLACKBURN
       position at B.5.d.70.35
   "B" Battery TOMMY TRENCH between "Z"
       trench & M.G trench
   "C" Battery Disused part of KENT ROAD
       N of M.G Trench.
   "D" Battery B.5.c. 35.25

4. Each Battery will supply 1 runner at Group Hdqrs. The 2 runners of 93 M.G Coy will report at CLAYTON on "Y" day. Each battery will also supply 1 runner who will report to the D.M.G.O Hdqrs 11th Yorks ABERGELE dug out at 9 a.m. on Z day. This runner will know the route from ABERGELE to his battery position. ABERGELE is near the junction of HUDSON & NEW BRUNSWICK trenches in T.22. D Battery Commanders will arrange to supply these

runner

5. S.A.A. & stores all necessary will be taken to Battery positions as detailed in Appendix A

6. Separate orders will be issued for the withdrawal of the guns of 92 M.G. Coy from their defensive to battery positions.

7. Batteries will remain in position on "Z" day until they receive the code word "AUSTRALIA". They will then move in accordance with the orders issued by their respective company commanders.

8. Battery commanders will arrange to connect their batteries by telephone as follows :-
"A" Battery to Right Bn Hdqrs direct.
"B"   "   "   BOLTON DUG OUT.
"C"   "   "   "   "   "   "
"D"   "   "   "   "   "   "

9. Two signallers will be at each battery position. Sgt Raymond (92 M.G. Coy) will be in charge of signal arrangements at BOLTON DUG OUT. All signallers of 92 & 93 M.G. Coys not employed at Battery positions will report to Sgt Raymond at BOLTON DUG OUT at 9 am on "Z" day.

2

6. Separate orders will be issued as to the date & zero hour of operations and as to the synchronization of watches. If possible there will be a watch in the possession of each gun commander.

N. A. Johns Capt.
O.C. No 1 Group.

4. 11. 17.

3.

Orders with reference to operations on Nov: 8th 1917   App 4.

A. Moving from defensive to battery positions

(1) ALTON, ASHFIELD and the 4 guns of No 4 Section will form "C" Battery (LT WOODS & LT HARLEY)

AMBLESIDE and the 5 RED LINE GUNS will form "D" Battery (LT DUNLOP & LT ARROWSMITH)

(2) Battery commanders are responsible that their guns are in a position by Zero hour, guns will not move from their defensive positions before dusk on Y/Z night.

ALTON will send 8 belt boxes to KENT R^D prior to moving and will be responsible for moving the balance of their gun stores at dusk on Y/Z night.

ASHFIELD (LT WOODS) will send 4 men to help ASHFIELD move their gun stores to KENT R^D. LT HARLEY will notify LT WOODS of the time when these men are required.

Belt boxes of above two teams will be moved full.

AMBLESIDE (LT ARROWSMITH) will supply 2 guides to take team & stores to Battery positions. Cpl Snowden will proceed with this team. Guides will report at AMBLESIDE at 4-30 P.M.

AMBLESIDE may empty belt boxes before moving the S.A.A. being carefully stored and handed over as trench stores.

Remaining guns & stores will be moved to battery positions under arrangements to be made by battery commanders.

B. Handing over to 93 M^y. G. Coy

(3) During the morning of 7th inst a representative of 93 M^y. G. Coy will visit each gun position and take over trench stores. Lists of these will be prepared & signatures obtained. Section Officers will retain these receipts relating to positions under their charge and hand them in at the Orderly Room M^T ST ELOY on the morning of the 9th. A representative of 93 M. G. Coy will be at each position during Y/Z night to guard stores when teams move to their battery positions, but teams need not delay their move if this representative has not reached their position by dusk on Y/Z day.

Food containers, waterproof ration bags & gas blankets for guns will be handed over as trench stores. Yukon packs will be taken out.

C. Move to M^T ST ELOY.

(4) On receipt of code word "AUSTRALIA" batteries will prepare for moving guns & stores to M^T ST ELOY under arrangements to be made by battery commanders.

(5) LT FAULKS will send five limbers to report at Coy Hdqrs on the evening of Nov: 8th and will ensure that they reach Hdqrs as soon after dusk as is possible with safety. There will be six mules per limber if he considers it advisable. Two limbers will be available for each battery, battery commanders will send 2 guides to Coy Hdqrs to guide these limbers to battery dumps. The remaining limber will be loaded up with stores etc at Coy Hdqrs under the supervision of C.S.M. Crookes.

(6) Teams will be sent to DURHAM CAMP MT ST ELOY under arrangements to be made by battery commanders. Trains are available at DAYLIGHT SIDING at 3-30 p.m. 5-0 p.m. & 7-0 p.m.

(7) Cooks at DURHAM CAMP will have hot tea and if possible bully rissoles ready for teams on their arrival.

(8) Battery commanders will send a report to Coy Hdqrs at CLAYTON when their guns & teams are clear.

(9) LT FAULKS will make the usual arrangements for moving stores, transport etc to DURHAM CAMP.

(10) SGT RAYMOND will arrange to reel in special wires laid to 92 M.G. Coy battery positions. This wire will be sent down with gun stores.

6-11-17

app 5.

UNIT.	DATE.	PLACE.	TIME.	NATURE OF WORK.	REMARKS.
92nd M.G. Coy	9-11-17	PARADE Ground below Durham Camp	9-30 – 12-30 afternoon	Kit Inspection checking of Guns + stores Baths	
	10-11-17	do do do do do + Range	9 – 10 am 10 – 11 am 11 – 11-45 11-45 – 12-30 afternoon	Physical training Belt filling Revolver Practice Judan pack training Football + 1 section Range	
	11-11-17			Divine Service	
	12-11-17	do do do do do + Range	9 – 10 am 10 – 10-30 10-30 – 11-30 11-30 – 12-30 afternoon	Company drill Use of clinometer Gas drill Care + cleaning Guns and stores Football + 1 section on Range	
	13-11-17	do do do do do + Range	9 – 10 am 10 – 11 11 – 11-45 11-45 – 12-30 afternoon	Manage drill Belt filling Physical training Stoppages Football + 1 section on Range	
	14-11-17	do do do do do + Range	9 – 10 am 10 – 11 11 – 11-45 12-30 – 5-11 afternoon	Company drill Fitting of + spare parts + use of trilling spare parts box Care + cleaning of Guns + stores Football + 1 section on Range	

NO 92 MACHINE GUN COMPANY

Copy

UNIT.	DATE.	PLACE.	TIME	NATURE OF WORK.	REMARKS.
92 K.G. Coy.	15-11-17	Parade Ground Durham Camp	9 - 10 a.m. 10 - 11 a.m. 11 - 11-45 11-45 - 12-30 afternoon	Physical training Bayonet drill Revolver practice stoppages football	
	16-11-17	do do do do	9 - 10 a.m. 10 - 11 " 11 - 11-45 " 11-45 - 12-30 afternoon	Company drill Bayonet drill stoppages stripping football	
	17-11-17	do do do Huts	9 - 10 a.m. 10 - 11 " 11 - 11-45 " 11-45 - 12-30 afternoon	Physical training Fitting of spare parts & use of spare parts box Gas drill Lecture football	

OPERATION ORDER BY CAPT G.S. KING COMMD^G 92 M.G. COY. app 6.

(1) (a) N° 2 Section (2nd/Lt ARROWSMITH) & N° 4 Section (LIEUT WOODS) will relieve two sections of 142 M.G. Coy in the GAVRELLE Sector on the afternoon of the 18th inst.

(b) No 2 Section as detailed, will take over the Battery Position in THAMES ALLEY (B.29.b.77).

No 4 Section as detailed will take over the Battery Position in NORTH TYNE ALLEY. (B.24.a.60)

(c) Sgt Raymond will arrange for one signaller with instrument to accompany each Section.

(d) Each Section Officer will detail two runners to report to H.Q. for duty as soon as relief is complete.

(e) The detail will be under the command of LIEUT. FLOYD of N° 243 M.G. Coy – H.Q. at EAST BAILLEUL POST (B.23.b.1000)

(2) STORES

(a) Guns, Tripods, F.A. Cases and 1 Spare Parts box per Section will be taken in.

(b) 10 Belt Boxes per gun will be taken over at the position.

(c) Maps, T. Bases, Aiming Posts and all trench stores will also be taken over. Receipts will be given and duplicates sent to H.Q. at EAST BAILLEUL immediately on completion of relief.

(3) RELIEF

(a) Details will parade at a time to be notified later in marching order. Overcoats (to be rolled & strapped under the haversack) will be taken, but packs will not be carried. They will proceed by train leaving MONT ST ELOY at 10.30 a.m.

(b) N° 2 Section will proceed to GUN JUNCTION at which spot they will be met by a guide who will conduct them to the position. This guide will be at the rendezvous at 12-15 p.m.

(c) N° 4 Section will detrain at PLATEAU JUNCTION and proceed via OUSE ALLEY to the junction of OUSE ALLEY & RED LINE, where they will be met by a guide. They should reach the rendezvous by 1 p.m.

(4) TRANSPORT

(a) A complete fighting limber per section will be packed with stores & Rations for one day.

(b) N° 2 Section limber will be met at ECURIE CROSS ROADS by a guide detailed by the T.O. and proceed to GUN JUNCTION.

(c) N° 4 Section will proceed to SKY LINE POST. Limbers will be at the rendezvous by 12 NOON and on return will report to 2/Lt FAULKS at the Transport Lines.

(5) RATIONS

The T.O. will make arrangements with 243 M.G. Coy as to the sending up rations with their limbers each night.

N° 2 Section will require 6 tins of water each night

(6) CODE

Code word for completion of relief will be – SOMERSET.

(7) GENERAL.

All possible information will be obtained from outgoing teams and every effort will be made to secure continuity in the night firing programme. To assist in this, one man per Gun team from 142 M.G. Coy will remain behind on the night following relief.

Copy No 9

OPERATION ORDER No 201   20.11.17   App 7.

BY CAPT G.S. KING   COMMDG 92 M.G. COY

1. No 4 Section (LT WOODS) will relieve a section of JUSTICE in the front line to-morrow 21st inst.

The following positions will be taken over
    F.1. C.25 C. 1025
    F.2. H.6. b. 1550
    F.3. B.24. d. 5618
    S.1. B.30. C. 4585

Section H.Q. will be at the dugout in NAVAL TRENCH at H.6.a.68.

STORES

1. Tripod, 10 Belt Boxes per gun, and all trench stores will be taken over at each position.

Receipts will be sent to Rear H.Q. in RAILWAY CUTTING immediately on completion of relief.

Teams will be up in their new positions by 11 a.m. The teams at present at TYNE BATTERY will be made up to 1. N.C.O and 6 men.

2ND/LT. ALLEN will arrange for the necessary reinforcements to arrive at TYNE BATTERY not later than 9.30 a.m.

LT WOODS on completion of relief will detail one man to proceed to Coy H.Q. for duty as runner.

Completion of relief will be notified to H.Q. at the RAILWAY CUTTING by code word SOMERSAULT.

Until the necessary Signal arrangements have been made, Coy H.Q. will remain at RAILWAY CUTTING.

2. No 1 Section under 2/LT HARLEY will go into Brigade Reserve at ROBERTS CAMP. Special instructions have been issued to 2/LT HARLEY.

    COPIES
        1 D.M.G.O.
        2 LT WOODS.
        3 O.C. JUSTICE.
        4 GAGE.
        5 RETAIN.

Copy No 5

OPERATIONS FROM 22-11-17 to 30-11-17 (INCLUSIVE)   App. 8.

22-11-17 No rounds were fired last night
          No rounds fired.
23-11-17 A trench is being constructed at THAMES battery position,
          working parties being sent up every night.

24-11-17 No rounds fired

25-11-17 Two M.gs fired a total of 3.000 rounds on C.26.b.4340.
          No other guns fired.
          A new place for ammunition has been built at THAMES
          BATTERY and the trench to the actual battery position is now
          completed. Work has been progressing on gun positions round GAVRELLE

26-11-17 2. M.gs from THAMES Battery fired 1.000 rounds (In accordance
          with S/9/27.
          Improvement of trenches near all M.G. positions.

27-11-17 2. M.gs from THAMES BATTERY fired 1.250 rounds.
          No other gun fired. Trench to battery position of THAMES widened.

28-11-17. THAMES BATTERY fired 2250 rounds (In connection with S/9/27 also
          engaging TARGETS 94, 148 and 145).

29-11-17 THAMES BATTERY
              1. Gun fired 1.000 rounds at C.19.d.9314
              1   "   "   1.000   "   " C.25.b.7072
          At intervals during night 2 guns fired 1.000 rounds in
          connection with S/9/27.
          Trenches were cleaned in neighbourhood of gun positions

30-11-17 The 4 M.Gs in THAMES BATTERY fired 10.000 rounds at the
          F.F. area.
          Each gun fired 1 belt per hour commencing at 7 P.M.
          and continuing till 5 A.M this morning.
          No other guns fired.

OPERATION ORDER No. 202 BY CAPT G.S. KING. **App 9.**
Commd_g_ 92 M.G. Coy.

On 25-11-17 the following intersection relief will take place.

SECTION.	FROM.	TO.	REMARKS
No 1	ROBERTS CAMP.	THAMES BATY.	1. N.C.O. & 3 men per team will be taken into the positions the rest going to the RAILWAY CUTTING
No 2	THAMES BATY.	FRONT LINE.	Teams to be made up to 1. N.C.O. & 6 men
No 4	FRONT LINE.	ROBERTS CAMP.	2ND LT ALLEN will take command of the section on relief.

<u>No 1 Section</u> under 2/Lt HARLEY will proceed by travel route to THAMES BATTERY. Route - GUN JUNCTION, TOWY TRACK, TOWY ALLEY, THAMES ALLEY, arriving at THAMES BATY by 12 noon. A guide will be at the commencement of TOWY TRACK at 11 a.m. Details beyond 1. N.C.O. and 3 men per team will report to Coy H.Q. in RAILWAY CUTTING.

<u>No 4 Section</u> Lt WOODS will arrange for a guide from each gun team to be at the junction of MARINE TRENCH and THAMES ALLEY at 12 noon, to conduct the teams from No 2 Section to their positions. As soon as relieved, teams will proceed independently to Coy H.Q. where a meal of hot soup will be provided. They will subsequently proceed to ROBERTS CAMP under 2/Lt ALLEN, who will report on arrival to O.C. CAMP.

<u>No 2 Section</u> - Reinforcements to make up teams to 1. N.C.O. and 6 men will proceed to THAMES BATY arriving there before 11 a.m. Immediately on arrival of No 1 Section 2/Lt ARROWSMITH will hand over 2ND/LT HARLEY and proceed to take over from Lt WOODS. Care will be taken to prevent any congestion at the rendezvous.

<u>STORES.</u>

Guns, spare parts, tripods &c and all trench stores, will in every case be handed over and receipts taken, which will be sent to Coy H.Q. as soon as possible. The unconsumed portion of this days rations will be carried out in every case. Officers mess crockery will be handed over.

<u>TRANSPORT</u>

1. Half limber will report to ROBERTS CAMP at a time to be arranged by 2/Lt HARLEY and the T.O. to take up kit & rations &c. This limber will remain at MAISON DE LA COTE and take out the kit &c of the outgoing section.

Completion of relief will be wired to Coy H.Q. by code word GENERAL POST.

REPORT ON OPERATION under 31 Div/O.2.3.

App. 10

92 Inf Bde 0.184   28/11/17

No. 2 BATTERY

Location of Battery B.29.b.04.

Target C.26.a.39 — C.26.a.51.

The position selected, a disused trench, was reconnoitred in company with Section Officers on original Z. day and guns were in process of getting into position when the postponement of the operation was notified.

On Z. day 28-XI-17 guns were in position and laid by Section Officers by 1-15 P.M.

Depression stops were used.

Rapid fire was opened at Z. Hour and maintained for 10 minutes.

At Z.+10 guns ceased fire but were kept in readiness in case any suitable target presented itself. As no such target was seen and things seemed fairly quiet at 2'30 the order was given for guns to return independently at intervals to their Battle positions.

News that normal conditions had been resumed was received at 5. P.M.

    Casualties :- Nil
    Retaliation :- Nil
    Rounds fired :- 7.500

STOPPAGES

No important stoppages occurred and no breakages reported.

A few No. 3 thick Run stoppages were caused by K.N. 16 S.A.A.

Confidential

Volume xxiv.

Vol 20

War Diary.

92nd Machine Gun Company. 31st Division.

December 1917.

WAR DIARY

VOLUME 24
PAGE 1

INTELLIGENCE SUMMARY.
(Erase heading not required.)

Army Form C. 2118.

DECEMBER 1917

Place	Date	Hour	Summary of Events and Information	Remarks and references to Appendices
	1-12-17		Company in lines. 7000 O.Rs fired.	Appen 1
	2-12-17		1 O.R. transferred on Cookery Course. 1 O.R. from hospital. 1 O.R. to U.K. (Munitions).	
	3-12-17		5000 O.Rs fired.	
			1 O.R. wounded in action.	
	4-12-17		4000 O.Rs fired.	
			12 O.Rs to trenches.	
			Strength of Coy 143 O.R.	
	5-12-17		5000 O.Rs fired.	
			Capt JONES rejoined from CAMP CAMIERS and took over command of Coy from CAPT KING.	
			1 O.R. to hospital. 1 O.R. from hospital.	
	6-12-17		5000 O.Rs fired.	Appen 2
	7-12-17		5000 O.Rs fired.	
			Coy witness a demo by 165 M.G. Coy.	
			1 O.R. rejoined from travelling course. 1 O.R. from leave to U.K.	Appen 3
	8-12-17		Cleaning of all Guns & Stores (Coy Training).	Appen 4
			1 O.R. to hospital.	
	9-12-17		Coy training as per programme.	
			3 O.Rs from leave to U.K.	
	10-12-17		Coy training as per programme.	Appen 5
			CAPT KING proceeded on leave to U.K. 1 O.R. to C.C.S.	

Army Form C. 2118.

VOLUME 24   WAR DIARY   *or*   **INTELLIGENCE SUMMARY**   DECEMBER 1917

PAGE 2

Instructions regarding War Diaries and Intelligence Summaries are contained in F.S. Regs., Part II. and the Staff Manual respectively. Title pages will be prepared in manuscript.

(Erase heading not required.)

Place	Date	Hour	Summary of Events and Information	Remarks and references to Appendices
	11.12.17		Coy training & infantry training	appx 6
	12.12.17		Coy training & infantry training 2/O.R.	✓
			2/O.R. reported to V.K.	
	13.12.17		Coy training	✓
	14.12.17		Coy evening tactical scheme with 12 N.F. Bathn	✓
			2/O.R. rejoined from Base Depot	
			1/O.R. to Hospital	
			2/O.R. to Base (Signals) attached	
	15.12.17		Coy training	
			1/O.R. rejoined from C.C.S.	
			2/O.R. to Base (Signals) attached	
			2/O.R. to hospital	
			2/O.R. to V.K. S/O.R. from there to V.K.	
	16.12.17		Coy training	✓
			1/O.R. to V.K. S/O.R. from there to V.K.	
			1/O.R. from hospital	
			C.S.M.S. CAINES promoted to 2/Lt M.G. Coy and posted to C.S.M. (W.O. Class II)	
	19.12.17		Coy training	✓
			1 Officer & 2 O.R. rejoined from Base area course	
	20.12.17		1 Officer to Hospital	✓
			Sgt. MC DOUGALL recommended for CROIX-DE-GUERRE	
			Strength of Coy 14 Y O.R.	

Army Form C. 2118.

WAR DIARY
or
INTELLIGENCE SUMMARY.
(Erase heading not required.)

VOLUME 24 DECEMBER 1917
PAGE 3

Place	Date	Hour	Summary of Events and Information	Remarks and references to Appendices
	19.12.17		Coy training	appx C
	20.12.17		1.O.R. on leave to U.K. from leave to U.K.	✓
	21.12.17		Coy training	
			Coy training	
			1.O.R. on leave to U.K.	appx 7
	22.12.17		Reported from a. to R. Camp	
			1.O.R. on leave to U.K.	appx 8
	23.12.17		Coy training	
			3 O.R. on leave to U.K.	
			SGT JONES proceeded to U.K. Cadet School	✓
			1 O.R. to Hospital	
	24.12.17		Coy training	✓
			1 O.R. from leave to U.K.	
	25.12.17		Coy xmas	
			1 O.R. from leave to U.K. CAPT KING returned from leave to U.K.	✓
			1 O.R. to Hospital 1.O.R. from Hospital	
	26.12.17		Coy training	✓
			1 O.R. to Hospital 1 O.R. from Hospital	
	27.12.17		Coy training	
			No 1 Copt Hunter wounded in airplane. Two casualties	

WAR DIARY
INTELLIGENCE SUMMARY

Volume 94 — Army Form C. 2118.
DECEMBER 1917 P.4

Place	Date	Hour	Summary of Events and Information	Remarks and references to Appendices
	28.12.17		Coy training. 1 O.R. from leave to U.K. 1 O.R. from hospital. 1 O.R. from leave.	Appen 8
	29.12.17		Coy training. 2 O.R. proceeded on leave to U.K. 1 O.R. from leave. Capt King proceeded on leave. 1 army school also C.S.M. Crookes. 1 O.R. rejoined from C.C.S.	
	30.12.17		Coy training.	
	31.12.17		Coy training. 1 O.R. from leave. A complete new section which had previously processed were reported to complete and which had previously processed were reported from unit the strength. (2 officers + 35 O.R.)	Strength 2 off 160 O.R.

OPERATIONS FROM 1-12-17 TO 7-12-17 (INCLUSIVE).   Appen 1

Vol 9.

1-12-17 2 Guns fired 8000 rds at C.19d.4.1 to C.20c.10.15 + C.25 to 3500 to C.25 G.0.60
         400 rds from R4 & R5 at A.A.
         There was no retaliation.

2-12-17 2 Guns fired 5000 rds at C.C. (1 belt per hour per gun) from
         7 p.m. to 5 a.m.

3-12-17 2 Guns fired 4000 rds at R.R. (between 7 p.m. 11 p.m.
         and 1 a.m. - 6 a.m.
         New shelters completed.

4-12-17 2 Guns fired at intervals during the night 12000 rds
         at D.D.

5-12-17 2 Guns fired 5000 rds at F.F. at intervals throughout
         the night.

6-12-17 No rounds were fired.

7-12-17 No rounds were fired.

OPERATION. ORDER. N° 205 BY CAPT. G.S. KING.
COMMD° 92 M.G. Coy.

Ypres Nov 19

(1). The 169. M.G. Coy will relieve 92 M.G. Coy and 3 Guns of 243. M.G. Coy. in the line on the morning of the 7th inst.

(2) The following positions will be handed over:-

F.2.H.6.b. 1550. — 2. Guns.
THAMES. BATY. B.30.a.1275. 6. Guns.
CAMIERS } B.29.a.1772. 1. Gun.
CULE.
CLIPSTONE. H.5.a.95.55. 1 Gun.

(3.) STORES. 10 Boxes. S.A.A., all petrol tins and all Trench Stores, MAPS, orders etc will be handed over at each position. Tripods will be taken out.
At present it is arranged that Belt Boxes will also be taken out. — In the event of it being decided to hand them over, the code word CAMIERS will be sent to Section Officers, when 10 Belt Boxes per gun will be handed over.

(4) GUIDES. 1 Guide per team will be on the Road at the commencement of TOWY TRACK B.26.C.37. at 10-45. The C.S.M.

- 2 -

will meet the incoming teams there with the guides.

(5) <u>TRANSPORT</u>. All men & Stores will be taken to ANZIN by bus, which will be at MAISON de la COTE at 3.p.m.

(6) <u>RECEIPTS</u>. will be taken and handed in to Coy. H.Q. on relief.

Particular care will be taken that positions are handed over in a clean & sanitary condition, and a certificate obtained to that effect from incoming teams.

Acknowledge.

ht.
For O.C. 92 M.G. COY.

Company Orders N   Aot 2-12-17
by Capt N A Towne   Commdt OC HC M

Orderly Officer   2Lt Arrowsmith
Next for Duty   S/Sgt Allen
Routine.

         Reveille   7.0 a.m.
         Breakfast   7.30 a.m.

9.15 a.m. Company Parade for Sports

    Pick [?] Stores will be [?] on
    [?] a parade [?]
    [?].
    And [?] for [?] [?]
    to be [?] direct [?] T.O.

2.0 p.m. Pay.

COMPANY ORDERS. No. 6. FOR: 9-12-17
By. CAPT N.A. JOHNS. COMMD 92 MGC

ORDERLY OFFICER   2/Lt W.H. ALLEN *Appr 4* *Vol 19*
NEXT FOR DUTY.   2/Lt W. HARLEY
DUTY SECTION.   No 4 Section.
ROUTINE.

   Reveille 7.0 a.m.
   Breakfast 8.30 a.m.

9-30 a.m. Inspection Parade.

4-0 — 4-30 p.m. C of E. Service.

Fire Orders
 Attention is called to Fire Orders issued tonight. These will be posted up in the billets and read by all ranks. N.C.Os are responsible that they are strictly observed at all times.

       N. A. Johns Capt
       Commd 92 MG Coy.

COMPANY ORDERS. No 63. FOR. 10-12-17.
BY. CAPT. N.A. JOHNS. COMMD'G 2 M.G.C.

ORDERLY OFFICER   LIEUT. H.V. WOODS.
NEXT FOR DUTY.   2/LT. ARROWSMITH.
DUTY SECTION.   No 2 SECTION.
ROUTINE.

    Reveille 7-30 am.
    Breakfast 8-0 am.

9-0 - 10-0 a.m. Route march under
       2/LT ARROWSMITH + 2/LT ALLEN.
10-0 - 11-0 a.m. under Section Officers.
11-0 - 11-30 a.m. Cleaning of guns & Stores.
11-30 - 12-30 p.m. Physical Training.

1-0 pm   Dinners.

Afternoon   Football.

UNIT.	DATE.	PLACE.	TIME.	NATURE OF WORK.	REMARKS.
92 M G Coy.	12·12·17	ANZIN.	9·0 - 10am 10·0 - 11 11·5 - 12 12·5 - 12·30p.	Infantry drill Platoon Practice Barrage drill Cleaning of Guns & Stores.	Football G 5/11. 11·12·17.
	13·12·17	do.	9·0 - 10·30am 10·30 - 11·30 11·30 - 12·30	Bombing Barrage drill Physical training.	Football
	14·12·17	do.		Tactical scheme with 1st E.Yorks Regt. Cleaning of Guns & Stores.	Football
	15·12·17	do.		P. Bombing Practice/manance of Barrage Battery. Cleaning of Guns & Stores.	Football
	16·12·17	do.		Divine Service.	Football
	17·12·17	do.	9·0 - 10 am 10·0 - 11 am 11·45 - 12·30p	Immediate Action Physical training Reparation of Guns & Stores for relief.	Football
				M A Phee. Capt comdg 92 M G Coy.	

COOPERATION OF M.G.s WITH A VANGUARD.
SCHEME IN CONJUNCTION WITH 12th EAST YORKS.

GENERAL IDEA. The enemy have broken through our lines in the VIMY SECTOR as far south as the LA SCARPE RIVER.
Great confusion prevails and it is very uncertain how far or in what numbers he has advanced, but reports have been received that his Tanks and Cavalry with some Machine Guns has reached and hold the LENS - ARRAS ROAD.

SPECIAL IDEA. The 92nd Inf. Bde. is advancing from ACQ. with orders to seize and occupy the high ground running through F.23 & 29 and the 12th EAST YKS. REGT. have been detailed to form the advanced guard.

COMPANY EXERCISE. Each of three Coys "A" "B" & "D" will in turn act as the vanguard to the advanced guard and will deal with situations which will be pointed out to them by the umpires at F.27.b.69.

Each Coy. will be allotted 1 Section of the 92nd. M.G. Coy.

No 1 Sec. 92.M.G. Coy. will co-operate with "A" Coy.
No 2 " " " " " " " " "B" "
No 4 " " " " " " " " "D" "

Coys. will start from the Battn Parade Grounds (L.11.a.27.) at the following times

"A" Coy - - - 9.15 a.m.
"B" Coy - - - 9.45 a.m.
"D" Coy - - - 10.15 a.m.

ROUTE. St. AUBIN, MAROEUIL. Right at F.28.c.11. Left at F.28.c.25. Right at F.27.d.60.

DRESS. Fighting Order with steel helmets.

UMPIRES. LT. COL. C.H. GURNEY. D.S.O.
CAPT. N.A. JOHNS. 92.M.G.Coy.
Officers Commdg. "A" "B" & "D" Coys.
Umpires mounted, will assemble at Battn. H.Q. at 9.15 a.m. 14th inst.

ENEMY. will be represented by Signallers in Caps.

RENDEZVOUS. Sections will reach L.11.a.56. at the following times:-
No 1 Sec. 9.0 a.m.
" 2 " 9.30 a.m.
" 4 " 10.0 a.m.

They will there pick up guides of 12th E.YKS. REGT. who will take them to the parade grounds.

LIMBERS. 2 fighting limbers per section have been ordered as follows:- No 1 Section on road outside mens billet at 8.0 a.m.
No 2 " " " " " " " " " 8.30 a.m.
No 4 " " " " " " " " " 9.0 a.m.

OPERATION ORDER FOR 22-12-17
BY CAPT. N. A JOHNS COMMDG 92 MG Coy

1. The Company will move from its present billets to ROBERTS CAMP.

2. All transport (animals with one day's feed) inclusive of mules for water cart + 3 fighting limbers will report at Coy H.Q. at 8.45 a.m. where they will be packed as follows. (allocation will be made by C.S.M.)

   (a) 3 limbers will be allotted respectively to the 3 Sections.
   Section Officers Kit will be packed on these.

   (b) 1 limber will be allotted to the Orderly Room + Signallers.

   (c) 1 limber will be allotted for canteen. This will be used also for Shoemaker, articifer + Sergts mess.

   (d) 1 limber will be allotted for mess + H.Q. baggage.

   (e) The G.S. Waggon + remaining limber will be for C.QMS Stores and anything left over.

3. The cooks will be responsible for packing cooks cart

4. The packing of section limbers will be superintended by section officers.

— 2 —

The CSM will detail 4 men for (a)
4 men for (b) 6 men for (c) the servants
and 2 men for (d) and 6 men for (e)
+ will personally supervise their work.

5. A clearing up party of 1 Sgt and 15 men will report to the orderly officer at 9.a.m. A billet warden will report to the orderly officer before Coy. moves + the necessary certificate from him that everything has been left in a clean + sanitary condition will be obtained.

6. Blankets will be rolled in bundles of 10. immediately after reveille and stacked neatly outside the main gate by the orderly room (under the guard)

7. The guard will be dismissed at 9.a.m.

8. Lt. DUNLOP together with Sgt Raymond + 2 signallers on Cycles will leave at 8.30 a.m. and take over new billets. He will arrange to meet + guide the Company in. The cooking arrangements for the midday meal will also come under him.

10. When packed the Transport will move out on to the road.

11. Coy parade in full marching order at 9.45 a.m ready to move off.

9. Contents of limbers at present in Transport lines will be removed by

T.O. before limbers are despatched.
1. OR representative from each section will be sent to report to T.O. to look after their sections stores.

For O.C. 82 M.G. COY.

Appendix 8
Vol 15

NO 80
MACHINE GUN
COMPANY
No. 6/11
Date 22-12-17

UNIT	DATE	PLACE	TIME	NATURE OF WORK	REMARKS
7th M.G. Coy	23-12-17	Rabat Camp	9.0 to 10 a.m	Divine Service	
			10.30 - 11.15	Route march to ... hill	
	25-12-17	do	9.30 - 11.30	Dismounted action	
			10.30 - 11.30		
	26-12-17	do	9.0 a.m	Shelter trench	
			11.30 -	Saddlery drill	
			2.0-3.0 P.M	Musketry practice	
			8.30 - 10.30 am	Dismounted action	
	27-12-17	do	10.30 am	Tactical scheme	
			12.30 - 1.10		
	28-12-17	do	9.0 - 10	Lecture T.O.E.T.	
			10.10 - 11.30	Musketry practice (route)	
			12 - 1	2 Sections dismounted training	
			2 - 3	saddlery drill	
			3.30 - 5.30	Mounted action officers	
	29-12-17	do	9.30 am	1 Section T.O.E.T.	
			9.30	2 Sections tactical schemes	
			10.30	1 section mtd ... attack & cleaning guns	
			12.30	1 Section...	
	30-12-17	do	9.0 - 10.30	Inspection of ... harness etc	
	31-12-17	do	9.0 - 10.30 pm		
			9.0 - 10.30	1 section mtd about turns & changing leads	
1 - 1-18	do	9.0 - 11.30 pm	1 Section T.O.E.T.	
			10.30 -	1 Section mtd action off ...	
			11.30 - 1.0pm	1 section... mounted action & lecture	
2 - 1-18	do	9.0 - 10 am	Tactical scheme	
			10 -	1 Section mtd about turns & changing guns	
			10 - 11	1 Section mtd action with lecture + Tactical	
			11 -	1 Section mtd ... off ...	
			1.0 - 4.0 pm	saddlery... off ...	
3 - 1-18	do	9 - 10 am	Dismounted training	
			10 -	Bayonet ...	
			12.30 pm	Preparing ...	
4 - 8-18	do		...	

(... at Aleer all today - Special programme)

Army Form C. 2118.

WAR DIARY

~~INTELLIGENCE SUMMARY~~

(Erase heading not required.)

Vol 21

WAR DIARY
OF.
92 MACHINE GUN COY.
FOR MONTH OF
JANUARY. 1918.

Army Form C. 2118.

VOLUME 25
PAGE 1.

WAR DIARY
or
INTELLIGENCE SUMMARY.
(Erase heading not required.)

No 92 MACHINE GUN COMPANY
JANUARY 1918.

Place	Date	Hour	Summary of Events and Information	Remarks and references to Appendices
Company at ROBERTS CAMP.	1-1-18		Preparating for line. 1. OR rejoined from anti-gas Course.	App. 1.
	2-1-18		Company proceeded to line relieving 93 M.G. Coy in Right Bde Sector, relief being complete by 2 p.m. 1. OR. rejoined from leave to UK.	
	3-1-18.		2. OR proceeded on leave to UK. 1. OR. from leave. 1. OR. to Gas Course.	
	4-1-18.		2,500 rounds were fired on Road in U.25.a. at intervals during the night.	
	5-1-18.		3,000 rds. expended on tracks in U.26.a.37.	
	6-1-18.		2,000 rds were fired from C.2a.00 to C.14.a.50. 1500 rds. on HENIN WETARD ROAD from U.25.a.21. 2,000 rds from C.1.d.47. to C.1B.23. and 2,000 rds at U.25.c.53, making a total of 7,500 rds expended throughout the night. CAPT. H.A. JOHNS proceeded to 31st Divisn Scool for duty on 9/P.M.G.O. LIEUT W.N.V. DUNLOP took over command of Company. 1. OR rejoined from leave to UK.	
	7-1-18.		1500 rds fired at C.1B.60.70. 4500 rds on OPPY SUPPORT C.T.D. and 1500 rds at H.Q. C.17.b. Total fired 7,500 rds. 2/Lt. G.H. ARROWSMITH proceeded on leave to UK. 1. OR. to M.G. Course CAMIERS. 4. OR on leave U.K.	
	8-1-18.		Junction of tracks and trenches in C.1B.60.70 received 4,000 rds during the night, also 750 rds were fired from C.2a.00 to C.14.a.00. Total rds fired 4,750.	
	9-1-18.		1500 rounds were expended from C.1B.20 to C.1B.95. 2500 rds H.Q. and centre of activity in C.1a.60. 2500 rds. at C.7.a.45. and 1250 rds at C.7.a.28. Total fired 7,750 rds.	
	10-1-18.		2500 rds fired at C.1.a.46. 2500 rds. on RAILWAY C.19.a.88. 2500 rds on trenal C.2.d.34.5. C.2.d.47. Totals fired 7,500 rds. 1. OR returned from leave.	

WAR DIARY

VOLUME 25. PAGE 2.

No 92 MACHINE GUN COMPANY
JANUARY 1918

Army Form C.-2118.

Place	Date	Hour	Summary of Events and Information	Remarks and references to Appendices
	11-1-18		Tools in C.1.b.60.70. received 2500 rds. HQ at 4.19.d.88 1500 rds. Trench from C.2.a.34 to C.2.d.77 2000 rds. MG posts at C.7.a.45 and C.7.a.28 1250 rds. A total of 7,250 rds being fired during the night.	
	12-1-18		3. OR proceeded on leave. 1 OR returned from leave. 2000 rds were expended at Gaps in enemy wire C.1.b.18 & C.1.b.03. 2000 rds T.30.a.69 to T.30.b.48 2000 rds T.30.d.25 to T.30.d.69. 1000 rds C.7.a.80 to C.7.a.45.60. Total fired 7,000 rds.	
	13-1-18		2. OR proceeded on leave. 6500 rds were fired at Gaps in enemy wire throughout the night. 2. OR proceeded on leave.	
	14-1-18		9,200 rds were fired at Gaps in wire.	
	15-1-18		12,250 rds expended in Keeping open gaps in enemy wire. 1 OR returned from leave.	
	16-1-18		Harassing fire was carried out during the night on selected targets. 11,250 rds were fired. Company relieved in the line by 93. M.G. Coy. Relief was completed at 8 pm. and Company proceeded to ROBERTS CAMP, where owing to the bad condition of the trenches, the last party arrived about midnight. 2 OR to hospital.	App. 2.
	17-1-18		1 OR returned from leave. 2 OR to hospital. General cleaning up of Guns stores and equipment.	
	18-1-18		Checking of Gun stores and inspection of Kit. 2 OR from leave. 1 OR proceeded to Base Depôt. No. H. Section under 2/Lieut. W.H. ALLAN proceeded to LANCASTER CAMP for training with 10 EAST YORKS REGT.	
	19-1-18		Company training as per programme. 1 OR admitted to Hospital. 1 OR from Hospital.	App. 3.
	20-1-18		Coy Training. 3 OR proceeded on leave. 1 OR to Hospital.	
	21-1-18		Coy training. 4 OR returned from leave.	

VOLUME 26.
PAGE 3.

Army Form C. 2118.

WAR DIARY
INTELLIGENCE SUMMARY.
(Erase heading not required.)

No 92 MACHINE GUN COMPANY
Month: JANUARY 1918

Place	Date	Hour	Summary of Events and Information	Remarks and references to Appendices
	22-1-18		Coy training. 1 O.R. from Hospital. 1 O.R. proceeded on leave.	
	23-1-18		Coy training. 1 O.R. from leave. Party of 30 O.R. under 2/Lt W. HARLEY proceeded to line to consolidate shell holes for M.G. positions. 2/Lt G.H. ARROWSMITH returned from leave to U.K. 3 O.R. from leave. 1 O.R. from hospital.	
	24-1-18		Coy training. Party of 30 O.R. under 2/Lt ARROWSMITH proceeded to line and continued work on shell hole positions. 1 O.R. to Hospital. 2 O.R. from leave.	
	25-1-18		Coy training. 1 O.R. to Hospital.	
	26-1-18		Coy training. 2 O.R. proceeded on leave.	
	27-1-18		Preparation for line. No 1 Section returned to ROBERTS CAMP. 2 O.R. reinforcements arrived from Base depot. 1 O.R. from leave.	
	28-1-18		Coy relieved 93 M.G. Coy in line Relief was complete by 6 p.m. At 11.30 p.m. enemy were observed approximately 30 strong approaching post at B.6.a.45. They were easily dispersed by bombs and rifle fire. 1 O.R. reinforcement arrived. 1 O.R. proceeded on leave. 1 O.R. from leave.	App. 4.
	29-1-18		1500 rds. were fired on selected targets throughout the night. 2 O.R. returned from leave.	
	30-1-18		1500 rds. were fired on Enemy U.26.a. 2000 rds. on C.8.b.6.18. 1500 rds. on C.8.C.40.70. Total of 5000 rds during the night. 1 O.R. reinforcement arrived. 2 O.R. proceeded on leave.	
	31-1-18		1500 rds were spd on Enemy U.26.a. 2000 C.8.O.40.80. 500 rds were fired at E.A. over BREUX at midday (30') with no observed effect. At 11.15 p.m. enemy put down barrage on forward area in vicinity of OPPY. 500 rds were fired into left of OPPY WOOD. Total fired 4500 rds. 1 OR proceeded to U.K. for special course of instruction. 1 O.R. from leave. Battle Coy Cte Crafter throughout the month.	

Monoath Lt.
For O.C. 92 M. G. COY.

"OPERATION ORDERS BY CAPT N.A. JOHNS COMMD 92ND M.G. COY"

APP: No 1

1. 92 M.G Coy will relieve 93 M.G Coy in the line on Jan 2nd
2. No 4 Section will take over ALTON, ASHFIELD, AMBLESIDE & BLACKBURN
   No 2   -   -   -   - CANT, CROSSLEY, CLAYTON & CAMBRIDGE
   No 1   -   -   -   - CARDIFF, CREWE, CHESTER, & CORTY
3. Guides for all positions and Headquarters will be in TOMMY ALLEY at SKYLINE POST at 11 am.
4. Tripods & belt boxes will be taken over from 93 M.G Coy.
5. 1½ limbers will proceed to SKYLINE POST arriving at 11 am. One half limber is allotted to each section for its Gun stores. No 1 & 4 section will pack in a fore half limber. No 2 section will pack in rear half limber. One O.R will be detailed from each section to proceed with these stores.
6. Reveille to-morrow will be at 6.30 am, packs will be packed by 7 am. Breakfast 7 am. Stores will be packed and Camp cleaned by 8 am. The Orderly Officer will inspect the Camp at 9 am.
7. Two blankets per man will be taken into the line, leather jerkins will be worn. Blankets and overcoats will be rolled in waterproof sheets and strapped to the back of the belt.
8. Sections will march to SKYLINE POST independently:-
   No 4 Section will leave Camp at   9.30 am.
   -   2   -   -   -   -   -   -   9.35 am
   -   1   -   -   -   -   -   -   9.40 am
9. Section Officers will send a list of the names of their teams at each position, to the Q.M.S and also to Coy Hdqrs
10. Officers Kits will be packed by 8 am
11. Sgt. RAYMOND will make the necessary arrangements for taking over from the signallers of 93 M.G Coy
12. On completion of relief No 2 & 4 Sections detail 1 O.R to act as runner at CARDIFF position. Daily reports will be sent to CARDIFF position. No 1 Section will detail a runner to take messages to rear Hdqrs as required.
13. Coy Hdqrs will be at CARDIFF position. Rear Hdqrs at B 14.D.5.4
14. List of trench stores will be sent to CARDIFF by 9 am 3rd inst
15. Code for reporting relief complete. YOUR MESSAGE HAS ARRIVED.
16. 2Lt. FAULKS will send 1 G.S waggon, 1 cooks cart & 5 limbers to ROBERTS CAMP at 8 am 2nd Jan. He will also arrange to move Water cart and 1½ fighting limbers to the TRANSPORT LINES.
17. The unconsumed portion of rations for 2nd inst will be carried. Rations for Jan. 3rd will be sent up by limber on night of Jan 2nd
18. The Orderly Room papers etc will be sent up by limbers on night of Jan 2nd

Copy.

A Woods Lt.

For O.C. 92 M.G. COY.

OPERATION ORDER No 207 BY LIEUT. W.N.U DUNLOP COMMᵍ 92ⁿᵈ M G Coy

APP. 2

1. The 93 M.G. Coy will relieve 92 M.G. Coy in the Right Bde sector on the 16th inst.

2. A guide will be sent by every gun team except those at CANT and CROSSLEY, to be at DAYLIGHT RAILHEAD at 11 am.

3. Maps, S.O.S. lines and all information tactical and administrative will be carefully handed over by section Officers. Particular attention is drawn to the fact that there are new S.O.S. lines. Receipts will be obtained that particulars of these S.O.S. lines have been explained and understood. All tripods, belt boxes, & trench stores etc. will be handed over and receipts obtained. These receipts will be handed in to Orderly Room at ROBERTS CAMP immediately on arrival.

4. All stores brought out of the line will be carried as far as DAYLIGHT RAILHEAD and will be left there under a guard, to be provided by O.C N°3. Section
N° 1, 2 & 3 Sections will be marched from there to ROBERTS CAMP under their section Officers, and will not move off independently.
N° 4 Section will proceed to MOUNT ST ELOY. O.C section will obtain special orders for this from Coy H.Q on his way to DAYLIGHT RAILHEAD

5. Two complete limbers will be detailed to be at this dump at DAYLIGHT RAILHEAD at 5.30 pm. The T.O will obtain the necessary pass to use the concrete road

6. For the removal of H Q stores etc 1 complete limber and the Cook's cart will be on the road at B.14.a at 5.30 a.m. The C.S.M and Orderly room Cpl will accompany this limber. LIEUT WOODS will leave H.Q in time to take over ROBERTS CAMP by 9.0 am. He will be responsible for moving the C.Q.M stores from Transport Lines, for allotting billets, and providing hot meals for sections on arrival.

Copy DNWood Lt.
For O.C. 92 M.G. COY.

APP N° 3

TRAINING PROGRAMME

DATE	PLACE	TIME	NATURE OF WORK	REMARKS
19.1.18	Roberts Camp	9.0 - 9.30 am 9.30 - 10.30 10.30 - 11.30 12.0 - 12.45pm	Inspection parade followed by S.B.R. drill Company drill under Orderly Officer Cleaning ammunition & Belts Laying, setting	
20.1.18	do		Divine Service	
21.1.18	do	9.0 - 9.30 am 9.30 - 10.30 10.30 - 11.30 12.0 - 12.45pm	Inspection parade followed by S.B.R. drill T.O.E.T. I.A. Revolver Competition	
22.1.18	do	9.0 - 9.30 am 9.30 - 10.30 10.30 - 11.30 12.0 - 12.45pm	Inspection parade followed by S.B.R. drill Return on Barrage Elementary Fire Direction I.A.	
23.1.18	do	9.0 - 9.30 am 9.30 - 10.30 10.30 - 11.30 12.0 - 12.45pm	Inspection parade followed by S.B.R. drill Company drill under Orderly Officer Elementary Fire direction T.O.E.T.	
24.1.18	do	9.0 - 9.30 am 9.30 - 12.30pm	Inspection parade followed by S.B.R. drill Route march	
25.1.18	do	9.0 - 9.30 am 9.30 - 10.30 10.30 - 11.30 12.0 - 12.45pm	Inspection parade followed by S.B.R. drill 1 Section System back training do do	Elementary Fire direction
26.1.18	do	9.0 - 9.30 am 9.30 - 10.30 10.30 - 12.30pm	Inspection parade followed by S.B.R. drill Barrage drill Map reading	
27.1.18	do	9.0 - 9.30 am 9.30 - 10.30 10.30 - 11.30 12.0 - 12.45pm	Inspection parade followed by S.B.R. drill Barrage drill I.A. T.O.E.T.	
28.1.18	do	9.0 - 9.30 am 9.30 - 12.30pm	Inspection parade followed by S.B.R. drill Route march	

Copy.

Winsor Lt.
For O.C. 92 M.G. Coy.

OPERATION ORDER Nº 208. BY LIEUT. W.N.U DUNLOP
COMMD^G 92ND M.G Coy.   APP. 4

1. 92. M.G Coy will relieve 93rd M.G Coy in the Right Bde sector on 28th inst.

2. Positions will be taken over by sections as follows:—

ALTON - ASHFIELD	LT. GALLON
KENT ROAD POSITIONS	2/LT. ARROWSMITH
CLAYTON	2/LT. ALLEN
CARDIFF	2/LT. HARLEY
BOSTON - BARNSTAPLE	LT. JENKINS

3. Guides for ALTON, ASHFIELD, BARNSTAPLE & BOSTON will be at JUNCTION of TIRED & TOMMY (Near Bde HQ) to meet incoming teams at 4.0 pm. The teams for ALTON - ASHFIELD will be taken as far as KENT ROAD by the first guide. There they will obtain, after a rest if necessary, two more guides to take them to their destination.

4. All maps, papers, trench stores Belt Boxes S.A.A. etc will be taken over. Receipts will be obtained and forwarded to Coy H.Q through CARDIFF not later than 6.0 pm on 29th inst.

5. When relief is complete, each section or sub section under an officer, will send one runner to CARDIFF. These runners will be on CARDIFF ration strength.

6. Relief complete will be wired by code words. "Your message received at ---- pm."

7. <u>SIGNALLERS</u> The CSM will see that the duties of this section in the line are properly allotted by Pte Linger.

8. <u>TRANSPORT</u> 2 limbers will be provided on morning of 28th inst and packed with gun stores etc for line by 11 am.

9. <u>BLANKETS</u> 2 per man will be carried. They will be rolled and strapped underneath the haversack.

Copy   HVWoods LT/
For O.C. 92 M.G. COY.

VOLUME. 26.

Army Form C. 2118.

WAR DIARY
~~INTELLIGENCE SUMMARY~~
(Erase heading not required.)

WAR DIARY

OF

92ND. MACHINE GUN COY.

FOR MONTH OF

FEBRUARY 1918.

WAR DIARY

INTELLIGENCE SUMMARY

Army Form C. 2118.

No 92 MACHINE GUN COMPANY
Date: FEBRUARY 1918.

VOLUME 26
PAGE 1.

Place	Date	Hour	Summary of Events and Information	Remarks and references to Appendices
	1-2-18.		At the commencement of month Company were in line in ARLEUX (Right Bay) Sector. S.O.S. signal was received at 8.2 p.m. Guns opened fire on S.O.S. lines and short bursts were maintained for 2 hours. A small party of enemy were observed approaching ASHFIELD position (B.6.d.45). They were fired on by M.G. and forced to take cover. Four wounded prisoners were captured by Infantry. 9,225 rds were expended during the night. 2 O.R. proceeded on leave to U.K. 1 O.R. to Tunnelling Coys. 1 O.R. sent to CCS.	
	2-2-18.		1500 rds were fired into Square U.26.a. 2500 rds on FOOT ALLEY. 3050 rds on C.8.C.45.25. Total rds expended 7,000 during the night.	
	3-2-18.		2,500 rds were fired on C.7.d.82.06. 750 rds were fired at E.A. which crossed our lines at 3.30 pm. A total of 3,250 rds were expended. Fire was limited owing to patrols being out and movement in the open. 2 O.R. from CAMIERS. 2 O.R. from CAMIERS. 1 O.R. from Sanitary Corps. CAPT G.S. KING rejoined from CAMIERS. 2 O.R. to hospital.	
	4-2-18.		1500 rds were fired on U.26.a. 1500 rds on FOOT ALLEY in C.I.C. 1500 rds on CONNIE TRENCH in C.I.d. E.A. we engaged at 10 a.m. 200 rds being fired without observed effect. 4,700 rds were fired throughout the night. CAPT. G.S. KING proceeded to 243 T.G. Coy on appointment O.C. 1 O.R. wounded. 1 O.R. to hospital.	
	5-2-18.		500 rds were expended on CONNIE TRENCH, 750 rds on Light Rly in C.I.b. 3 O.R. rejoined from leave to U.K.	
	6-2-18.		In conjunction with artillery following harassing fire was carried out C.I.B.60.15 & C.2.a.50.50 on light Rly. 4,000 rds Harassing from C.2.a.10.50 & C.2.a.02.50 3000 rds from C.2.a. to U.26.C. 1500 rds on enemy C.T. in U.19.a. ARLEUX CHEZ BONTEMPS ROAD from U.25.a. to U.19.a.10.5 including BOIS VILAIN + MONTREAL ROAD on both sides. E.A. were engaged at 10.30 am & 4.30 pm. over ARLEUX with 500 rds. Total of 12,500 rds were expended during the night. Coy were relieved by 93 M.G. Coy and proceeded to ROBERTS CAMP. Relief was complete by 8.0 pm. CAPT. N.A. JOHNS rejoined from Divisional Wagons and took over command of company.	App. 1.

VOLUME 2b
PAGE 2.

WAR DIARY
of
INTELLIGENCE SUMMARY.
(Erase heading not required.)

Army Form C. 2118.

No 92 MACHINE GUN COMPANY
Mo. FEBRUARY
Date 1918.

Place	Date	Hour	Summary of Events and Information	Remarks and references to Appendices
	7-2-18.		General cleaning up of Guns, Stores & Equipment. 2. OR reinforcements joined. 1 OR from Course CAMIERS. 2 OR proceeded on leave to UK.	
	8-2-18.		Coy training.	
	9-2-18.		Coy training. LIEUT. BL. N. V. DUNLOP proceeded on leave to UK. 2/LT. R.B. FERGUS joined from Base Depôt.	
	10.2.18.		Coy training. Work was done on improvement to Camp & Transport Lines. 2/LT. G.H. ARROWSMITH proceeded on P. BT. Course ST. POL.	
	11-2-18		Coy training. 2. OR rejoined from leave to UK.	
	12.2.18.		Coy training. Work continued on Camp and T. Lines. 1. OR to Hospital.	
	13.2.18.		Coy training. 1 OR to Hospital.	
	14.2.18.		Coy training. 20 OR transferred from Infantry. 1. OR evac to C.C.S. (a.o.k)	
	15.2.18.		Coy training. Work continued on Camp and T. Lines. 3. OR proceeded on leave to UK. 1. OR to Course CAMIERS. 1 OR to Hosp.	
	16.2.18.		Coy training. 1 OR rejoined from leave to UK.	
	17.2.18		Divine Service. Preparation of Guns & Stores for line. 1. OR accidentally injured evac to C.C.S. 1. OR rejoined from leave. 1 OR from hospital.	
	18.2.18.		Company relieved 243 M.G. Coy. in line in ACHIVILLE (Left Bde) Sector. Relief was complete by 9.20 p.m.	App. 2.
	19.2.18.		3,750 rds were fired at Cross Roads U.13.C.40.23. 3000 rds on Road & Tracks in U.25.6.14.83. 3 OR proceeded on leave to UK. 1 OR rejoined from Tunnelling Course.	

VOLUME 26
PAGE 3.

Army Form C. 2118.

WAR DIARY

NO 92 MACHINE GUN COMPANY
" " FEBRUARY 1918

Place	Date	Hour	Summary of Events and Information	Remarks and references to Appendices
	20.2.18		All Guns opened rapid fire on receipt of S.O.S. Signal at 9.0 p.m on enemy raiders, who were repulsed with losses. 42,500 rds were expended. 1 Gun fired 1000 rds U.25.6.14.23. 750 rds U.13.c.4.23. Total of 44,250 rds were fired throughout the night. 2/Lt FAULKS proceeded on leave to UK. 4 OR on leave.	
	21.2.18		4500 rds were expended on Junction of Road & Tracks in U.25.b. 20.80. 3000 rds on Track U.24 & 45.65 to U.13.c.76. 5000 U.19.a.21.15 U.19.b.35.65. Total fired 12,500 rds. 1 OR wounded.	
	22.2.18		11,000 rds were fired at intervals at Cross Rds. T.18.a.75, 65. 4000 rds at T.18.a.95.60. 250 rds fired at EA at 1.30 p.m. Total rds expended 15,250. 2 OR proceeded on leave to UK. 1 OR to Sanitary Course. 1 OR returned from Hospital. 1 OR on leave.	
	23.2.18		5,500 rds were expended in harassing fire on Junction of Tracks U.25.c.20.83. 4000 rds on T.18.d.74.62. 4000 rds on T.18.a.95.60. Total 13,500 rds. fired throughout the night. 2 OR proceeded on A.A. Course. 2 OR on leave.	
↳	25.2.18		4,800 rds were fired on Junction of Road & Tracks U.13.C.2500 rds on Sunken Road T.24 & 45.50 to U.13.C.38.35. Total 13500 rds. 1 OR to Hosp. 1 OR from leave.	
	24.2.18		6,000 rds were expended on Cross Roads T.18.a.75 & 75.65. 3000 rds on Road U.13.C.85.78. 2750 rds on Roads U.13.a.41.01. harassing fire. Total of 11,750 rds expended.	
	26.2.18		3000 rds were fired in harassing fire on Roads & Tracks in U.13.C. 6000 rds on Trenches & Tracks in T.24.b.9.2. and T.18.d.40.75. Total expended 9,000 rds.	
	27.2.18		4,000 rds were fired on Sunken Road U.25.c.38.35. 4,000 rds on Road & Tracks U.13.a.80.78 & U.13.a.44.01. at intervals throughout the night. 1 OR to Hospital. Coy were relieved in the line by 243 M.G. Coy. & proceeded to ROBERTS Camp. Reliefs	App. 4.
	28.2.18		was complete by 2.0 p.m. 1 OR proceeded on leave to UK. 1 OR reinforcement joined. Coy proceeded to BRUNEHAUT FARM prior to move to back area.	

WDFood Lt.
O.C. 92 M.G. Coy

OPERATION ORDER No 209 BY CAPT. N. A. JOHNS
COMMDG 92 M.G Coy

No 92
MACHINE GUN COMPANY
16-2-18

SECRET

1. The 92nd M.G Coy will relieve 243 M.G Coy in the left Bde sector on Feby 18th.

2. Groups:—
ANDREWS, ALNWICK, & ALDERSHOT.   2/LT. HARLEY at ALDERSHOT.
ASTON, ACTON and 3 guns. BRISTOL   LIEUT. JENKINS at BRISTOL
(1 gun team of No 1 section attached)

BULFORD, BASINGSTOKE, BRIGHTON, & BRIXTON. LIEUT GALLON at BRIGHTON.
AYR, ANGLESEA, ABERGELE, & BINGHAM.   2/LT. ALLEN at ANGLESEA

3. Guides have been arranged as follows:—
1 guide for ANDREWS, ALNWICK, ALDERSHOT, ASTON & ACTON at Brickstacks at 4-45pm.
1 guide for No 2 section at Brickstacks at 5-0pm
1   "   " No 4   "   -   5-0pm
1   "   " Hdqrs & BRISTOL guns.   -   5-15pm
Seperate guides for each gun position will be picked up at the junction of HUDSON. C.T. & VANCOUVER ROAD.

4. TRANSPORT.— for gun stores, rations & water
1 limber for ANDREWS, ALNWICK, ALDERSHOT, ASTON, and ACTON to junction of WINNIPEG ROAD and HUDSON C.T.
1 limber for No 2 section to BRIGHTON
1 limber for No 4 section to junction of SASKATCHEWAN. RD & HUDSON. C.T.
1 limber for BRISTOL guns to BRISTOL.
Limbers will not cross the ridge till after dusk. 2 O.Rs to be detailed to proceed with each limber.

5. HANDING OVER. Tripods, belt boxes will be taken over at all positions. Belt filling machines will be taken over at ANGLESEA, BASINGSTOKE & BRISTOL. List of trench stores taken over will be forwarded to Coy Hdqrs with morning report on 19th inst.

6. SIGNALLING ARRANGEMENTS Fullerphones will be taken over at BRIGHTON & BRISTOL. DIIIs are required for ANGLESEA, ALDERSHOT, BRIGHTON & BRISTOL

7. RATIONS will be sent up as follows while the Coy is in the line.
1 limber:— Packed in fore part of limber ANDREWS, ALNWICK, ALDERSHOT, ASTON & ACTON. to junction of WINNIPEG Rd & HUDSON. C.T.
Packed in rear part of limber No 2 sections rations to BRIGHTON
1 limber:— Packed in fore part of limber No 4 sections rations to junction of SASKATCHEWAN RD & HUDSON. C.T.
Packed in rear part of limber rations for 3 gun teams at BRISTOL & Hdqrs to BRISTOL.
— Drinking water.

8. LIEUT JENKINS will hand over the camp to 243 M G Coy

9. Section Officers will send two copies of the teams detailed for their positions to Coy Orderly Room by 12 noon on 17th inst

10. 1 Runner per section will be detailed for Coy Hdqrs.

11. Code for reporting relief complete "SITUATION NORMAL"

12. 1 Blanket per man will be taken into line. Packs will be packed and remaining blankets rolled in bundles of 10, by 8.0am on 18th inst. Officers kits to be packed by 10am. Dinner at 12.30pm. Camp to be ready for inspection at 2pm.
Leather jerkins will be worn and the blanket and overcoat will be rolled in waterproof sheet and strapped to the back of the belt

13. G.S. wagon & 2 limbers at 10am. } To report to ROBERTS CAMP
Cooks Cart at 1pm   }
        H.Woods Lt f/w Capt
        COMMDG 92 MG Coy

App. 3.

OPERATION ORDER NO. 210 BY CAPT. N.A. JOHNS
COMMDG 92nd M.G. Coy.
Copy No. 11

SECRET

1. INFORMATION. The 243 M.G. Coy. will relieve 92 M.G. Coy in Left Brigade Sector on the 27th inst.

2. GROUPS.

| ANDREWS ALNWICK ALDERSHOT | } LT JENKINS at ALDERSHOT | AYR ANGLESEA ABERGELE BINGHAM | } 2/LT ALLEN at ANGLESEA | BULFORD BASINGSTOKE SASKATCHEWAN RD.(2) | } LT GALLON at BRIGHTON |

BRIXTON(2) } 2nd LT FERGUS
BRISTOL(3) } at BRISTOL

3. GUIDES. Guides for LT. JENKINS Positions   WINNIPEG DUMP
   "   "   2/LT ALLENS   "   Junction of HUDSON and SASKATCHEWAN
   "   "   LT. GALLONS   "   "   " CANADA and HUDSON
   "   "   2/LT FERGUS   "   BRISTOL
   "   "   BRIXTON   at Junction of OTTAWA and HUDSON

All Guides to be detailed under arrangements to be made by Officers in charge of the various positions and to be at various dumps at 5.45 pm.

4. HANDING OVER. 1 Gun to be handed over by 2 LT. FERGUS at BRISTOL to 243 Coy. All Tripods, Belt-Boxes, Trench Stores, S.O.S. & Defence Lines, Barrage & Work Programme & R.E. material will be handed over. All Drinking Water Cans will be brought out. All Telephones will be brought out except one Fullerphone and one D III belonging to 243 Coy. which will be handed over at BRISTOL. All Belt Filling Machines will be handed over. Maps and papers taken over from 243 Coy will be handed over to them.

5. POSITIONS. All Positions will be handed over in a clean and sanitary condition. Empty tins &c. within a 25 yd. radius of Guns will be buried.

6. TRANSPORT (1) One half Limber to WINNIPEG DUMP for ANDREWS, ALNWICK, ALDERSHOT at 7 pm. Rear half to be left at BRISTOL for BRISTOL & BRIXTON (2) One half Limber to Brighton at 7 pm for BULFORD, BASINGSTOKE, SASKATCHEWAN RD. Rear half to HUDSON C.T. for AYR, ANGLESEA, ABERGELE, BINGHAM (3) One Limber to BRISTOL for HDQRS. at 6.15 pm.

7. SECTIONS will march back under Section Officers independently to ROBERTS CAMP.

8. TAKING OVER. 2/LT HARLEY will arrange to take over ROBERTS CAMP at 2 pm. He will arrange to have a hot meal ready on arrival in Camp. List of Trench stores handed over will be handed in to the Orderly Room immediately on return to Camp.

9. CODE WORD for reporting Relief complete "ALL OFF."

Copies. NO.1   OC
   " 2   2/ic
   " 3
   " 4   2
   " 5   3
   " 6   4
   " 7   T.O.
   " 8   OC.243
   " 9   D.M.G.O.
   " 10 File
   " 11 War Diary.

H.P. Woods FOR Capt.
COMMDG. 92 M.G. Coy.

App. 4.

OPERATION ORDER N⁰ 208 BY LIEUT.
DUNLOP W.N.U.
COMMDG. 92 M.G. Coy.

1. 93 M.G. Coy. will relieve 92 M.G. Coy. in the Right Brigade Sector on the 6th inst.

2. No Guides will be required.

3. All Trench Stores, S.A.A., maps, documents &c. will be handed over, receipts obtained and handed in to Orderly Room without fail on same night.

4. TRANSPORT :-
   Limbers will be detailed as follows :-
   1 Limber at CARDIFF   5.0 pm for 2/Lt HARLEY
   1   "   "   "   5.0 pm for HDQRS.
   1   "   "   "   8.0 pm " BOSTON & BARNSTAPLE
   1   "   " CLAYTON   5.0 pm " CLAYTON and KENT RD. Positions
   1   "   "   "   8.0 pm " ALTON & ASHFIELD.

5. LT. WOODS will take over Camp from 93 M.G. Coy and provide a hot meal for Sections on arrival.

6. SECTIONS will proceed to Daylight Railhead and march by sections to ROBERTS CAMP - not independently.

Copy.

H.R. Woods Lt.
for O.C. 92 M.G. Coy.

31ST DIVISION
92ND INFY BDE

TRENCH MORTAR BTY
MAY - AUG 1916

31ST DIVISION
92ND INFY BDE

WAR DIARY

INTELLIGENCE SUMMARY of 92/2 Trench Mortar Battery In the field

Army Form C. 2118.

Place	Date	Hour	Summary of Events and Information	Remarks and references to Appendices
COLINCAMPS TRENCHES. Continued.	1916. May 11th		Visiting position K34 B95 Wicker Trench an old disused dug-out 10 yds. to the right of gun emplacement was found to have been knocked in by German cannisters, this was apparently in retaliation for our firing of the 11/5 inst. No shots were fired from this position until dusk, when 5 were sent over the enemy instantly retaliated with 2nd and light artillery and cannisters, nothing fell into our emplacement but a good number were near. So I decided to vacate the position next day, thinking that the enemy had spotted it. From position K34 B95 Wicker Trench 2 rounds were fired. Ammunition expended 7 Rounds Casualties Nil	
	12th		A new temporary position was found at K34 D89 this was a communication trench leading to the front line, this position was excavated and the gun put in, 2 shells were fired into the "Quad" in order to range and register, they both fell into the front line of the Quad. It was afterwards reported by the Coy. holding the front line D Coy 11th E.Y.R. that the 2 shells had been effective, arms and legs having been blown in the air by our shells. Capt. Williams C. Coy 11th (S) Bn E.Y.R. having arranged to fire rifle grenades into the Quad. asked the T.M.B. to co-operate, this was arranged. Guns at K34 693 fired 20 shells (falling into the wire and 14 into the trenches, the Coy observers in saps reported that groans were heard when our shells exploded. Ammunition expended 22 Rounds Casualties Nil	
	13th	P.M. 7.30	2 shells was fired from each position during the morning, as soon as these were in the air of open was blown in the German lines, evidently a signal to take cover or to observe in order to locate our guns. Each Gun fired 10 shells into the "Quad" with good results. A few cannisters were sent back after us, but these fell wide evidently our new position in Wolf Trench was also our position in Wolf Trench was Secure. Ammunition expended 26 Rounds Casualties Nil	
		P.M. 6.45		

WAR DIARY

INTELLIGENCE SUMMARY of 92/2 Trench Mortar Battery In the field

Army Form C. 2118.

Place	Date	Hour	Summary of Events and Information	Remarks and references to Appendices
COLINCAMPS TRENCHES Cont'd.	May 14th 1916	—	D. Coy of the 11th (S) Bn E.Y.R having been warned during the night by eavesdroppers I fired 15 shells from R.R. temporary position at K.3 + D.89, the shells fell into the trench ("Quad") and there was no reply from the enemy. From K.34 & 9.5 Wicker Trench 5 shells were fired, the enemy replied with eavesdroppers.	
		1 P.M.	T.M.B. 93/2 arrived with 2 guns in charge of 2nd Lt Battey who took over from me and the relief being completed, my battery proceeded to Bus-les-Artois (R.C. Camp). During the period my battery occupied the trenches on the whole good work was done. The infantry did not take kindly to the gun at first, regarding it with suspicion, but after seeing the effect of its shells they had more confidence in it, and came to the conclusion that in the event of an advance it would be very useful. The gun when being moved along the trenches was at first carried shoulder high, thus drew the fire of German snipers, who were able to follow its course along our trenches. This caused me to think that a carrier would be necessary, so I wrote to the 92nd Inf. Bde on the subject, suggesting a stretcher and enclosing a sketch for same. This gun was spent in chiefly degree ranging etc.	
	15th to 24th		On the 19th great co-operation with T.M.B. 93/2 experimentally in wire cutting was carried out. It was found that the shells was most effective against thin wire; thick wire rather destroyed the idea that the stakes was useless against wire. A full report of tests was sent to 92nd Inf Bde.	

WAR DIARY or INTELLIGENCE SUMMARY

2/2 Trench Mortar Battery
Army Form C. 2118.

Place	Date	Hour	Summary of Events and Information	Remarks and references to Appendices
COLINCAMPS TRENCHES (Continued)	May 1916. 24th	1 p.m.	Lt Ock with ½ battery and 2 guns, relieved TMB 93/2 Lt Tufford. The same arrangement as before i.e. 2 guns in front line, 2 in Reserve in COLINCAMPS. Positions of guns as before i.e. K34 B95, K34 B95, K34 D89. The position at K34 B95 Wolf Trench had been greatly improved by TMB 93/2 good head cover having been added. The two former positions were used shells being fired at various intervals all aimed at the "Quad". Ammunition Expended 18 Rounds.	
	25th		Flagstaffs Taken Hostons were very active all day, also their artillery was very busy on our front line trenches. Each gun fired 8 ten shells during the morning in the afternoon I was informed that a 6" howitzer would bombard the "Quad" So I thought that it would be a good opportunity for my two Stokes to join in. I gave orders that each gun was to fire as soon as our howitzer shell was heard passing overhead. This was done and the bombardment was quite successful the enemy did not retaliate. Ammunition Expended 56 Rounds Casualties NL.	
	26th.		The morning was rather a trying one for the battalion holding the left sector of our Brigade Frontage, the German heavy guns was shelling our front line for two hours and in that time did some very accurate shooting, traversing the trenches time after time causing many casualties. No. 4 our two gun positions throughout the day. Ammunition expended 16 Rounds Casualties NL	

WAR DIARY
INTELLIGENCE SUMMARY

Army Form C. 2118.

1/V2/2 Trench Mortar Battery — In the Field

Place	Date	Hour	Summary of Events and Information	Remarks and references to Appendices
COLINCAMPS TRENCHES Continued	May 1916 27th		At the request of Battalion commanders holding our sector, I ordered our guns to keep quiet all details of necessary things was very little to report excepting the number of our Aeroplanes which were over the German lines, at one time 15 was counted. It was reported by one of my Gunners that at 4 a.m. an aeroplane was seen to fall into the German lines, the distance could not state if it was one of ours or not. Ammunition Expended 4 Rounds Casualties nil.	
	28-		The night had been very quiet, also there was very little artillery activity during the day. Leaving 2 men to each gun I took the remainder to dig ammunition recesses and dug outs having been informed that in a short time we should be shifting from our present area. Day and night digging parties. A certain number of casualties were sent over by the enemy, our guns replied. Ammunition Expended 23 Rounds Casualties nil.	
	29-	12:30 PM	2nd Lt Burnet arrived with the left half battery to relieve the right half Relief over right half proceed to COLINCAMPS. Day & night digging parties. Ammunition Expended 16 Rounds Casualties nil.	
	30-		Fresh temporary emplacements were found and positions were pegged off to excavate them, this Emplacement being near the front line the work had to be done at night. The men in myself were sent to the trenches to continue the work at the dug-outs. The 2" T.M. fired in the afternoon in order to register on the enemy wire, the two Stokes fired at the same time. Ammunition Expended 16 Rounds Casualties nil. 200 are verlid Candles	

Army Form C. 2118.

WAR DIARY
INTELLIGENCE SUMMARY of 9/2/2 Trench Mortar Battery
(Erase heading not required.)

Sir. the field

Remarks and references to Appendices

(6)

Place	Date	Hour	Summary of Events and Information
COLINCAMPS Trenches Continued	May 1916 31st		Work at emplacements and dug-outs continued. Lt Oaks visited Trenches Things were very quiet, altho' enemies continued to worry us. I was observing the German "Quad" with my glasses when I saw 2 puffs of smoke, immediately after I saw 2 canisters in the air, the canisters appeared to have been thrown from the spot of the puffs of smoke suggesting to my mind that the puffs of smoke were used as a "blind" in order to prevent our spotting the German mortar. Ammunition expended 12 rounds casualties nil. During our shell in the trenches our emplacements having been completed we were able to fire frequently and worry the German "Quad" considerably, altho the absence of the "Red" cartridge was felt. the "Green" cartridge only confining our range to 200y so that we could only reach the "Quad", whereas had we been able to obtain the "Red" cartridge our range would have been increased to 430y and we could then have reached other parts of the German line.

R. Oaks Lt
o/c 9/2/2 T.M Battery

92 INF BDE 32 DIV

Army Form C. 2118

WAR DIARY
or
INTELLIGENCE SUMMARY
(Erase heading not required.)

Trench Mortar Battery 92/1

Vol 1

Box 2136

Place	Date	Hour	Summary of Events and Information	Remarks and references to Appendices
BUS LES-ARTOIS	6/5/16	8 AM	Battery moved up to COLLINCAMPS under 2nd Lt D. UNNE. Remainder of Battery left there at COLLINCAMPS	No LTM's to be put in advanced gun position of support trench Map 57.D NE 3&4 1: 10,000
COLLINCAMPS	7/5/16		Battery Limbers from K23d34 – K35a49. (Ref Inch 57D NE 3&4). Day of urgent labour to dig Emplacements & repair others. Res in trees km K29 C 54. Capt Horsley visited trenches	
TRENCHES	8/5/16		Carrying up stokes Gun Ammunition. Setting Emplacements & digging. Very quiet digging Empacements. Capt visited trenches Very quiet. Emplacements finished. 4 rounds from Blairs an air in retaliation for Caunetin at 10.15 am.	
	9/5/16 10/5/16		At 6.15 Capt Horsley with right half Battery relieved 2nd Lt Dunne & left half then latter took over on half at COLLINCAMPS.	
	11/5/16		Working line of old advanced gun trap placed 2 guns in position in front line at K23d21 just left of Pne 15 & K23d 1700 right of 14 Pne & retaliated line at 11. am. on K29 & 79. All the shots both Eleven shots on German line about the parapet & comm; trench falling in the trench or about the parapet & comm; trench. At 11.30 am Officer in chf in front line reported a man in German line apparently looking & firing rifle grenades. Two shots were fired by Gun & other Guns & fell a few yards above & the left of the Path & Le town. Throwing up. He took then ceased. About 12.30 pm. 3 German H.E. shells fell within a few yards of his firing position. He only slightly damaged parados. Night very quiet.	

Army Form C. 2118

WAR DIARY
or
INTELLIGENCE SUMMARY
(Erase heading not required.)

Instructions regarding War Diaries and Intelligence Summaries are contained in F. S. Regs., Part II. and the Staff Manual respectively. Title Pages will be prepared in manuscript.

Place	Date	Hour	Summary of Events and Information	Remarks and references to Appendices
	12/5/16		Right company reported sniper very active at about point K29 a 25. Enemy front line was traversed by our "Stokes", at this point for about 50 yards. Enemy very active all the afternoon, appeared to be sheltering the new gap entrance.	
	13/5/16		Enemy fired 14 "Minnys" into 15 Post "D" Company and blew in a fire bay burying a man. Company asked for retaliation, & at 4.10 p.m. we fired 39 rounds from Puckle type into enemies 2nd line trench at point K29 d 47. 35 from 4 guns. Fire spread over about 40 yds of enemy line and was very effective, timber, stakes, chalk etc. being hurled into the air. Battalion observation post reported extensive damage to the enemy line.	
	14/5/16		Enemy very quiet indeed and as a relief was to take place during the afternoon, were requested not to fire whilst the conditions remained so. Were relieved by 93/1 French Mortar Battery at 2.45 pm. Battery moved back to BUS by motor transport.	
BUS-LES-15/5/16 ARTOIS.	16/5/16		Thoroughly cleaning and overhauling guns etc. after coming out of trenches. Pte. Cooper sent on leave.	
	17/5/16		Exercises & Drill. Ranging with dummy shell.	

WAR DIARY or INTELLIGENCE SUMMARY

(Erase heading not required.)

Army Form C. 2118

Place	Date	Hour	Summary of Events and Information	Remarks and references to Appendices
	18/5/16		Exercises, digging and ranging. Practice at wire cutting. Very good shooting and results quite satisfactory. A shell falling among wire entanglements would appear to clear a cut about away in an area of 8 feet × 6 feet. Moderate wind blowing.	
	19/5/16		Drill digging etc.,	
	20/5/16		Capt. W. G. Horley proceeded to Heston Trench Mortar School on an advanced course of "Stokes 3"	
	21/5/16		Church parade	
	22/5/16		2nd Lieut. H. W. Dunne returned from leave. Drill & Exercises.	
	23/5/16		Drill digging & ranging with dummy shells.	
	24/5/16	8.0am	Battery moved up to COLINCAMPS. ½ Battery going into the trenches with ½ guns under 2nd Lieut. Dunne. Remainder into billets at COLINCAMPS.	
	25/5/16		No 1. Sub-section proceeded to VALHEUREUX to witness a Mortar demonstration. Owing to an accident at the school, this was abandoned.	
	26/5/16		Pte. Cooper returned from leave	

Army Form C. 2118

WAR DIARY
or
INTELLIGENCE SUMMARY
(Erase heading not required.)

Instructions regarding War Diaries and Intelligence Summaries are contained in F. S. Regs., Part II. and the Staff Manual respectively. Title Pages will be prepared in manuscript.

Place	Date	Hour	Summary of Events and Information	Remarks and references to Appendices
	25/5/16	7am	Sniper reported very active at point K35 a 6.9, Company asked for retaliation, fired 15 shots fired between 27 & 28 bays, making use of small trench, and observed same to fall in enemies trench. No further trouble from sniper. Right Company troubled with enemy trench mortar emplaced at point K35 a 6 3. Fired 3 shots which failed to silence mortar, then in conjunction with the Artillery fired 17 shots which were very effective doing considerable damage to reported emplacement. Enemies front line.	
	26/5/16		Enemy trench mortars & rifle grenades very quiet & were requested not to fire whilst this prevailed. Working party during night making new trench & clearing old one.	
	27/5/16		Fired 1 shot in reply to rifle grenade which immediately ceased. Carrying ammunition to the trenches.	
	28/5/16		Fired 1 shot as previous day in reply to rifle grenade and as before grenades ceased. Also shots & cries were heard directly after it was reported that party to retaliate in receiving Company and groans in emplacements. Guns in emplacements were night working parties digging emplacements, wires.	

1875 (Wt. W593/826 1,000,000 4/15 J.B.C. & A. A.D.S.S./Forms/C/2118.

WAR DIARY
or
INTELLIGENCE SUMMARY
(Erase heading not required.)

Army Form C. 2118

Instructions regarding War Diaries and Intelligence Summaries are contained in F.S. Regs., Part II. and the Staff Manual respectively. Title Pages will be prepared in manuscript.

Place	Date	Hour	Summary of Events and Information	Remarks and references to Appendices
	29/5/16	7 am	Bentie company trenches with rifle grenades, fired 2 shots from point K 29 c 5. 4. & grenade caught.	
		4:30pm	Capt. Hovley and right half battery relieved left half under 2nd Lt. Dunne (2 guns in trenches, 2 in/ reserve at COLINCAMPS, according to Brigade Orders)	
		8.0 pm	Fired 3 shells from point K 29 c 5.4. into enemy trench	
	30/5/16		In retaliation for enemy rifle grenades, fired 9 shells from K 29 c 5.4. and at 9.0 pm fired 21 shells from extreme right of Battalion frontage on to enemy trenches left of quadrilateral. Enemy had been active during the afternoon & evening with small "minnenwerfers". No reply to our fire be thinks several cannisters but ceased as we continued firing. Damage to enemy trenches was considerable; 40 R.G's were fired from our lines in conjunction with our Stokes fire. Night very quiet. All the battery employed either digging or changing ammunition.	

Army Form C. 2118

WAR DIARY
or
INTELLIGENCE SUMMARY
(Erase heading not required.)

Instructions regarding War Diaries and Intelligence Summaries are contained in F. S. Regs., Part II. and the Staff Manual respectively. Title Pages will be prepared in manuscript.

Place	Date	Hour	Summary of Events and Information	Remarks and references to Appendices
	31/5/16		At request of "C" Coy. Commander, retaliated for R.G's. with 10 rounds, first left of Guadalthenal, enemy replied strongly with artillery to which own replied. W.P. Horsley Capt. O.C. T.M.B.S. 92/1 92/1 Trench Mortar Battery whilst in the trenches do duty with the 10th and 12th East Yorkshire Regiment.	

1375 Wt. W593/826 1,000,000 4/15 J.B.C. & A. A.D.S.S./Forms/C. 2118.

WAR DIARY

INTELLIGENCE SUMMARY

Army Form C. 2118.

XXXI

X/92/2 Trench Mortar Battery
In the field

Vol 1

Place	Date	Hour	Summary of Events and Information	Remarks and references to Appendices
BUS-LES-ARTOIS	May 1916 6th	8 AM	Battery moved to COLINCAMPS 2nd Lt Burch taking 2 guns and half the battery into the trenches the remainder with 2 guns being left in billets at COLINCAMPS. The half battery in the trenches relieved T.M.B 94/1. The relief having been completed. Working parties were told off to improve emplacements at K34 B95 and K34 B93. (Ref. Trench Map HEBUTERNE 57 NE 3 & 4 parts of) with the object in view of making these emplacements permanent. The working parties were unable to do much work by day owing to the activity of German snipers, and also rifle grenades were both numerous and accurate.	
COLINCAMPS TRENCHES Ref TRENCH MAP - HEBUTERNE 57D NE 3 & 4 (parts of) Second edition Scale 1:10000	7th 8th		Day and night working parties to improve positions.	
	9th		Emplacements completed from these we could reach the Quadrilateral in the German lines, this place to my mind was used by the enemy chiefly for the purpose of firing his Trench Mortars. 1 gun fired from (K34 B95) into the Quadrilateral about K35 A33 4 shells were fired they all fell well with the trench, and the point was registered. From K34 B93 Wieter Trench 4 shells at the "Quad" point K35 A 32. 2 shells fell into the wire and the last one into the trench, this point was also registered. There was no retaliation on the part of the enemy. Ammunition expended 8 rounds Casualties Nil. 2nd Lt Oaks visited trenches	
	10th		The two guns fired 6 rounds each from the above emplacements. The orders I received were to range & register, but not bracket, because the trenches were filled with working parties who had a great deal to do in order to improve the trenches which were very bad. I could retaliate if necessary. Ammunition expended 12 rounds Casualties Nil. 2nd Lt Oaks with the left half battery relieved 2nd Lt Burch from emplacements K35 B.95 and K35 B93. each gun fired 2 rounds. Ammunition expended 4 rounds Casualties Nil	

WAR DIARY
INTELLIGENCE SUMMARY of 92/2 Trench Mortar Battery
In the field

Army Form C. 2118.

Place	Date	Hour	Summary of Events and Information	Remarks and references to Appendices
COLINCAMPS TRENCHES, Contd.	1916. May 11th		Visiting position K34.B.9.5 Wieler Trench, an old disused dug-out 10 yds. to the right of gun emplacement was found to have been knocked in by German canisters. This was apparently in retaliation for our firing the 10" mortar from this position until dusk when 5 were sent over. The enemy instantly retaliated with light artillery and canisters, nothing fell into our emplacement but a good number were near, so I decided to vacate the position next day, thinking that the enemy had spotted it.	
	12th		From position K34.B.9.5 Wieler Trench 2 rounds were fired. Ammunition expended 7 Rounds Casualties A new temporary position was found at K34.D.8.9. This was a communication trench leading into front line. The position was excavated and the gun put in. 2 shells were fired into "the Quad." In order to range and register they both fell wide of the Quad. It was afterwards reported by the Coy. holding the front line, D Coy. 11th E.Y.R. that the 2 shells had been of sufficient range and had been blown down in the air.	
		P.M. 7.30	Capt. W. Williams C. Coy 11th (S) Bn. E.Y.R. having arranged to fire rifle grenades into the Quad, asked that T.M.B. to co-operate, this was arranged. Gun at K34.D.8.9 fired 20 shells, 6 falling wide, the rest 14 into the trenches the Coy observers in Saps reported that groans were heard when our shells exploded. Ammunition expended 22 rounds Casualties Nil. 2 shells were fired from each position during the morning as soon as there was in the air O haven was seen in the German lines, evidently a signal to take cover or to observe in order to locate our guns.	
	13th	P.M. 6.45	Each gun fired 11 shells into the "Quad." with good results. After canisters were sent back after us, but these fell wide evidently our new position had not yet been located I also our position in Wolf Trench was seeing Ammunition Expended 26 Rounds Casualties nil.	

WAR DIARY

Army Form C. 2118.

INTELLIGENCE SUMMARY of 92/2 Trench Mortar Battery. In the field.

(3)

Place	Date	Hour	Summary of Events and Information	Remarks and references to Appendices
COLINCAMPS TRENCHES Contd.	May 1916 14th		D. Coy of the 11th (S.) Bn. E.Y.R. having been worried during the night by enumerated(?) fired 15 shells from our temporary position at K.34.d.8.9, the shells fell into the trench ("Quad.") and the ruins; there was no reply from the enemy. From K.34.a.9.5 Wicker Trench 5 shells were fired; the enemy replied with enumerators(?).	
		1 P.M.	T.M.B. 93/2 arrived with 2 guns in charge of 2nd Lt Batty who took over from me and the relief being completed my battery proceeded to Bus les Artres (Rest Camp). During the above my battery occupied the trenches on the whole good work was done. The Infantry did not take kindly to the gun at first, regarding it with suspicion, but after seeing the effect of the shells they had more confidence in it and came to the conclusion that in the event of an advance it would be very useful. The gun when being moved along the trenches was at first carried shoulder high, this drew the fire of German Snipers (who were able to follow its course along our trenches), thus caused us to think that a carrier would be necessary, so I wrote to the 92nd Inf. Bde. on the subject suggesting a stretcher and enclosing a sketch for same. This time was spent in drill digging ranging etc.	
	15th to 24th	8 A.M.	On the 19th inst in conjunction with T.M.B. 93/1 exploded to ascertain in what cutting was tried. It was found that the 2 lb 4 lbs Shells was most effective. Though was thus against thick wire. They rather destroyed the idea that the shells was useless against wire. A full report of tests was sent to 92nd Bd. T.B.	

WAR DIARY
INTELLIGENCE SUMMARY

Army Form C. 2118.

of 92/2 Trench Mortar Battery In the field

(4)

Place	Date	Hour	Summary of Events and Information	Remarks and references to Appendices
COLINCAMPS TRENCHES. (Continued)	May 1916. 24th	1 P.M.	2 Officers with ½ battery and 2 guns, relieved T.M.B 93/2 L.T.T.M.Bd. The same arrangement as before i.e. 2 guns in front line, 2 in Reserve in COLINCAMPS. Positioned guns as before i.e. K34 B93, K34 B95, K34 D80. The position at K34 B95 Wolf Trench had been greatly improved by T.M.B 93/2 good head-cover having been added. The two former positions were used shells being fired at various intervals all aimed at the "Quad". Ammunition expended 18 Rounds Casualties Nil.	
	25th		The German Trench Mortars were very active all day, also their artillery was very busy on the front line trenches. Each gun fired a few shells during the morning in the afternoon I was informed that a 6" howitzer would bombard the "Quad." So I thought that it would be a good opportunity for my two Stokes to join in. I gave orders that each gun was to fire as soon as our howitzer shell was heard passing overhead. This was done and the bombardment was quite successful the enemy did not retaliate. Ammunition expended 56 Rounds Casualties N.L.	
	26th		The morning was rather a trying one for the battalion holding the left sector of our brigade frontage the German heavy guns were shelling our front line for two hours, and in that time did some very accurate shooting, traversing the trenches time after time, causing many casualties. We used our two gun positions throughout the day. Ammunition expended 16 Rounds Casualties N.L.	

WAR DIARY

INTELLIGENCE SUMMARY

Army Form C. 2118.

1/92/2 Trench Mortar Battery
In the field

(Erase heading not required.)

Instructions regarding War Diaries and Intelligence Summaries are contained in F. S. Regs., Part II. and the Staff Manual respectively. Title Pages will be prepared in manuscript.

Place	Date	Hour	Summary of Events and Information	Remarks and references to Appendices
COLINCAMPS TRENCHES Continued	May 1916 27th		At the request of battalion commanders holding our sector, I ordered our guns to keep quiet altho' retaliate if necessary. There was very little to report excepting the number of our Aeroplanes which were over the German lines, at one time 15 were counted. It was reported by one of my gunners that at 4 a.m. an aeroplane was seen to fall into the German lines, the observer could not state if it was one of ours or not. Ammunition expended 4 Rounds. Casualties Nil.	
	28th		The night had been very quiet, also there was very little artillery activity during the day. Leaving 1 man to each gun I took the remainder to dig Ammunition recesses and dug-outs having been informed that in a short time we should be shifting from our present area. Day and night digging parties. A certain number of casualties were suffered by the enemy, our guns replied. Ammunition expended 23 rounds. Casualties Nil.	
	29th	p.m. 12.30	2nd Lt Burch arrived with the left half battery to relieve the right half, relief over, right half proceeded to COLINCAMPS. Ammunition expended 10 Rounds. Casualties Nil.	
	30th		Day & night digging parties. Fresh temporary emplacements were found and parties were told off to excavate them, these emplacements being near the front line the work had to be done of night. The men in mufti were sent to the trenches to continue the work of the dug-outs. The 2" T.M. fired in the afternoon in order to register on the enemy wire, the two shots fired at the same time. Ammunition expended 16 Rounds. Casualties Nil. L.E.O are nitro cellulose.	

WAR DIARY
INTELLIGENCE SUMMARY

of 92/2 Trench Mortar Battery Su-the field

Army Form C. 2118.

Place	Date	Hour	Summary of Events and Information	Remarks and references to Appendices
COLINCAMPS Trenches Continued	1916 May 3rd		Work at emplacements and dug-outs continued. L/Oakes visited trenches. Things were very quiet, altho' canonnitures continued to worry us; I was observing the German "Quad." with my glasses when I saw 2 puffs of smoke, immediately after I saw 2 cannisters in the air, the cannisters appeared to have been thrown from the right of the puffs of smoke, suggesting to my mind that the puffs of smoke were used as a "blind" in order to prevent our casualties nil. Expended 12 rounds. During our shell in the trenches our emplacements having been completed we were able to fire frequently and worry the German "Quad" considerably, altho' the absence of the "Red" cartridge was felt, the "green" continuing our range to 200y so that we could only reach the "Quad" whereas had we been able to obtain the "Red" cartridge our range would have been increased to 430y and we could then reach other parts of the German line.	

R.J.Oakes Lt.
O/C 92/2 T.M Battery

Army Form C. 2118.

WAR DIARY
INTELLIGENCE SUMMARY

(Erase heading not required.)

Instructions regarding War Diaries and Intelligence Summaries are contained in F.S. Regs., Part II. and the Staff Manual respectively. Title Pages will be prepared in manuscript.

X 92/2 Trench Mortar Battery In the field

Place	Date	Hour	Summary of Events and Information	Remarks and references to Appendices
BUS-LES-ARTOIS	May 1916 6th	8 AM	Battery moved to COLINCAMPS 2nd Lt Burch taking 2 guns and half the battery into the trenches the Remainder with 2 guns being left in billets at COLINCAMPS The half battery in the trenches Relieved T.M.B 94/1. The relief having been completed working parties were told off to improve emplacement at K.34 B 95 and K.34 B 93. (Ref: Trench Map HEBUTERNE 57 NE B 94 parts 8) with the object in view of making these emplacements permanent. The working parties were unable to do much work by day owing to the activity of German snipers, and also rifle grenades were both numerous and accurate.	May '16
COLINCAMPS TRENCHES Ref TRENCH MAP — HEBUTERNE 57 NE B.4 (Parts) Second edition Scale 1:10,000	7th 8th		Day and night working parties to improve positions Emplacements completed from these we could reach the Quadrilateral in the German lines, this place to my mind was used by the enemy chiefly for the purpose of firing his trench Mortars. 1 gun fired from K34 B 95 with Wolfrimm into the Trench, and the point was registered. From K34 B 93 Wicker Trench 4 shells were fired they all fell point K35 a 33 [*] 3 shells fell into the wire and the last one into the Trench, this point was also Registered. There was no retaliation on the part of the enemy. Ammunition expended 8 rounds Casualties Nil. L⁰ Col a visited Trenches	Cay '16
	9th		The two guns fired 6 rounds each from the above Emplacements The orders I received were to range & Register, but not permit [?] , because the trenches were filled with working parties who had a great deal to do in order to improve the trenches which was very bad. I could retaliate if necessary. Ammunition expended 12 Rounds Casualties Nil	
	10th		2nd Lt Oakes with the left half battery relieved 2nd Lt Burch. From Emplacements K35 B 95 and K35 B 93 each gun fired 2 Rounds. Ammunition expended 4 rounds Casualties Nil.	

2449 Wt. W14957/M90 750,000 1/16 J.B.C. & A. Forms/C.2118/12.

21/12 Vol 2

War Diary of 92 TMB.
from the 1/6/16 to 30/6/16

WAR DIARY or INTELLIGENCE SUMMARY

Army Form C. 2118

Trench lu ota B.G 92/1

Place	Date	Hour	Summary of Events and Information	Remarks and references to Appendices
Trenches E. of COLLINCAMPS	1/6/16	5:30 AM	Fired a hanging shot from front line S.E. of MATTHEW COPSE & late in the morning sent twenty bombs (Stokes) in or about enemy line at K.29.d.01 from portion at K.35.a.49 was fire opened.	Ref: Trench Map. HEBUTERNE 57.D. N.E. 30.4. Part of The B.G was doing duty with 10 G.B." 2 yrs R.
		2.pm	From portion opposite North of German Quadrilateral (K.35.a.63) my battery in conjunction with T.M.R.G 92/3 bombarded the German portion & henches at this point firing on the works & 2nd line of henches, on the front line in a line on 2" henches T.M's also fired about ten rounds at the emplacement, & one on Lewin & Vickers gun emplacements kept up same line of fire. During this time on portion to prevent him spotting on portion shafts burst in place, & henches taken down & taken up. the effect of the bombardment was great as the enemy was seen investments being hurled into the air. Walk we seen tranel in some damaged place & reached them during the night were damaged shelters. Also the Battalion stretcher claim at least some success at intervals. The 2 from of my B.G fired by watching there places for enemy. 48 rounds during the bombardment. In the evening fired ten rounds in German front line & communication trenches.	
	2/6/16		In the evening fired ten rounds in German front line & communication trenches opposite K.35.a.49. Went of the bombs passing into the trench. Sgt Wader went or leave to U.K. Enemy was very quiet, & no retaliation asked for.	
	3/6/16	3 AM	Enemy mortar & Rifle Grenades which were active during "Stand to" fired Replying to enemy mortar bombs from Perry St. Emplacement (K.35.a.49) along enemy front, twenty bombs firing into the German Trabulateral in reply. At this line my other guns were firing on the enemy Carmi ators.	

Continued

WAR DIARY
or
INTELLIGENCE SUMMARY
(Erase heading not required.)

Army Form C. 2118

Place	Date	Hour	Summary of Events and Information	Remarks and references to Appendices
Continued	3/6/16	3 p.m.	German Artillery heavily shelled my Perry gr emplacement will HE. (K35a 49) & I decided to withdraw gun & team to a back position a few yards off. We went few sheets blew up the emplacement in which & he what on the old dummy hack where my position was. I neared the gun to take along to the left of R. Future & set up for use there in close proximity to my other gun which was situated opposite the Gradientical in a dummy trench wall at WICKER.	
		5 p.m.	Registered from WICKER & after getting the target had ten rounds into his trenches. While relaying on fresh target enemy opened a heavy Artillery fire onto the Emplacement & I again decided to withdraw a short distance — the Emplacement was completely blown up. Gun hurled, ammunition scattered, but to dare sheets, we were again sheered. he got a new position close to where the gun was when – whilst digging in hurried size of In artillerist at the gun we were shelled.	
		9 p.m.	2/Cpl Penn went on leave to U.K. bombarded German line to which he replies with both guns.	
	10 (midnight)		On Artillery put a barrage on enemy lines, & at abt 12 a barrage on rem, & at abt	
	4/6/16	2 AM.	2 AM. when it had died down I took the remainder of my battery to dig out wounded & dead. The day was exceptionally quiet & I was relieved by the 93rd B.S.B. at 2 pm. returning with my battery to Bun.	

1875 Wt. W593/826 1,000,000 4/15 J.B.C. & A. A.D.S.S./Forms/C. 2118.

Army Form C. 2118

WAR DIARY
or
INTELLIGENCE SUMMARY
(Erase heading not required.)

Instructions regarding War Diaries and Intelligence Summaries are contained in F.S. Regs., Part II. and the Staff Manual respectively. Title Pages will be prepared in manuscript.

Place	Date	Hour	Summary of Events and Information	Remarks and references to Appendices
Continued B in	4/6/16		2nd Lt. Dunne (the other officer of my B.S.) who had been on leave in reserve at COLLINCAMPS, proceeded in the evening to 29th Casualty Clearing Station with wife on the scene.	
	5/6/16		Checking equipment, overhauling gun etc	
	6/6/16		Training etc. L/Cpl. Hunte went on leave to U.K. Drew books from Field Cashier. During the period of time from 4th inst. in the trenches from 21/5/16 – 4/6/16 the work done by Pits Crné (59) Suivez (1062) & Reup (421) was specially worthy of praise, under a heavy fire from enemy artillery.	

Place	Date	Hour	Summary of Events and Information	Remarks and references to Appendices
BUS-LES-ARTOIS	11/6/16		Orders received that in future 92/1, 92/2 and 92/3 Trench Mortar Batteries, the latter battery being a newly formed battery, are to be amalgamated together and named 92nd Trench Mortar Battery and divided into three sections and commanded by Capt. W. P. Horsley.	
COLINCAMPS	12/6/16		Battery moved up to COLINCAMPS and relieved the 93rd T.M.B. relief completed at 12.15 pm. Capt Horsley, Lieut Orke, 2nd Lieut Burch with No 1 Section and half of No 2 and 3 sections in the trenches having seven guns. Fired 57 rounds during afternoon as follows:- 3 bombs from K.29 & 8.9 - 6 rounds from K.29a 8.2 - 9 rounds from Rile Copse - 33 rounds from Wolf Trench and 6 rounds from Beef Street. Considerable damage was reported to have been done with trench mortars and rifle grenades. Enemy very quiet. Enemy sent over a few concentos to which we immediately replied with our Stokes	
"	13/6/16			

WAR DIARY or INTELLIGENCE SUMMARY

Army Form C. 2118

Place	Date	Hour	Summary of Events and Information	Remarks and references to Appendices
	14/6/16		During the day we fired 111 rounds, made up as follows:- 53 rounds from the left sector, 42 rounds from the centre sector and 16 rounds from the right sector. Majority of shots fired being effective. Enemy scored a direct hit on our emplacement in Beef Street. Capt Horsley attended a Brigade conference at COURCELLES. Lt Dunnin took over our right sector and the 10 East York Regt. were relieved by the 12 York & Lancs Regt.

The Brigadier-General complimented the battery on standing by the guns and still firing them under heavy shell fire. 2nd Lieut Burch & 2nd Lieut Hunt and 4 guns in centre sector and left sector. 1 gun at point K29c 4.2. off flag. 1 gun in Leeds Trench about K29c 6.5. 1 gun at point K29c 7.7. front line and 1 gun at point K29a 7.0. in front line. Fired 6 shells at enemy trench mortar emplacement and scored 1 direct hit, point aimed at being K35a.6.4. | |

WAR DIARY
or
INTELLIGENCE SUMMARY
(Erase heading not required.)

Army Form C. 2118

Place	Date	Hour	Summary of Events and Information	Remarks and references to Appendices
	15/6/16		Fired 52 rounds during the day doing considerable damage to enemies emplacements and trenches.	
	16/6/16		4 new guns Mark 2 Tubular mounting were sent into the trenches in exchange for the old guns. Fired 45 rounds in retaliation to enemy mortars	
	17/6/16		Enemy sent about 30 canisters over, causing some trouble. Replied back in the ratio of about 3 to 1. Expended 92 rounds from 4 guns which effectively silenced enemy trench mortar	
	18/6/16		Enemy trench mortar observed at pt. K 35 a. 6.4. Fired 6 rounds at emplacement and observed 1 shell to fall right into emplacement doing great damage. Fired a total of 79 rounds.	
	19/6/16		In retaliation for enemy rifle grenades we fired 22 stells, which proved very effective & during the afternoon fired 49 shells in reply to enemy trench mortars which were reported to have done considerable damage.	

WAR DIARY or INTELLIGENCE SUMMARY

Army Form C. 2118

Place	Date	Hour	Summary of Events and Information	Remarks and references to Appendices
	20/6/16		Fired a total of 75 shells during the day chiefly in retaliation for rifle grenades and trench mortars	
	21/6/16		Fired 12 shells from K.29.c.77.m. to enemy snipers position which proved effective. Fired 33 shells in reply to enemy trench mortar and during the evening fired 24 shells from K.29.a.7.0. on to enemy machine gun emplacement. 2nd Lieut Bunch returned from the trenches to COLINCAMPS. Section 2 relieved Section 3 under 2nd Lieut Pte E. Smith wounded by M.G. fire	Shot through the lung.
	22/6/16		Fired a total of 85 shells during the day chiefly in retaliation for trench mortars. 2/W. Retteman returned from leave.	
	23/6/16		Fired a total of 72 shells during course of day. Capt. Horsley and 2/Lts Bunch and Henson spent the morning going around the front line emplacements to and inspecting Sap. 2/Lt Hicks + No 2 Section withdrawn in the evening.	
	24/6/16		Bombardment of Enemy's positions commenced at 5.0 A.M. half a dozen 5.9 shells fell in COLINCAMPS during	

WAR DIARY
or
INTELLIGENCE SUMMARY

Army Form C. 2118

Place	Date	Hour	Summary of Events and Information	Remarks and references to Appendices
	24/6/16		the morning; remainder of day nothing important occurred, except the continuation of bombardment of the Enemy lines.	
	25/6/16		Bombardment very heavy in early morning and a fair number of Whiz-Bangs & 5.9 H.E. were fired into COLINCAMPS only doing slight material damage.	
	26/6/16		Bombardment continued during night & whole day. The Enemy fired about 50 H.E. & 20 Whiz Bangs into COLINCAMPS. No damage; though some of the craters were only 20 yds from the HQ an Rieul.	
	27/6/16		Bombardment continued.	
	28/6/16		Enemy fired some 5.9 H.E. into COLINCAMPS, Hutting a Field in which were some men of Section 3. The damage was slight except for 1 gun being placed out of action & 4 bicycles slightly damaged.	

WAR DIARY
or
INTELLIGENCE SUMMARY

Army Form C. 2118

Place	Date	Hour	Summary of Events and Information	Remarks and references to Appendices
	29/6/16		Bombardment continued. COLINCAMPS fairly badly damaged, but no men were killed or wounded. Nos. 1 & 2 Sections moved up to Sap C, leaving COLINCAMPS at 5.45 p.m.	
	30/6/16		No. 3 Section moved up to URIAH TRENCH at 6.0 p.m. It was found inadvisable to attempt to go up to front line before dark, the Trenches being too badly damaged & in view of Enemy trenches. Capt. Horsley & Lt. Batt went to reconnoitre the way up & to site places in the front line for the guns to fire from. After dark the Section was safely brought up in spite of Enemy shelling. 40 Ammunition carriers & 20 ratios carriers were employed in follow on & were supplied 15 from Pearl battalion in the Bde. left in trenches under Battery H.Q.S. in COLINCAMPS 20 guns of ratios & 40 bringing up stretchers for carrying ammunition for the Battery. Except the No. 3 Section who were in reserve in men of Battery, except the No. 3 Section who were in reserve in URIAH head were employed	

Place	Date	Hour	Summary of Events and Information	Remarks and references to Appendices
Continued	30/6/16		Throughout the night digging out ammunition which had been buried by German shelling & carrying ammun: from the Sap to gun position in front line & adapting a & ate here to gun position that in use be any Every few & was fine Pack B4. Cutting on wire seemed to draw it where Germans employed observed down the Sap was very difficult owing to infantry taking place in the ammunit: was it for even & was obliged to get the Officer i/c Sap (R.E.) to intervene.	

hP Horley Capt.
OC 92 W T M B 5

92nd Bde.
31st Div.

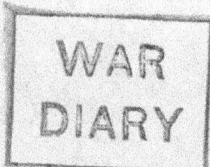

92nd BRIGADE

TRENCH MORTAR BATTERY

1st to 31st JULY 1916.

Confidential   Vol VII 3

War Diary
of
92nd J. Mortar Battery

1st July to 31st July
1916

WAR DIARY
or
INTELLIGENCE SUMMARY

Army Form C. 2118

92nd Trench Mortar Battery

Place	Date	Hour	Summary of Events and Information	Remarks and references to Appendices
Trench E.4 COLINCAMP	1/7/16	2 AM.	When dawn came the work of digging out the ammunition which had been buried by enemy shelling was held up at the first line or what of remained of it, it had not been completed. This work was carried on & finished under a heavy fire, & it was during this time that Pte Butler one of the carriers was wounded.	
		5:30 AM	About 5:30 AM L/Cpl Dalton & Pte Halliday were wounded whilst digging their gun positions & adopting shell crater for use, & Shortly afterwards Pte Leveson was wounded.	
		7.20 AM.	At 7.20 AM our 2 Stokes guns in the Sap Replacement about 40 yards from the Penma front line opened rapid fire at the Bangi Gun & 3rd line trenches, & the remaining 2 guns of No 1 Section with the 4 guns of No 2 Section opened rapid fire at the German 1st line, during this rapid burst the attacking Infantry had got out of our front line & started the advance. Artillery which had been shelling heavily were developed on the German trenches from also fired in [?] effective, a barrage in [?] fire on our front line, & these appeared to be barrages on our [?] put on our front line & on "No Man's Land." In spite of this our Stokes are continued firing through the 10 minutes allowed us, & at 7.30 AM when our Infantry had to cease some 800 rounds had been fired by our 8 guns in action — About 7.30 one of our guns was buried by a shell, he was not caused & it was remove about an hour late	

Place	Date	Hour	Summary of Events and Information	Remarks and references to Appendices
Continued	1/7/16		Acting on my orders the guns had been withdrawn into the S of A.P. to the rapid burst of to minute, to avoid development of attack, & to try & draw loss. The six gun firing from one place line herden or in rear of the gun line in place where it did not skirt were very exposed to both fire & the teams of are gun that to them were gallantly in that they had a splendid example yet by 2nd Lt Hine who put in charge of 3 guns made them backwards & forwards, encouraging them both during the bombardment by 3 others & freer ranks where Situs place or for the secting them & disposing of their ammunition.	
	After-noon		At about 9 AM I received orders from Colonel Rickman, Comm'd'g 11 East Lanc to stand by in readiness to move, later an information reaching the position of our attacking troops was almost an my battery was under the orders of the 92 ne Infantry Bg, it was arranged between us to wait for further developments later on I decided in consultation with Colonel Rickman to get up my guns again in our front line ready to fire at Redan a few line if it should be necessary, & it proved that on our men were not holding it	

Army Form C. 2118

WAR DIARY
or
INTELLIGENCE SUMMARY
(Erase heading not required.)

Place	Date	Hour	Summary of Events and Information	Remarks and references to Appendices
Cuinchy			It was during this time & about 3.30 pm, when 2nd Lt Hunt was wounded in several places by shrapnel whilst setting his gun set up, & Pte. Harrison was wounded in wrist late whilst carrying ammunition to the gun. At 4 pm 1/Cpl Swift & Pte Kirby became casualties of were suffering from shock due to the intense "barrage" placed on our front line by the enemy. It would appear that the enemy discovered the forward gun emplacement which was 3 in galvanised iron off the Sap going to the German wire, & brought up to the surface & thence at about 40 yards from the German wire a whizzbang during a visit with one of my officers to observe the German wire being gone - & a lot of part of their sheer fire elsewhere to the enemy barrage in the Sap. Hits fr: a dem, & getting ammunition were difficult an pm on to the attack in fact pm 10pm 30/6/16 the shells other before its assault the Sap was crowded with infantry, it being almost the only cover available & also wilt wounded men, & after the assault had taken place the congestion of caused by wounded men, became worse, & evacuation of the wounded over the parapet was lat, the barrage being very severe, the communication trenches being impassable, & the shelter heaven being fairly terrified in the trenches behind.	

Place	Date	Hour	Summary of Events and Information	Remarks and references to Appendices
Continued			Towards evening our firing line & any Scof of cure were full of wounded & men of my Battery assisted in getting away of the wounded to Stretcher ambulance & in visiting the Stretcher bearers. Orders given to my section of 4 guns to deserve at "Wheat" farm to "Stand by" in preparation for an advance by 92nd Inf. B'de., did not reach us in time & the advance was later cancelled.	
			Before dark the danger of leaving the S. of the open up by the German line & also the Entrenchment was taken into account & my line panicaded up the Entrance with Sand bags in running a B-ade which was afterwards taken on by the Infantry.	
			The night passed with only average shelling by the Enemy till dawn when heavy fire was again directed onto our trenches.	
	2/7/16	1 A.M.	At about 1 A.M. orders were received to withdraw & march back to bivouac at Bus-les-Artois. The B.5 were clear of the trenches by 4 p.m. The following Officers & men were specially praised for their conduct throughout — Continued	

WAR DIARY
or
INTELLIGENCE SUMMARY

Army Form C. 2118

(Erase heading not required.)

Place	Date	Hour	Summary of Events and Information	Remarks and references to Appendices
Continued	2/7/16		Lieut D. Brake, 2nd Lt Hime, L/cpl Burr.C. & Pte Petty (in charge of Sun.) & Pte Hire & Allum J.S. who carried ammunition up to the gun after 4 men had been knocked out doing the same thing. Pte Haigh who carried messages from the front line to the section in reserve & to Bn.s H.Q. here & there during the day, though very heavy fire. In conclusion O.R. of Battery worked splendidly. 9th Bn. went into Corps Reserve.	Route
	3/7/16		The Brigade went out for a route march — WARNIMENT. WOOD. AUTHIE. VAUCHELLES. LOUVENCOURT BUS. The weather was very pleasant. Had orders late in the evening to Stand-By for a move. As a move was impending.	
	4/7/16		Received orders that the Brigade was moving back its wad deys. Detailed orders came later. The Bn. would move on the morning of the 5th to BERNAVILLE resting one night on the road at BEAUVAL. The T.M.B. was to have the use of a Motor Lorry which meant that all the stores etc

1875 Wt. W593/826 1,000,000 4/15 J.B.C.&A. A.D.S.S./Forms/C. 2118.

WAR DIARY
or
INTELLIGENCE SUMMARY
(Erase heading not required.)

Army Form C. 2118

Instructions regarding War Diaries and Intelligence Summaries are contained in F.S. Regs., Part II. and the Staff Manual respectively. Title Pages will be prepared in manuscript.

Place	Date	Hour	Summary of Events and Information	Remarks and references to Appendices
	4/7/16		had to be pulled by hand on the hand carts suffered. Route. AUTHIE, SARTON, TERRAMESNIL, BEAUVAL CANDAS, FIENVILLERS, BERNAVILLE.	
	5/7/16		Paraded 6.30 A.M. Was told that the Corps Commander would inspect us at SARTON. The head of the 92nd M.B. passed the X Roads at EAST end of AUTHIE at 7.30 and overtook the Column 1 mile W. of AUTHIE. The whole column halted on the side of the road while the Corps Commander, Sir A. Hunter-Weston, rode down the line & said a few words of congratulation & praise to each unit. The column then continued its march reaching BEAUVAL shortly after Noon. The march was very trying as the Head carts were heavy & extremely difficult to pull, owing to the heat & steepness of the hills. The Brigade left BEAUVAL at 8.30 A.M. in the morning and reached BERNAVILLE at 12.30 P.M. Remainder of day spent in resting.	
	6/7/16			

WAR DIARY
or
INTELLIGENCE SUMMARY
(Erase heading not required.)

Army Form C. 2118

Place	Date	Hour	Summary of Events and Information	Remarks and references to Appendices
	7/7/16		The day was spent in cleaning guns; handcarts etc & inspecting kits.	
	8/7/16		Received orders to entrain at AUXI LE CHATEAU. ½ Battery to be at station at 3.0 p.m. ½ Battery to be at station at 6.0 p.m. took the following PROUVILLE, MAIZICOURT, AUXI LE CHATEAU. Lt OAKE & 2/Lt BURCH with No 2 Section and half of 2 & 3 Section consisted of the 1st party. Capt Hartley and 2/Lt Hunt with the remainder of the Battery the 2nd. The 1st party reached THIENNES the station of detrainment at about 9:30 and marched to ROBECQ reaching the latter place at about midnight.	
	9/7/16		The 2nd Party arrived at THIENNES at about 4.0 AM and reached ROBECQ at about 7.0 AM. The men worked splendidly — pulling very heavy loads with extraordinary cheerfulness. Remainder of day spent in washing.	

WAR DIARY
or
INTELLIGENCE SUMMARY
(Erase heading not required.)

Army Form C. 2118

Place	Date	Hour	Summary of Events and Information	Remarks and references to Appendices
	10/7/16		Most of day spent in inspections and getting guns harness etc clean.	
	11/7/16		Various drivers were put in charging gun drives. A few men were returned to their Battalions. The Corps Commander saw all officers at 11.0 AM and gave a short lecture	
	12/7/16		The day included Bayonet fighting – Physical drill – gun drill – Distance Judging and Battery. More gun drives + lectures.	
	13/7/16		Received orders to be ready to move in a few hours.	
	14/7/16		The 11th EAST YORKS had some swimming sports in the LA BASSÉE Canal. Starting at 11.0 AM. They were a great success and were well attended – the men particularly being very keen. Received detailed orders at 6.0 PM to move to RIEZ BAILLEUL at once and Bivouac there for one night. Route to be followed CAROMME - MEURILLON - LAGORGUE - RIEZ BAILLEUL. The Battery did not move off until 8.0 PM as the G.S. wagon provided for our use did not turn up. The Battery moved off at 8.0 PM under W DRAKE – Capt Horsley remaining behind to see after the transport which had not turned up.	

1875 Wt. W593/826 1,000,000 4/15, J.B.C. & A. A.D.S.S./Forms/C. 2118.

WAR DIARY
or
INTELLIGENCE SUMMARY
(Erase heading not required.)

Army Form C. 2118

Place	Date	Hour	Summary of Events and Information	Remarks and references to Appendices
	14/7/16		The majority of the stores etc were on the knock-carts – the men pulling very well and cheerfully. The Battery reached RIEZ BAILLEUL at about 12.0 midnight and settled down for the night at on a field at pt. M/D 2.4. The G.S. wagon with Capt HORSLEY did not arrive until 4.0 A.m.	
	15/7/16	11. A.m	Capt HORSLEY and Lt OAKE went to inspect the trenches at leaving 2/Lt BURCH in charge of the Battery. They went a wire back at 4.30 p.m ordering No 1 Section under 2/Lt HUNT to move up to the trenches leading Capt Horsley at ESTAIRES Church. The men arrived of the battery to when to billets at PONT. DU. HEM when they woned met 2/Lt OAKE. This message failed to arrive as the signal office of the 6th WARWICKS did not deliver the message – the non consequents was delayed nearly 3 hours. The battery left RIEZ. BAILLEUL at 9.0 p.m. No 1 Section going to the trenches, No 2 Section going to PONT. DU. HEM which was reached.	

WAR DIARY
or
INTELLIGENCE SUMMARY
(Erase heading not required.)

Army Form C. 2118

Place	Date	Hour	Summary of Events and Information	Remarks and references to Appendices
	15/7/16	10.0 p.m.	No. 1 Section relieved 182nd T.M.B.y, took over 24 rounds of ammunition & right emplacements. 4 guns were put into the line under Capt Horsley and 2nd Lt Hunt.	Ref: Map Name 36 S.W. Trench Map 28: 7a.
		8 p.m.	Smoke bombs were placed all along the front line, gas was let off to the North.	
	16/7/16		16 rounds fired from M 30 c 11, 9 rounds from M 30 c 16, 29 rounds from M 30 a 25, 23 rounds from M 24 d 15. Total 77. Lieut Oake & 2nd Lt Bench visited the trenches in the afternoon.	Guns number from S to N
		10.45 p.m.	Guns were withdrawn & set up 200 yds in rear of & to cover front line.	
	17/7/16	5 am	Guns commenced firing from our front line. Stern emplacement (M/30 c 11) received direct hit from small "Minenwerfer" which fell inside the emplacement, badly damaging the gun, wounding Pte Barker A.100. & Pte Reed J. 374. (10 KO/137 E. Yorks Regt C) as well as smashing six rounds of ammunition which also detonated did not explode. 9 other small Minnies fired at this emplacement one after the other, falling a little short but in a 10 yd. group. Nos. 2 & 3 guns retaliated at once. New Emplacements constructed at M30 a 03	

WAR DIARY or INTELLIGENCE SUMMARY

Army Form C. 2118

(Erase heading not required.)

Place	Date	Hour	Summary of Events and Information	Remarks and references to Appendices
	18/9/16		Enemy front line & communication trenches were shelled throughout the day. 111 rounds being expended. All spare men carrying up ammunition to front line, remainder of Battery at PONT-DU-HEM also employed carrying ammunition. German line to north was being bombarded by our artillery, wirecutting etc. Stokes fire distributed on enemy line as follows:- No 1 gun 43 rounds about M 36 a 34 No 2 gun 10 rounds at M 30 a 52. No 3 gun 20 rounds at abt M 30 a 55. 16 rounds at abt M 30 a 41 & some at M 30 a 42 05 registered. No 4 gun 39 rounds at M.G. emplacements etc abt. M 24 d 6530. F.O.O. reports enemy machine gun knocked out by this gun. Total of rounds fired being 131.	
	19/9/16		Artillery bombardment continued. "Stokes" fire distributed along enemy front. At 6 pm the time for the attack by 61st Div. on our North flank & 5th Australian Div. on field nearby. At 7.55 pm message received to cover retirement of 61st Div. by all available means Infantry fire, Lewis & Vickers guns, Rifle Grenades & Stokes. All ammunition in the	

WAR DIARY or INTELLIGENCE SUMMARY

Place	Date	Hour	Summary of Events and Information	Remarks and references to Appendices
	20/4/16	8am	trenches was therefore fired by us with good effect. Q/New 4th of Battery immediately put in carrying ammunition from the dump & detonating it. At 10.15pm Nos 1 & 2 Guns placed in position at M.29.1. & from then onwards starred enemy line persistently. At 12.30am the time for raiding party to enter enemy trenches, these two guns placed a barrage just South of M.30.c.58 for 15 minutes. Ammunition expended 424 rounds. No 1 Section carrying up ammunition to front line. Lieut Oake & 2nd Lt Burrell with No 2 Section relieved No 1 Section, who marched back to PONT-DU-HEM. The 61st Division expressed their appreciation of the support given them by the 92nd T.M. Battery. No 2 Section having relieved No 1 Section found that in these trenches we held the upper hand and decided to keep it. The rate of retaliation arranged by the outgoing section was	

WAR DIARY
or
INTELLIGENCE SUMMARY
(Erase heading not required.)

Army Form C. 2118

Instructions regarding War Diaries and Intelligence Summaries are contained in F.S. Regs., Part II. and the Staff Manual respectively. Title Pages will be prepared in manuscript.

Place	Date	Hour	Summary of Events and Information	Remarks and references to Appendices
	2/7/16		adhered to & found to be most effective. Our four guns were in action throughout the day and gun at M 30 c 1.2 fired on a mine crater, two days old at M 30 c 5.4. Sandbags & timber were blown in the air. The guns were withdrawn at night & set up in the support line in order to fire into our front line in the event of an attack. Ammunition expended 330 rounds. Casualties Nil. The guns were brought back to their emplacements in the front line at "stand to". An officer on parapet duty mounted out a German dug-out at M 30 a 4.5. 6 rounds were fired on this point completely destroying the dug-out. A "Minenwerfer" was observed to be flying from M 24 d 6.3. 20 rounds were fired thereon & it was assumed that an emplacement had been badly damaged. The gun at M 30 c 1.6. disposed of numerous working parties during the day. All guns were set up in the front line at night to assist in keeping open gaps in the enemy wire & to prevent him repairing	

WAR DIARY or INTELLIGENCE SUMMARY

Army Form C. 2118

Place	Date	Hour	Summary of Events and Information	Remarks and references to Appendices
Trenches	22/1/16		Gun at M.24.d.1.5. was shifted to another emplacement, having been subjected to rather heavy artillery fire, this probably in retaliation to our effective firing during the morning. Ammunition expended 268 rounds. Casualties nil. Guns were ordered to remain in our front line all night to keep gaps in the wire open. Foot work was done by gun at M.24.d.1.4. This gun having traversed German front line, firing 30 shells & doing considerable damage. The enemy retaliated with light artillery causing some casualties in our front line & getting very near to our emplacement. Gun with night company at M.30.c.1.2. fired on a ruined farm house at M.30.c.7.5. work was being carried out by enemy at the front, the working party was dispersed & hits of the wall knocked down (no doubt). Brigadier having arranged with artillery that short rapid bursts were to be fired at enemy during the night, ordered our guns to co-operate. Upper Section was ordered to remain in front line during the night and fire five rounds rapid at 11 p.m., 1 and 1.20 a.m., the time specified for the artillery bursts.	

WAR DIARY or INTELLIGENCE SUMMARY

Army Form C. 2118

Place	Date	Hour	Summary of Events and Information	Remarks and references to Appendices
	23/7/16		Enemy put a barrage on support trench, but nothing came into the front line. Ammunition expended 241 rounds. Casualties Nil. It was found during the day that in the new gun not tubular mountings the legs had become bent. Apparently they are not lasting enough for the gun. Orders having been received that the 184 Trench Mortar Battery would relieve no, no special targets were engaged, the guns fired periodically on the enemies front line. Relief completed at 7.30 pm. Ammunition expended 59 rounds. Casualties Nil.	
	24/7/16		The Battery moved from PONT Du HEM at 12 noon to RICHEBOURG ST VAAST which was reached at 1.30 PM. No 1 Section with 2/Lt HUNT and HEWSON proceeded immediately to the trenches, relieving the 184 TMA. The relief was completed by 4.30 PM. The frontage was from VINE ST to QUINQUE RUE. The guns (4) were sited up in the existing emplacements and immediately opened fire. No 1 Mortar S.16.a 25 26, No 2 Mortar S.10.c 30, No 3 Mortar S.10.c 37 10, No 4 Mortar S.10.c 50 18. During the evening went and examined the line and decided to build a new emplacement at S.16.a.24. All the guns were taken out of the line at 10.30 pm and moved to the support trench.	

Place	Date	Hour	Summary of Events and Information	Remarks and references to Appendices
	25/7/16		Enemy Mortars and Artillery were quite a lot of good work was done by us against the Enemy, support + front line trenches up to 11.0 A.M. Total number of rounds expended 134.	
	26/7/16		Two guns were kept in the front line and fired during the night. Guns were placed in the front line at 4. A.M. and traversed the Enemy's front line from S16a 6.5 to S16a 8.7 and traversed from S16a 85 to S16a 7.3. effectively. The enemy's rifle grenades and trench mortars were silent all day. At 12 Noon the enemy bombarding our line from S16a 24 to VINE ST. with 5.9" shells and Shrapnel to which we replied with 15 rounds from 12 4" Mortar. No damage was done. The Boulevard was shelled about 3/4 hr. Rounds expended to the at 11. A.M. 290. All guns were ordered to be set up front line at night - and that two were to cover our own men in civilobe trail in to remain by guns were taken back. This was done; the support line.	
	27/7/6		At 4.0 A.M. two men of N˚2 Mortar heard shots from the Enemy trenches. On looking over they discovered someone of the Enemy standing on his own parapet.	

WAR DIARY or INTELLIGENCE SUMMARY

Army Form C. 2118

Place	Date	Hour	Summary of Events and Information	Remarks and references to Appendices
	27/7/16		Shaking his fist in our direction. They were heard to say in English "you English B----ds, we'll give you it---- tonight". A machine gun at that moment discharged ---- and 6 stokes bombs were immediately sent over to that spot. A sniper reported that he saw a Stokes bomb fall amongst a German working party killing 4 men. Two extra guns were sent into the line Bay order of the Divisl ads and took up positions at S22c.02.52 and S22a.01. They spent the day improving and building emplacements. No of wounds received our up to U.O. Ahn was, 270. The Enemy bombarded our line bn. between BOND ST. and VINE ST. for 2 hr from 2.0 pm to 2.30 pm. He was otherwise looking for our emplacements which he did not hit. the however considerably damaged the parapel and wounded one man; Pte C.W. Pope Aurel 12.69. slightly in the shoulder. Our artillery reply was extremely weak. Capt Horsley 1/DAKE and 2/L/Suckett	

Place	Date	Hour	Summary of Events and Information	Remarks and references to Appendices
	27/7/16		hurried us in the evening and just as the enemy arrived at 9.20 p.m. the enemy opened a violent bombardment about 2000 yds on the left. The guns got safely into their night position and all got ready to cover our offence. There was no barrage on our line however and the bombardment slackened at about 11.30 P.M. and died away altogether at about midnight — The remainder of the night was calm.	
	28/7/16		The enemy were particularly quiet all day. We did good work against the enemy's fire and second lines — a large number of tanks etc were seen to fly into the air — so a considerable amount of damage must have been done. The two extra guns doing good work from S22 C 7.3.6 S22 C 7.9. Caway during the day a slight explosion probably a Smeed bomb store. Number of rounds fired up to — 11. 0 A.m. 257.	

WAR DIARY or INTELLIGENCE SUMMARY

Army Form C. 2118

Place	Date	Hour	Summary of Events and Information	Remarks and references to Appendices
	29/7/16		Number of rounds fired up to 11.0 A.m. were 294. The morning was very quiet on the Enemy's part. Capt HORSLEY and 2/Lt BURCH with his gun team relieved No 1 Section at 12 Noon.	Bde. Order that 2 guns are to be in the line. W.P.H.
	30/7/16		Two guns were withdrawn from the line & kept at H.Q. in reserve on account of an establishment being reduced from 12 to 8 guns. This left 4 guns in the Bde. frontage, 2 in back breakwater. During the day Enemy trench mortars, rifle & communication headers were continually subjected to cover fire at any point along his line. A M.G. was at S22c56 in parapet was badly damaged & M.G. range 212 rounds turned on the spot for bursts of fire during the night. 2YR were fired opposite to 125, R. R. York R & 82 opposite to 135 2.Y.R. 199 rounds were fired at various parts of German line. Notably at "Boar Head" FME DU BOIS and at S22c85. were 4 direct hits were observed in a suspected M.G. Emplacement.	
	31/7/16		Target engaged during the day were trenches in S16a. The line in front of S16.4 & all trenches from about S22c 79 – S22c 85 Enemy being quiet. The only retaliation being on trench sector with 77mm field Gun. 269 rounds fired during day.	Ref. Trench map 1/1000 FME DU BOIS SECTION W.P. Horsley Capt. OC 92nd Trench mortar Bty.

Confidential

War Diary

of

92nd Trench Mortar Battery

August 1916.

Vol VIII
4

Army Form C. 2118

92nd Trench Mortar Battery

WAR DIARY
or
~~INTELLIGENCE SUMMARY~~
(Erase heading not required.)

4/8/16

Instructions regarding War Diaries and Intelligence Summaries are contained in F.S. Regs., Part II. and the Staff Manual respectively. Title Pages will be prepared in manuscript.

Place	Date	Hour	Summary of Events and Information	Remarks and references to Appendices
RICHEBORG ST VAAST.	1/8/16		20 rounds distributed S 22 C 7.8. 16 rounds on S 22 C 8.3. 31 rounds abt S 22 C 8.7 mls were common at no trench and 9 rounds fired into the Torpe bomb d'home, making a total of 76. About 7.30/am A 4 inch mortar was fired at Rope trench evidently a lighter minenwerfer than the first T.M. fired into this sector since the Brigade took over, it also fired into our more during early morning, our Stokes retaliated. Our two guns in our right sub-sector had evidently been sifted where therefore moved. In left sub sector 67 rounds were distributed about the "Bomb head", 58 rounds abt S10 a.00. Smoke was seen coming from about S16 A 0.9, whenever a minenwerfer was fired, 28 rounds were fired at this point. An officer from the Left Brigade pointed out a spot that were the enemy were carrying and working their bundles, 10 rounds were fired at this target and damage was done, men wounded was flung into the air. Total rounds for the day 239.	Ref: Trench Map 1/10000 FERME DU BOIS SECTOR
	2/8/16			
	3/8/16		Lieut Oake and 2nd Lieut Hunt and No 1 Section relieved Capt Conoley & 2nd Lt. Birch with No 2 Section at midday. Fire was distributed along enemy front line at point S 22 C. 35.75 to S 22 C. 6.1 and from S 22 a. 65.20. to S 22 a. 55.40. The enemy retaliated rather heavily about 4 pm. Attention was paid to enemy line at S 16 a 65.40 and 16 at S 16 a 50.78 and emplants immediately behind these points, 2 shots fired on to point S10 C 95.30. Three up a large quantity of new planking etc. Total number of rounds for the day 139. The guns were removed to the support line & kept up so as to fire into "No man's land" at night if necessary.	
	4/8/16		Fire distributed from S 22 a 65.20 to S 22 a 55.40. from S10 c. 0.8. to S10 C. 90.15. A suspected emplacement was pointed at + we obtained 2 direct hits, doing considerable damage. Total number of rounds for the day 210. Enemy very quiet except for a few rifle grenades, which were vigorously replied to.	
	5/8/16		Bombed enemy front line between S22 C 40.75. and S 22 a 50.95. and from S22 a. 65.20. S22 a 55.40. and on front of the Island. We also bombed between S10 C 92.10. and S16 a 50.80. and between S16 a 50.80. and S16 a 55.55. Total of rounds fired 188. During the afternoon enemy bombarded our front line with minenwerfer and small H.E. to which fire immediately replied with 25m rounds effectively closing the enemy minenwerfer.	

1875 Wt. W 39/826 1,000,000 4/15 J.B.C. & A.J A.D.S.S./Forms/C. 2118.

WAR DIARY or INTELLIGENCE SUMMARY

Army Form C. 2118

Place	Date	Hour	Summary of Events and Information	Remarks and references to Appendices
	6/8/16		We fired at our usual targets & expended 202 rounds. Day very quiet. Enemy retired 6" temporarily evacuated the Bois head on account of our fire which has been very heavy.	
	7/8/16		Day went quiet except that the Bois & Ferme du Bois were 62 rounds during the day. 2 & 3 rounds on to that target.	
	8/8/16		Capt Moseley & 2 Lt Pearson with No 2 Section relieved Lieut Oake & 2 Lt Thynt with No 1 Section at midday. Day very quiet. Enemy sent over a few light grenades which were always replied to by our guns. Replied to fired 1862 rounds during the day.	
	9/8/16.		62 rounds fired from lime Street on to South of Bois head during the day and also on to Ferme of Sap, 40 rounds on to front line and communication trenches from S16a 50.60 to S16a 60.50, 30 rounds on to the Ferme du Bois & neighbourhood & 10 rounds on to Ferme Dou dame. At 10 p.m. a heavy burst of fire by our Stokes was carried out against the German sap and southern edge of Bois head, in all 40 rounds were fired. It took the enemy artillery 6 minutes to reply. Back he did with 16.77mm HE, at 10.16 we repeated this at same target, enemy replied at once with both HE and shrapnel on to our front line & support lines doing very little damage. The effect of our fire unknown, but the trenches were occupied owing to the number of lights sent up, also amount of machine gun fire. Total for day 242.	
	10/8/16		Targets were Artillery front "A", 5.22 a 65.70. S16 c 80.80. S16 a 40.60.6. S16 a 60.50. S16 a 60.60 to S16 a 65.80. S16 a 40.60. to S16 a 60.70. S16 a 70.70 to S16 a 90.75. S16 a 80.80.6 S10 c 00.15. Fire was opened out on to these places during the day. Total number of rounds fired 244 the day was very quiet except for a few trench mortars which mostly fell around Lockajen Sap. Our observer reports a sniper post and a M.G. emplacement were badly damaged at S.22 a.50.70. Another bomb fell in the middle of a working party at S10 c 00.10 and confusion was caused, advantage was taken of this to drop a few more in the same place. A Dug out was badly damaged at S.22 a 70.90 and all the planking on the top was fairly bare.	
	11/8/16		Trenches from S.16 c 80.90 to S16 a 90.40. & communication trench from S16 a 65.60 to S16 c 10.70. and from S.16 a 50.60. to S16 a 90.80. S16 a 65.55. to S16 a 70.35. S16 a 50.20.6. S10 c 00.30. were all fired on. The day was particularly quiet only a few minenwerfers coming over all in the same place. S/Lt Lockspen SO & selected flts of the enemy were fired on during	

1875 Wt. W3793/325 1,000,000 (4/15 J.B.C. & A. A.D.S.S./Forms/C.2118.

Army Form C. 2118.

WAR DIARY
or
INTELLIGENCE SUMMARY
(Erase heading not required.)

Instructions regarding War Diaries and Intelligence Summaries are contained in F.S. Regs, Part II. and the Staff Manual respectively. Title Pages will be prepared in manuscript.

Place	Date	Hour	Summary of Events and Information	Remarks and references to Appendices
	11/8/16		intermittent rapid bursts commencing at 12.5. Enemy staleton sight which consist of 77mm H.E.	
	12/8/16		Ferme du Bois & Ferme Cour d'Avoue were engaged as also German M.G. front and support lines & immediately south of it. Boars Head front & support lines north of it, trenches from 51Dc0030 to S16a9070. Total of rounds fired 190.	
	13/8/16		Ferme du Bois and vicinity were shelled. Between 1 and 2 o'clock the guns were shelled, the target was thrown well in front of guns, which was moved aft 75 yards, when Ferme Cour d'Avoue was engaged. South of Cot S16a 50.60 also north and enemy in front of enemy line for 40 yards to aft of Boars Head. Enemy system of trenches about S16a 80.88 were also dealt with. Total number of rounds fired 198.	
	14/8/16		Targets engaged were S16a 7050. Ferme du Bois and about S16a 7020. Enemy replied strongly with shelled on several occasions. Wire front line & communication trenches at abt S16a 5080. Enemy wire & system of trenches about S16a 7080. Fired a total of 235 rounds.	
	15/8/16		58 rounds were fired on & about Ferme du Bois & S16a 70.40. Suppd. M.G. emplacement at aft S16a 70.40. was engaged aft. Fired 28 rounds at about S16a 7080. & S16a 70.60. 72 rounds on wire & trenches at S16a 60.60. 61 rounds on & about wire & trenches at S16a 90.80. Enemy replied heavily about 8 am by minenwerfer as retaliation to our fire. Total fired 246 rounds.	
	16/8/16		Targets Ferme du Bois, S16a 7040. North of Boars Head were fired on. Fire was distributed between S16a 50.80. & S16a 30.80. A morning haze was fired into & dropped about S16a 7050. An observer reported that considerable were inflicted as a result. Total number of rounds fired 219.	
	17/8/16		Targets engaged were Ferme du Bois. Bois traversé d'Avoue & about the Boars Head. Were fired 211 rounds. Our observer says we sent a bomb or Th middletahl working & making a good deal of commotion	

Army Form C. 2118.

WAR DIARY
or
INTELLIGENCE SUMMARY
(Erase heading not required.)

Instructions regarding War Diaries and Intelligence Summaries are contained in F.S. Regs., Part II. and the Staff Manual respectively. Title Pages will be prepared in manuscript.

Place	Date	Hour	Summary of Events and Information	Remarks and references to Appendices
	18/8/16		We fired on to enemy cmp and Boms head, front line & supports around S16a 50.55. enemy support trenches from S16a 60.60. to S16a 95.95. & front line from S16a 80.20. to S18 a 00.30. Total number of rounds fired 239. The day was exceptionally quiet. No retaliation took place to this rapid burst of fire at 2.30 am. An emplacement or dugout was blown in at S16a 50.65. leaving a gap in the parapet.	
	19/8/16		Fired during day on enemy front line at S16a 80.00. and mire in front of this, on enemy front line & supports between S16a 65.50. & S16a 70.30. Boyau Leap & enemy front line at S16a 50.70. to S16a 60.65. & support line behind this. Total number of rounds fired 227.	
	20/8/16		Fired a total of 264 rounds mainly on to S16a 50.70 & S16a 70.80 and S16a 55.55. to S16a 95.25. The day was very quiet. The minenwerfer fired occasionally to which our Stokes replied & vigorously. The gander parapet was breached at S16 a 55.60. by our bombs.	
	21/8/16		Fired at enemy line at S16 a 90.10. Terme Cour d'Avoue, ceased enemy front line & supports between S16a 60.50 & S16a 40.60. & on to enemy line at S16a 70.55. Total number of rounds fired being 180. Enemy replied weakly with 77mm & small minenwerfer in retaliation to our bursts during the night.	
	22/8/16		Fired 232 rounds on to Ferme du Bois, Ferme Cour d'Arvie, Boms head & South pit. & on to enemies system of trenches from & about S16a 60.60. to S16a 95.95. Enemy retaliation only slight chiefly consisting of 77mm HEs.	

WAR DIARY or INTELLIGENCE SUMMARY

Army Form C. 2118.

Place	Date	Hour	Summary of Events and Information	Remarks and references to Appendices
	23/8/16		The day was very quiet and spent in registering for the evening's retaliation &	
	24/8/16		bombay of the (B)(3) Bn Roy Yorks Regt before to raid the enemy trenches at 12.34 am. It was left to the 2" Trench Mortars & our Stokes to deal with the enemy front line. We placed 6 guns so as to fire on to enemy front line & between S16a 50.75. and S10d 00.10. & opened fire for 35 minutes at 12.30 am extending 90 rounds. Our mortars immediately switched to the left & right two protecting the flanks of the raiding party 2 guns fired on to enemy front line & supports around S10d 15.05. firing 150 rounds in short bursts in 11 minutes & the other 2 guns fired 66 rounds at S16a 65.60. for 11 minutes. At 1:15 am fire was distributed around front S10c 05.05. & around points S16a 65.60. firing a further 110 rounds in short bursts & around place of entrance & exit. It fired 80 rounds on to pts S22c 55.70 to S22c 75.00. bombarding the intense bombardment the enemy was subjected to, his retaliation was very weak indeed, none of our emplacements were or guns were hit. On returning raiding party reported enemy front line practically levelled & not a living German was seen. Total number of rounds fired 561. From the Sors. S16a 70.60 S16a 90.70. S16a 90.90. were fired on to, we fired 149 bombs. Enemy small minenwerfer active but was always quickly replied to.	

WAR DIARY or INTELLIGENCE SUMMARY

Army Form C. 2118.

Place	Date	Hour	Summary of Events and Information	Remarks and references to Appendices
	25/8/16		The following targets were fired on support line from 516 f 10.90 to 516 a 55.55. trench running NE from 516 a 65.55. Ferme du Bois and vicinity. Ferme du Bois. 286 rounds were fired. At 10.10 pm a patrol returned & reported the enemy had a covering party out at 516 a 70.80 and a working party further South. At 10.20 pm 2 Stokes opened rapid fire for half a minute & the party 20 minutes later this was repeated as hammering could be heard, our field guns co-operated, results could not be observed, but some beautiful air bursts were obtained. 110 rounds were fired making the total 276.	
	26/8/16		Ferme du Bois & South of it & 516 a 70.70 were engaged. At 10.30 am enemy retaliated with howitzers (first firing small minenwerfer to draw our fire) off direction of our guns, then trying to knock them out, they shelled our parapet in several places. In two days the enemy fired 191 Howitzer shells at our emplacement at 516 a 25.15, but met with no success beyond breaking a few bays & only one man being slightly scratched. 50 rounds were fired at 516 a 90.45. were minenwerfer also thought to be firing from this was also located on the following points 516 L 90.60 & 516 f 90.40 B, 522 c 70.70. Total number of rounds fired 183.	
	27/8/16		Fine was distributed at about 516 a 80.60 & between 516 a 80.10 & 516 c 90.30. Enemy artillery was very lively during the morning retaliating with 77 mm HE & Shrapnel and some bigger Shrapnel w H.E. We fired 10 rds rapid from each of 3 guns in about 20 seconds into the Ferme du Bois drawing slight retaliation, we also paid attention to Ferme Cour d'Avoine & 522 c 70.40. Enemy shelled front line between Rife trench & Jumping trench burying one of our guns, we felt however, we had managed to bring near of 50 yds 5 of this position again worried him.	

Army Form C. 2118.

WAR DIARY
or
INTELLIGENCE SUMMARY
(Erase heading not required.)

Place	Date	Hour	Summary of Events and Information	Remarks and references to Appendices
	28/8/16		Fire was directed on to the following places between S.16.a.90.90. and S.16.a.70.50. Ferme du Bois, around S.16.c.90.60. Some bomb and trench mortar fire retaliation from the enemy. Fired a total of 248 rounds. Only slight retaliation from the enemy.	
	29/8/16		Targets engaged were S.16.a.70.70, trenches & wire north of the Bois Grenier in cooperation with the medium trench mortars in the afternoon; fired at intervals during the night as enemy were at the same point. Ferme du Bois attended with band round for 150 yards, & front line trenches from S.22.a.90.10 to S.22.a.60.80. Total number of rounds fired 283. Trenches very wet, most of our emplacements under water almost impossible to set up guns. Guns set up in the open on account of this.	
	30/8/16.		Our guns fired throughout the day on various targets. In the early morning D company of the 10(R)(S) In foot Yorkshire Regt. teased enemy with rifle grenades, bringing retaliation from enemy minenwerfer which was promptly knocked out by our Stokes mortars of minenwerfer S.16.c.90.10. Fired a total of 180 rounds.	
	31/8/16		We fired on enemy front line between S.16.a.70.80 & S.16.a.55. inclining 30 round at Gov 1-58am. Our mortars co-operated with artillery firing on our targets S.22.c.60.50 and S.22.a.80.10. Our bombardment ceased at 1-45 attended by the enemy retaliated mostly with light artillery & succeeded in knocking out a medium emplacement. Lieut. Querqui behaving R/Cpl. Tracey & Dufoit	

Army Form C. 2118.

WAR DIARY
or
INTELLIGENCE SUMMARY
(Erase heading not required.)

Instructions regarding War Diaries and Intelligence Summaries are contained in F. S. Regs., Part II. and the Staff Manual respectively. Title Pages will be prepared in manuscript.

Place	Date	Hour	Summary of Events and Information	Remarks and references to Appendices
			and the Officers & thirty one deserving of special praise for digging out an Officer & 4 men of the M.T.M.B. who were burned in their emplacement. Our bombardment severely damaged enemy trenches. We fired a total of 218 rounds.	
	NOTE		Owing to the nature of the line targets are very limited in this sector.	
			W. P. Horsley Capt O.C. 92 T.M. Battery.	

www.ingramcontent.com/pod-product-compliance
Lightning Source LLC
Chambersburg PA
CBHW080840010526
44114CB00017B/2340